TOURISM

TOURISM

Rob Davidson

Second Edition

LONGMAN

Pearson Education Limited
Edinburgh Gate, Harlow
Essex, CM20 2JE, England
and Associated Companies throughout the world.

First published in Great Britain 1989
This edition published in 1993
Reprinted 1994
Reprinted by Longman Group Limited 1995, 1996
Fourth impression 1997
Fifth impression 2000

ISBN 0 582 28854 1

British Library Cataloguing in Publication Data
A CIP record for this book is available from the British Library

Produced by Pearson Education Asia Pte Ltd
Printed in Singapore (B & Jo)

6292

CONTENTS

INTRODUCTION

Tourism's position as the world's largest industry has led to the widespread acknowledgment of the decisive role it plays in shaping the global economy and creating employment for many millions of people. More recently, attention has also been focused on the impact of tourism in other spheres, in particular on the physical and human environment of destinations, creating new, vitally important issues for consideration on the tourism agenda. As changing economic conditions, modified consumer behaviour and new technologies have created new tourism markets and the further expansion of this industry, its impact has become increasingly pervasive. Now, as this century draws to a close, there are few whose lives have not been touched by the worldwide spread of tourism, whether as consumers of this industry's products, as its employees, or as residents in cities or regions which have become tourism destinations.

Moreover, even in times of economic hardship, the forecasts for the continuing expansion of tourism remain buoyant. A 5% yearly growth rate for international tourist flows throughout the 1990s is widely predicted, with tourist expenditure likely to grow even faster in real terms. Wars, regional disturbances, and economic recession may temporarily check the rise of tourism, but have failed to make any significant impact upon its continuing global expansion.

The optimistic forecasts for the development of the tourism industry in the years ahead have given rise to a broad range of tourism courses in Britain and overseas. The 1980s in particular witnessed great advances both in the quality and quantity of educational provision for the tourism industry.

The recent growth in this field in Britain is most strikingly demonstrated in the following quotation by David Airey, of the Department of Education and Science: 'At the start of the 1970s, the only sector of tourism which had a well developed education and training system was hotel and catering. At the start of the 1990s, there is education and training at all levels for virtually all sectors of tourism. There are now some 2000 courses concerned with the three main sectors of tourism. These are currently enrolling about 30 000 new students each year . . . of which about 20% take courses in travel and tourism studies' (the others are in hotel and catering, and leisure studies courses). *Report to the 40th Congress of AIEST*, Berlin, August 1990.

Tourism has been written to provide essential background material for a range of vocational and non-vocational tourism courses in secondary schools and Colleges of Further Education. Its aim is to provide a sound and broad-based foundation in tourism, by examining the characteristics of the various sectors of the tourism industry, as well as the impact which that industry has in different domains.

The structure of the book presents a clear and logical introduction to its subject. After an initial chapter which defines tourist activity and demonstrates the extent to which this takes place throughout the world, the geographical context of tourism is examined. Chapters 3–7 then describe the different sectors of the tourism industry, followed by three chapters which illustrate the various impacts which tourism can have on the people and places where it takes place. The final chapter looks at the skills and attitudes of those employed by the tourism industry. The perspective of *Tourism* is essentially British, but the international character of tourism requires that a broader view be adopted at times, and throughout the text there are references to, and comparisons with, tourism in other countries.

The text of each chapter is liberally supplemented by stimulus material of various kinds: photographs, charts, diagrams, maps, and extracts from the Press, all of which serve to present graphically the given information on each topic. Detailed case studies further help to reinforce learning, by providing real examples drawn from the tourism industry, in order to illustrate the points being made in the text. Finally, vital features of *Tourism* are the exercises, tasks and assignments contained in each chapter. These have been designed to encourage an investigative approach to the subject, by inviting students to go beyond the content of this textbook and undertake personal or group projects which help them develop their own ideas and knowledge of the tourism industry.

The content of this book is highly relevant to the various travel and tourism-related schemes awarded by City and Guilds. It will appeal equally to students following the General Certificate in Secondary Education (GCSE) in *Travel and Tourism*, the first GCSE to be sponsored by industry, and the result of a highly successful partnership between educationalists and business partners, The American Express Foundation, Forte Hotels, the former International Leisure Group and the British Tourist Authority/English Tourist Board.

The book may also be recommended as an introductory text for those following GNVQs in Leisure & Tourism.

R Davidson

1

TOURISM AND TOURISTS

After reading this chapter, you should have a clear understanding of:
- the meaning of the words 'tourism' and 'tourists',
- the different forms of tourist activity and reasons for travelling,
- the history and development of travel and tourism,
- the scale of tourism throughout the world, Europe and Britain,
- the needs/requirements of tourists,
- the tourism industry today.

What is tourism?

'**Tourism**' and '**tourists**' are words that everyone reading this book will have heard and used many times. The word 'tourism' makes us think of travel, holidays and sightseeing. Most people have at some time seen visitors to their own area or elsewhere that they have thought of as 'tourists'. Many people have even thought of themselves as tourists, when they have been on holiday, for example.

Although both words are commonly used, there are many different opinions as to what *exactly* is meant by 'tourism', and who is – and who is not – a 'tourist'.

To begin the study of tourism, it is important to determine what is meant by the two words 'tourism' and 'tourist', in order to decide upon useful definitions of them which most people will accept, and which make the study of tourism easier.

For example, the Hoppers, are an American family who spend two weeks on holiday in Britain; one week in London and one week in Scotland. They stay in hotels, take a lot of photographs, visit the theatre and buy souvenirs.

Most people would agree that the Hoppers are tourists during their time travelling to, and around Britain and that their activities while on holiday are part of the tourism which takes place in Britain.

What is it about them that makes us think of them as tourists?

1 They are **away from their own home**: they have left their normal place of residence.

2 Their visit is **temporary and short term**: their time here is limited and they intend returning home to America, after a short time in Britain.

3 The **purpose** of their visit: a holiday is one of the activities normally associated with tourism.

Tourism is about people being away from their own homes, on short term, temporary visits, for particular 'tourism' purposes.

There are two points to consider at this stage:

First, this definition of tourism means that we can include people who travel to another place *in their own country* as tourists. For example, if someone travels 85 kilometres from London to Brighton for a weekend, then they become tourists while they are travelling to and while they are in Brighton.

Second, it means that people *on a day out* (away from home, on a temporary and *very* short-term visit) or 'day-trippers', as they are sometimes called, can also be included as part of the tourism that takes place at a particular location. Although people on a day out may not always think of themselves as tourists, we shall include them and their activities in our study of tourism. Day-trippers may, for example, visit a *tourist attraction* such as Edinburgh Castle and use a *Tourist Information Centre*, for advice.

What are the different purposes associated with tourism? The two main reasons for travelling which make people tourists are **leisure** and **business**.

Leisure tourism

Leisure tourism includes travel for various purposes. The following are examples of the main purposes:

Holidays

- a fortnight's trip to the beaches of Spain;
- a weekend in a country hotel in Scotland;
- a week in a farm guesthouse in Wales;
- 3 weeks cruising up the River Nile and visiting the Pyramids.

Sports (non-professional)

- a windsurfing weekend in the Lake District;
- a horse-riding tour of the Pyrenees;
- an English school football team's friendly match with a school team in Glasgow;
- a day out at the National Sports Centre at Crystal Palace, in London.

Cultural events

- attendance at the annual music festival in Aix-en-Provence;

- a holiday to see the Carnival in Rio de Janeiro;
- a day trip to Blackpool to see the Illuminations;
- a weekend in London, visiting special exhibitions in the museums.

Visiting friends and relatives

- a family wedding two hundred kilometres away;
- a weekend staying with friends in a neighbouring town;
- a six week visit of a retired English couple to their son and daughter-in-law's home in Australia;
- a Japanese father visiting his son who is studying at university in Oxford.

Business tourism

The second main purpose associated with tourism is people travelling on business. Business tourism consists of travel for various reasons, mainly:

Business meetings

People travel to meet each other in order to discuss business of some kind. For example:

- a British toy manufacturer flies off to Japan for five days, to meet Japanese toyshop owners and try to interest them in selling his products;
- a politician travels by train from London to Bristol and back again the same day, for a meeting with her supporters.

Exhibitions and trade fairs

Business people who offer a particular service of product may gather together for a few days at an exhibition centre to exhibit their service or product in the hope of attracting buyers. The following is an example of this:

> Hotelympia is an annual trade fair held at the Olympia Exhibition Centre in London. Hundreds of companies who manufacture equipment for hotels or who offer services, such as advertising for hotels, set up exhibition stands. The exhibition is attended by thousands of potential customers, such as hotel owners from Britain and overseas who come to examine, and perhaps purchase, some of the goods and services on offer.

Conferences and conventions

A group of people with something in common may gather together for one or more days, usually to discuss a range of topics of interest to them all. For example:

- 200 specialist doctors from all over the world gather together in a convention centre in Toronto, Canada, for a week to discuss better ways of caring for people with AIDS;
- the Labour Party holds its annual conference attended by thousands of its members, in Blackpool.

Other tourism purposes

Not all tourists are travelling for business or for leisure. Listed below are some of the other purposes associated with tourist visits:

Study

- an Argentinian student attending a college in Bournemouth for a month, to learn basic English;
- a week spent learning landscape painting at a residential arts centre in the Scottish Highlands;
- a doctor's daytrip to Manchester University to attend a special lecture on some research findings in his field of medicine;
- a one-week residential cordon bleu cookery course in Lyons.

Religion

- a Muslim's visit to Mecca;
- a French Roman Catholic visiting the Vatican to see the Pope deliver his Christmas Day message;
- a British Jewish family visiting Jerusalem's Wailing Wall;
- a pilgrimage to the Shrine of Our Lady, near Walsingham, in Norfolk.

Health

- a day trip to Bath, to drink water from the spa;
- a weekend spent at a health farm in the countryside;
- a visit to a Mediterranean sea water therapy centre, for relief from rheumatism;
- an Arab's visit to London for an operation in a private hospital.

EXERCISE

1 For each of the tourism categories above, suggest a further example of your own.

2 We have defined tourists as people who:

- are away from their own home
- are on visits which are short term and temporary

• are travelling for leisure, for business, or for other tourism purposes.

Using this definition, look at the following list of people and decide who is and who is not a tourist:

(a) Mr Miller travels to Lourdes in France, in search of a miracle.
(b) Ms Fowler flies off to Turkey for a two-week holiday in the sun.
(c) Mr Baker emigrates to Australia to settle there and begin a new life.
(d) Mrs Shamir travels from Glasgow to London to spend a week with her relatives there.
(e) Madame Boucher flies from Paris to America for three days to attend two business meetings in New York.
(f) Mr Singh takes his family from Swansea to Blackpool for a week's holiday.
(g) Miss Taylor spends a day out visiting a historic monument located on the edge of her town.
(h) Mr Patel spends six months working as a chef on an ocean-going cruise liner.
(i) Mrs Wheeler and her husband from Birmingham treat themselves to an evening's stay away from home in a country hotel.
(j) Herr Singer, a teacher, travels from Berlin to Frankfurt to attend a two-day conference on education.
(k) Miss Skipper spends a week at home studying French using a language cassette course.
(l) Señor Spanner comes to Britain for three years to study engineering at Brighton Polytechnic.

The rise of tourism

Throughout history, people have travelled all over the world for a variety of purposes – to trade, to fight in wars, and to educate themselves. Only in the last 40 or 50 years has tourism developed on the huge scale that we now know it, and this has only happened in certain countries in the world.

Until this century, only the very rich and leisured people in society had the free time and money required to travel outside their own immediate area. There are examples of this in every era in history. Wealthy Romans, in ancient times, travelled to seaside resorts in Greece and Egypt, for sightseeing purposes. In the 17th century, the sons and daughters of the British aristocracy travelled throughout Europe for periods of time lasting up to three years in order to improve their knowledge. This was known as the Grand Tour and was seen as a vital part of the education of this small but very privileged class. In the 18th century, travel for health became important when the rich and fashionable people of Europe began to visit the spa towns. The mineral springs, or spas, in these towns were supposed to have healing powers, and were bathed in, as well as drunk, by the visitors.

Leamington Spa, in England, and Baden-Baden in Germany, are examples of popular spa towns of those days, and even of present times. In the latter part of the century, sea water, too, earned a reputation for being medicinal, and as a result, many places on the coast were transformed from small fishing villages into thriving seaside resorts. Yet still only a small proportion of the population could afford the time and money to go there. Margate and Bognor Regis are examples of seaside resorts which grew popular in this way, often because some member of the Royal Family made them fashionable by spending time there.

As something which first became open to large numbers of ordinary working people, tourism has its roots in the sweeping social and technological changes of the 19th and 20th centuries. The Industrial Revolution in Britain created a new, more prosperous, class of working people who were able to afford to travel for pleasure. The amount of free time available for travel increased too, as more public holidays were created, followed by laws which made it possible, for the first time, for working people to have holidays with pay. At the same time, great advances in science and technology made possible the invention of rapid and relatively cheap forms of transport: the railways were invented in the 19th century and the passenger aircraft this century.

Figure 1.1 shows the main events of the 19th and 20th centuries which marked and contributed to the rise of tourism in Britain.

In Britain, in 1870, a typical holiday for a family would take the form of one day's trip to the seaside. The private companies who owned the new network of railways offered cheap-day excursions to seaside resorts from the cities where most people now lived. Each member of the family might pay half a crown (12½p) to travel from Manchester to Blackpool by train. They would probably take their own food for the day, but entertainment such as funfairs and sideshows would be available on the sea-front.

A century later, in 1970, many people in Britain were beginning to take advantage of good-value holidays abroad to places such as Spain. A typical family holiday might be a two week 'package tour' to the Costa Brava in Spain. One payment (about £50 each in 1970) would cover the payment of the whole package – the flight, the hotel and the meals taken on holiday. The family would drive their car to the British airport, leave it there for two weeks and collect it when they returned. During their holiday, they would enjoy the sand, sea and sun of Spain, perhaps taste foreign food for the first time, and meet tourists from other countries such as Germany and Scandinavia.

A similar pattern of development occurred in all industrialised countries of Europe and the USA, with more wealth and more free time for travel becoming available to ordinary working people. Technological developments in transport and new, economical ways of packaging travel and accommodation brought the price of tourism down to within the reach of ordinary people. By the middle of this century, '**mass tourism**', i.e., tourism

1830	The first passenger train service begins, between Manchester and Liverpool.	**1937**	Billy Butlin opens Britain's first holiday camp – at Skegness.
1837	The railway companies build the first large hotels at the railway stations.	**1939**	200 holiday camps around the coast of Britain provide holidays for 30 000 people a week in the summer. There are 2 million cars on the roads of Britain.
1840	The first steamship is built for leisure cruises by Cunard.		
1841	Thomas Cook opens the first travel agency.	**from 1950**	Cheaper air transport becomes available, with the growth of commercial airline companies.
1871	The Bank Holiday Act of Parliament creates four public holidays a year.	**1955**	The number of overseas visitors to Britain exceeds 1 million.
1879	Thomas Cook organises the first package tours to Europe and the USA.	**1957**	Due to cheaper air fares, transatlantic air travel exceeds sea travel for the first time.
1889 – 1899	The Savoy, Claridges, and Carlton hotels are opened in London, for European visitors and wealthy British people.	**1963**	The number of overseas visitors to Britain exceeds 2 million.
1901	Parliament passes the Factory Act, giving women and young people at least 6 days' paid holiday a year.	**1970**	6 million British people take holidays overseas. The number of overseas visitors to Britain exceeds 6 million.
1903	The first major hotel company – Trust Houses – opens a chain of hotels throughout Britain.	**1983**	77% of British workers have four or five weeks' holiday a year.
1910	The first hotel school opens, to train chefs for hotels and restaurants in London's West End.	**1987**	The number of overseas visitors to Britain exceeds 15 million.
1914	There are 130 000 cars on the roads of Britain.	**1990**	Overseas residents make a record 18 million visits to Britain.
1930	The number of British people crossing the English Channel for holidays on the continent exceeds 1.5 million.		

1.1 A summary major developments tourism in Britain

for a large proportion of the population of developed countries, was beginning.

Tourism today

Today, mass tourist activity is something which affects most countries in the world, either because people travel to them, or from them, or both. Most industrialised countries receive visitors from other countries, while some of their own population travel overseas or on visits around their own country. Developing countries are also affected by tourism. They do not produce many international tourists, for the same reasons that few British people travelled far from home in the 19th century: most of their populations have neither the time nor the money to travel. But more and more international tourist trips are being made *to* developing countries, as wealthy tourists seek out even more distant and unusual places to visit.

The division between the richest and poorest countries of the world is shown dramatically in terms of tourism by the fact that around 80% of the international tourist trips made in the world are made by people living in the 12 richest countries in the world, including Britain.

The majority of people in the world today still do not travel outside their places of residence. The populations of developing countries in particular spend all their time and effort satisfying their own basic human needs for food and shelter.

To arrive at a clear picture of tourism today and its scale on a global basis, it is necessary to look at the different types of tourism in more detail and to learn some new tourism terms.

Facts and figures about tourists and tourism usually use the word **origin** to describe where tourists come from, i.e. the country where their homes are, and the word **destination** to describe the place they are going to, i.e. the country where they intend to spend their trip.

EXERCISE

Give the origin and destination for the following tourists:

(a) James travels from Scotland to Greece, for a holiday.
(b) Susan flies from Birmingham to Amsterdam on a business trip.
(c) Maria arrives in Oxford for four weeks to improve her English, then she will return home to Sicily.
(d) Chandra has travelled to Calcutta from Madras for a family wedding.
(e) Pedro, who plays for Real Madrid, is in Barcelona for a football match.
(f) The Mayor of Arnhem in Holland is in Purley, near London, to arrange a town-twinning visit.

International tourism

Using the words origin and destination, there are two main ways to describe the movement of tourists from one place to another: **international** tourism which includes inbound tourism and outbound tourism and **domestic** tourism.

Inbound and outbound tourism are forms of international tourism, i.e. trips between one country and another. Inbound tourists are tourists entering a country from their country of origin, and outbound tourists are those who leave their country of origin to travel to another country. Any tourist who travels from his or her country of origin to a destination in another country can be described both as an outbound and as an inbound tourist at the same time, depending upon the point of view of the country describing them (*see* Fig. 1.2).

Fig. 1.2 The tourist leaves Country A to travel to Country B. From the point of view of Country A (the tourist's country of origin) he or she is an outbound tourist; but from the point of view of Country B, he or she is an inbound tourist

The words 'inbound' and 'outbound' only apply on the outward journey, at the beginning of the tourist's trip. On the return trip, the tourist is simply returning home.

Domestic tourism is the term used to describe tourist trips which take place in the tourist's own country. In other words, the country of origin and the country of destination are the same, for example, when someone from Newcastle takes a holiday in Devon. With domestic tourism, the tourist does not travel outside his or her own country.

EXERCISE

Look at the six tourists again in the previous exercise, and, from a British point of view, say whether each one is an outbound, inbound, or domestic tourist.

Figures which are produced to help measure the scale of tourism usually come in the form of two different kinds of information:

- figures showing the **number of trips made** by tourists: often called *arrivals*
- figures showing the **amount spent** by tourists at their destination: often called *receipts*

Both kinds of information are important to governments and to those responsible for measuring tourism and planning for it in their country, region, or town.

Figure 1.3 is in two parts. The first part (Arrivals) shows the total number of international tourist trips made throughout the world between 1980 and 1991, and the annual percentage change.

The first part may be interpreted as follows:

In the 12 years covered by the table, the number of international tourist trips made throughout the world has risen by approximately 160 million. The average annual percentage change over the previous year is approximately 4%. The general trend is upwards, and the years from 1987 to 1990 witnessed particularly impressive growth.

Year	Tourist arrivals (thousands)	Annual % change	Tourism receipts (million US$)	Annual % change
1980	287 906	4.0	102 372	22.8
1981	289 749	0.6	104 309	1.9
1982	289 361	−0.1	98 634	−5.4
1983	293 477	1.4	98 395	−0.2
1984	320 824	9.3	109 832	11.6
1985	330 471	3.0	116 158	5.8
1986	340 891	3.2	140 023	20.6
1987	367 402	7.8	171 352	22.4
1988	392 813	6.9	197 712	15.4
1989	427 660	8.9	211 436	6.9
1990	454 875	6.4	255 006	20.6
1991	448 545	−1.4	260 763	2.3

Fig. 1.3 Development of international tourism. Arrivals and receipts worldwide, 1980–1991
Source: World Tourism Organisation

EXERCISE

The second part of Fig. 1.3 (Receipts) shows the total expenditure on tourism throughout the world between 1980 and 1991. (Although this information is given in terms of American dollars (US$), it includes all spending in all currencies – £ sterling, French francs or Spanish pesetas etc.)

Using this information, write a paragraph similar to the previous one, describing the growth in spending on tourism in the world.

The bar chart in Fig. 1.4 shows clearly where most international tourists go and what are the most popular destinations.

In 1991, 61.8% of all international tourist trips had Europe as their destination. In other words, almost two out of every three international trips made that year were made to, or within, Europe. This makes our own continent the most popular region of the world for tourists.

It is not difficult to see what attracts so many tourists to Europe. The beaches and popular resorts of the Mediterranean; the spectacular scenery of Scandinavia and the Rhine; the rich history and culture of European cities, from Rome and Vienna to Athens and York; the thriving business centres of Geneva and London; and the natural and man-made sports facilities, from

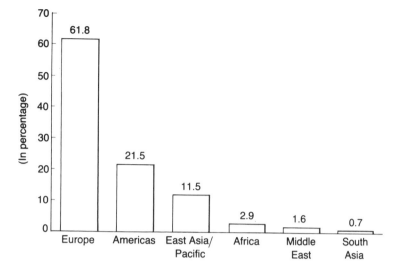

Fig. 1.4 Share of each region in international tourist arrivals (1991)

Source: World Tourism Organisation

Alpine skiing resorts to the golf courses of Scotland. Since mass tourism began, Europe has grown rapidly in popularity as a destination.

In 1960, only 50 million international trips were made to, or within, Europe. This figure doubled by 1970, and had doubled again, to 200 million trips by 1980. By 1990, over 450 million international tourist trips had European countries as their destinations. Yet, despite these phenomenal increases, Europe has been losing out during the 1980s and 1990s to other tourist regions of the world, and has not been able to hold on to its share of the total world market for tourism. In other words, the growth in international trips made to or within Europe has been slower than the total growth of international tourist trips throughout the world.

Europe's declining share of the world tourist market can be seen in Fig. 1.5.

	Shares (in percentage)				
	1950	*1960*	*1970*	*1980*	*1991*
Africa	2.07	1.08	1.51	2.54	2.90
Americas	29.61	24.11	22.95	21.32	21.50
East Asia/Pacific	0.75	0.98	3.04	6.82	11.48
Europe	66.60	72.66	70.76	65.55	61.84
Middle East	0.78	0.91	1.17	2.98	1.56
South Asia	0.19	0.26	0.57	0.79	0.71
World	100.00	100.00	100.00	100.00	100.00

Fig. 1.5 *Share of each region in international tourist arrivals (1950–1991)*
Source: World Tourism Organisation

From 1960, Europe's percentage share of international tourist arrivals fell by almost 10% during the following 30 years. During the same period, other world regions, notably East Asia and Pacific destinations increased their share of the total, at the expense of Europe and the Americas.

New, exotic destinations such as Singapore, Hong Kong and Thailand have been extremely successful in attracting business away from the more traditional European destinations. As long-haul (long-distance) air travel becomes more available and more affordable, Europe will face stiff competition from these newer destinations in the future, and its share of all tourist trips made throughout the world may continue to slide.

Country	Total amounts spent on travel abroad (million US$)	Population (thousand)	Average spending per capita US$
Europe			
Germany	31 650	63 230	501
UK	16 793	57 410	293
Italy	13 300	57 660	231
France	12 338	56 440	219
Netherlands	7 700	14 940	516
Switzerland	6 580	6 650	989
Austria	6 438	7 720	834
Sweden	6 245	8 600	726
Belgium	5 543	9 840	563
Spain	4 530	38 960	116
Denmark	3 347	5 140	651
Norway	3 207	4 240	756
Finland	2 739	4 990	549
North America			
USA	42 367	249 970	169
Canada	8 977	26 450	339
East Asia/Pacific			
Japan	23 942	123 610	194
Australia	3 882	17 090	227
Korea, Rep.	3 785	43 520	87
Malaysia	1 495	17 860	84
Singapore	1 381	2 690	513
New Zealand	1 332	3 350	398
Rest of world			
Mexico	5 379	86 150	62
Kuwait	2 315	2 140	1 082
Israel	1 600	4 660	343
Brazil	1 224	150 370	8

Fig. 1.6 *Leading generators of international tourism (1991)*
Source: World Tourism Organisation

At present, Europe is not only the *destination* for most of the world's international tourists, but also the *origin* of most international tourists.

Figure 1.6 shows the top 25 countries in the world in terms of how much they spend on international tourism, i.e. on tourism in countries apart from their own.

EXERCISE

1 List the European countries in rank order according to how much they spend on international tourism per capita.

2 From your list, discuss whether the amount spent on tourism differs between northern and southern European countries. Give two reasons why one half of Europe spends more on international tourism than the other half.

Tourism is clearly important to Europe as the origin and destination of most international tourists in the world, but what is the scale of tourism in Britain? Where does Britain appear in the international league of tourist destinations? Figure 1.7 shows the top ten destinations in the world in respect of how much they earn from inbound tourism, comparing the situation in 1981 with that in 1991.

1981		1991	
1 USA	12 163	1 USA	45 205
2 Italy	7 554	2 France	21 300
3 France	7 193	3 Italy	19 668
4 Spain	6 716	4 Spain	19 004
5 West Germany	6 227	5 Austria	13 967
6 Britain	5 938	6 Britain	12 588
7 Austria	5 690	7 Germany	10 947
8 Switzerland	3 035	8 Switzerland	7 030
9 Canada	2 552	9 Canada	6 741
10 Greece	1 881	10 Netherlands	4 300

Fig. 1.7 *International tourism receipts (in million US$)*
Source: World Tourism Organisation

From this you can see that over this period of ten years Britain has remained in sixth place. Austria and Germany have exchanged fifth and seventh places, but Britain remains behind the USA, France, Italy and Spain.

What makes Britain such a popular destination for tourists of all the countries in the world? Why is it an essential part of any European tour for anyone travelling around this continent? Britain has many features which are attractive to tourists:

The Royal Family and the aristocracy

- Buckingham Palace;
- royal weddings;
- stately homes.

Sporting events

- Wimbledon tennis championships;
- international rugby matches;
- golf championships.

Art and culture

- the Edinburgh International Festival;
- the British Museum;
- London's West End theatres.

History and tradition

- ancient monuments;
- historic churches and cathedrals;
- the Loch Ness monster.

Conferences and exhibitions

- the National Exhibition Centre, Birmingham;
- the Royal Highland Show, Edinburgh;
- the Ideal Home Exhibition.

Shopping and learning English

- Harrods;
- the Metro Centre, Gateshead;
- English language schools in Oxford and Cambridge.

All of these special features of Britain help to attract the millions of tourists who visit Britain every year, from overseas.

EXERCISE

For each of the six categories of special features of Britain, name two examples of your own, from anywhere in the country.

The number of overseas visitors to Britain is steadily increasing: Fig. 1.8 shows the number of visits to Britain made by inbound tourists between

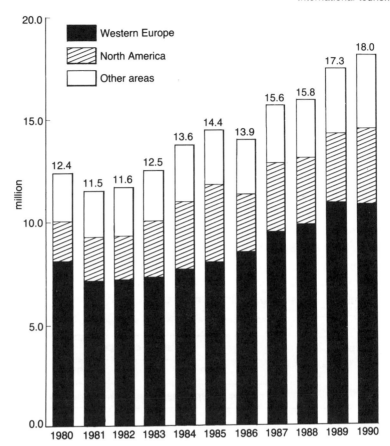

Fig. 1.8 Visits to the UK by overseas residents (1980–1990)

Source: International Passenger Survey

1980 and 1990. The bar chart clearly shows the importance of Western Europe as the origin of most of Britain's overseas visitors.

Figure 1.9 shows details of the top ten origins of inbound tourists to Britain, in terms of how many trips were made and how much was spent in 1990.

	Visits thousands	Spending £ mn
1 USA	3 048	1 661
2 France	2 309	463
3 West Germany	1 878	483
4 Irish Republic	1 317	383
5 Netherlands	993	207
6 Italy	714	343
7 Canada	701	283
8 Australia	629	415
9 Spain	605	283
10 Japan	571	309

Fig. 1.9 Countries of origin (1990)
Source: British Tourist Authority

America is the country from which most inbound tourists travelled to Britain. Americans also spend the most. Most of the other countries in the table are European countries whose residents can travel to Britain relatively quickly and easily and by a variety of different forms of transport.

Domestic tourism in Britain

So far, only the scale of inbound tourism to Britain has been examined but it is important to remember that domestic tourism also takes place in Britain on a large scale. Although British people are taking more holidays overseas each year, they still spend an enormous amount on tourism in their own country: on day trips, business tourism, short breaks, and visiting friends and relatives, as well as first and second holidays every year. Figure 1.10 gives details of British domestic tourism between 1989 and 1990.

Purpose	Number of trips			
	1989		**1990**	
	million	*per cent*	*million*	*per cent*
Holidays	65	59	58	61
Visits to friends and relatives	25	23	20	21
Business	14	13	12	12
Miscellaneous	6	5	5	5
Total	**110**	**100**	**95**	**100**

Purpose	Expenditure			
	1989		**1990**	
	£ million	*per cent*	*£ million*	*per cent*
Holidays	7 400	68	7 300	70
Visits to friends and relatives	1 000	9	900	9
Business	2 100	19	1 600	15
Miscellaneous	400	4	600	5
Total	**10 900**	**100**	**10 500**	**100**

Fig. 1.10 UK residents' trips and expenditure in the UK (1989–90) by purpose
Source: United Kingdom Tourism Survey

Further details of the spending patterns of Britain's domestic and overseas tourists are given in the pie chart in Fig. 1.11, which shows a breakdown of visitors' spending, item by item.

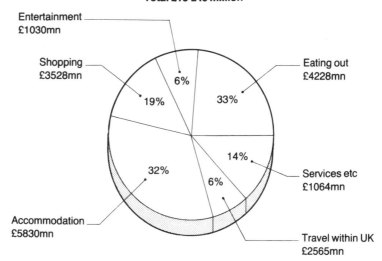

Domestic and overseas tourists
Total £18 245 million

Entertainment £1030mn

Shopping £3528mn

6%

19%   33%

Eating out £4228mn

14%

32%

6%

Services etc £1064mn

g. 1.11 Tourist *ending breakdown* .990)

urce: British Tourist *thority*

Accommodation £5830mn

Travel within UK £2565mn

EXERCISE

1 How would you compare the situation in 1989 and 1990 in terms of:
(*a*) the domestic tourist trips made, and
(*b*) the amount spent on domestic tourism in Britain?
Give as much detail as possible.

2 How does the total amount spent on domestic tourism in 1990 compare with the total amount spent by overseas visitors to Britain in the same year?

The tourism industry

Before any country, or any area within a country, can attract tourists on a large scale, there must exist certain important facilities and services for tourists, to cater for their needs from their time of arrival to their departure.

The businesses and organisations which provide these facilities and services make up what is known as the tourism industry. It is the tourism industry which looks after tourists and provides for their particular needs. Before looking at the tourism industry, therefore, it is important to consider what tourists' needs are.

At the beginning of this chapter, tourists were defined as people who:
- are away from their own home;
- are on visits which are short term and temporary;
- are travelling mainly for leisure or for business.

Travel and transport, and the retail travel trade

In order to get away from their own homes and out of the area where they normally live and work, people need some kind of transport to enable them to travel to their destination. Without travel and transport, there could be no tourism, so this is a vital sector of the tourism industry. The retail travel trade organises and packages travel and sells it to the public, most often through travel agencies.

Catering and accommodation

Unless they are day trippers or people staying with friends or relatives, tourists away from home need somewhere to stay and they need to be fed. The vast sector of the tourism industry which provides tourists with these services is known as the catering and accommodation sector.

Leisure, recreation and business facilities

Tourists need a reason for travelling in the first place. Leisure and business are the two main reasons which lead to tourist activity, and the businesses and organisations which provide leisure, recreation and business facilities make up another sector of the tourism industry.

Tourism promotion and tourist information

Detailed and well-presented promotional information on different destinations plays an important part in persuading the potential tourist to choose a particular city or country for their holiday or conference, for example. Tourist information also has a role in telling visitors what there is to do and see at a destination. Tourism promotion and information constitute, therefore, a key sector of the tourism industry.

Between them, these four sectors and the people working in them make up the tourism industry. The following chapters will examine each of these sectors in turn.

CASE STUDY

Tourism and India

India's population

India has the second largest population of all countries in the world, estimated at 821 million people in 1990.

Until recently, only the top 2–3% of the population could afford to travel. Now, with increasing prosperity, a large new class of people has formed, made up of prosperous farmers, people running their own small businesses, professionals, and the hundreds of thousands of Indians who work in oil-related industries in the Gulf. This new class makes up 10–15% of the country's population – approximately 100 million people – more than the total population of most developed countries.

The Indian population has a young age distribution. Around 40% of the population are under the age of 15 and another 20% are aged between 15 and 24.

Hindi is the official language of India, and the most widely spoken. But English is used as a language for many official purposes, and is understood by most educated Indians.

Indian travel overseas

In general, the most popular international destinations for Indian people are countries in East Asia and the Pacific: Singapore, Malaysia, Thailand and Hong Kong.

Britain, however, is the most popular European destination.

	Visits (000s)	% of all visits to Britain
1980	73	0.6
1981	91	0.8
1982	81	0.7
1983	103	0.8
1984	119	0.9
1985	122	0.8
1986	136	1.0
1987	136	0.9
1988	125	0.8
1989	139	0.8
1990	153	0.9

Fig. 1.12 *Visits to Britain from India (1980–1990)*

In general, Indian visitors stay longer in Britain than most overseas visitors. In 1990, they spent an average of 23 days, compared with an overall average of 11 days for *all* inbound tourists. But their longer visits do not lead to higher levels of spending. In 1990 Indian visitors spent an average of £432 per visit, compared with an average of £428 for all inbound tourists.

Purposes of visits to Britain

34% visits to Britain by Indian residents in 1990 were primarily holiday visits. A further 23% were to visit friends and relatives, while business visits accounted for 30% of all trips.

Indian visitors coming to Britain are twice as likely to be men than women. Only 33% of Indians visiting Britain in 1990 were women, as compared to 42% of *all* foreign visitors.

(Based on data from the BTA Tourism Intelligence Quarterly)

TASKS

1 State the reasons for international tourism becoming an increasingly common activity for Indian people, drawing parallels between India and events in 19th-century Britain.

2 Give two reasons why Britain is so popular with Indian visitors, explaining why so many choose this country rather than France, for example.

3 A large percentage of Indian visitors to Britain are here to visit friends or relatives. What is the link between this fact and the fact that although Indian visitors stay longer than average in Britain, their longer visits do not lead to higher levels of spending?

4 With visiting friends and relatives being the major purpose of so many Indian visitors to Britain, which regions of this country do you think benefit most from Indian visitors' spending?

5 How would you explain the fact that women are under-represented among the Indians visiting Britain?

6 Suggest an international destination for British people, where visiting friends and relatives is an important reason for tourism.

ASSIGNMENTS

1 Many factors affect the level of international tourism throughout the world. Conduct a class discussion on how each of the following can affect the volume of international tourism between one country and another, giving, wherever possible, actual examples.
(*a*) Terrorism, war and political unrest;
(*b*) A special occasion, celebration, or anniversary;
(*c*) The differences in exchange rates of currencies between the countries of origin and destination;
(*d*) Industrial action;
(*e*) Natural and man-made disasters.

2 Visitor survey

Conduct a mini-survey to find out what kind of visitors travel to your area. Draw up a questionnaire and use it to interview approximately one hundred visitors in the streets of your town or at a local tourist attraction. For example, you could find out:

- the visitors' place of origin;
- the length of their visit;
- the purpose of their visit;
- the type of accommodation used (if any);
- the type of transport used;
- whether this is their first or subsequent visit.

Remember to plan your survey well in advance: make sure that the questions you intend to ask can be clearly understood and easily answered. Test them on friends first to make sure of this. Be careful to avoid the possibility of obtaining biased results; for example, interviewing visitors near a car park could indicate an unrealistically high proportion of those who have travelled by car.

Remember also, that often people do not like to be stopped to answer survey questionnaires, so be polite and friendly and try to keep the number of questions to the minimum.

When you have completed your survey, combine the results of the whole class and represent the findings of the survey in the form of graphs or bar charts.

2

THE GEOGRAPHY OF TOURISM

After reading this chapter, you should have a clear understanding of:
- the meaning of the geography of tourism,
- the location of British tourists' destinations overseas,
- major routes in and out of, and around, Britain,
- the location of Britain's principal tourist destinations,
- how tourists reach their destinations,
- patterns of weather in Britain.

What is the geography of tourism?

Because tourism involves the movement of people between places, understanding tourism means having accurate knowledge of:

- where places are located in the world;
- the different routes between places;
- the different characteristics of places which are important for tourism, such as climate.

This type of knowledge forms part of the geography of tourism. Being acquainted with the geography of tourism is important for three different groups of people:

1 Students of tourism;
2 Consumers of tourism – people planning a holiday or a day trip, for example; and
3 People working in the tourism industry.

In the tourism industry, in particular, people are expected to know where places are, especially places in their own country and in their own locality. Anyone who works as a hotel receptionist, in a travel agency, or in a Tourist Information Centre, for example, is constantly asked questions about where destinations are and how they may best be reached. They are asked about the weather at destinations, and such questions as 'Where exactly is Alton

Towers?', 'Does it get too hot in Turkey in August?', or 'What is the best way of getting from Newcastle to the west coast of Scotland?'

If the travel agency counter clerk is unable even to find Turkey on a map of the world or the Tourist Information Centre assistant is unable to tell west from north, south, or east, then they lack the necessary knowledge and skills to do their jobs properly.

The same knowledge of the geography of tourism helps students of tourism to understand how that industry has developed as it has in different parts of the world, and helps consumers of tourism to plan holidays successfully and to appreciate important characteristics of their destinations.

Britain's inbound and outbound tourism

Ports and airports

Tourists entering or leaving Britain must use one of its many ports or airports. These are known as **points of entry** and **points of departure**, depending on whether inbound or outbound tourism is being discussed.

Figure 2.1 shows the main ferry routes leading to and from Britain's ports. In addition to these, points of entry or departure also include Britain's airports, 17 of which currently have more than half a million passengers passing through them every year.

EXERCISE _____

1 List the British ports that are important for connections with Scandinavian countries.

2 Where do most visitors come from when they arrive in Britain at ports on:
- the south coast of England?
- the coast of Wales?
- the south west coast of Scotland?
- the coast of East Anglia (Felixstowe and Harwich)?

3 Give four examples of British ports with four or more ferry routes leading to and from them.

4 Give one example of a British port which is a point of entry and departure for travel to and from another continent.

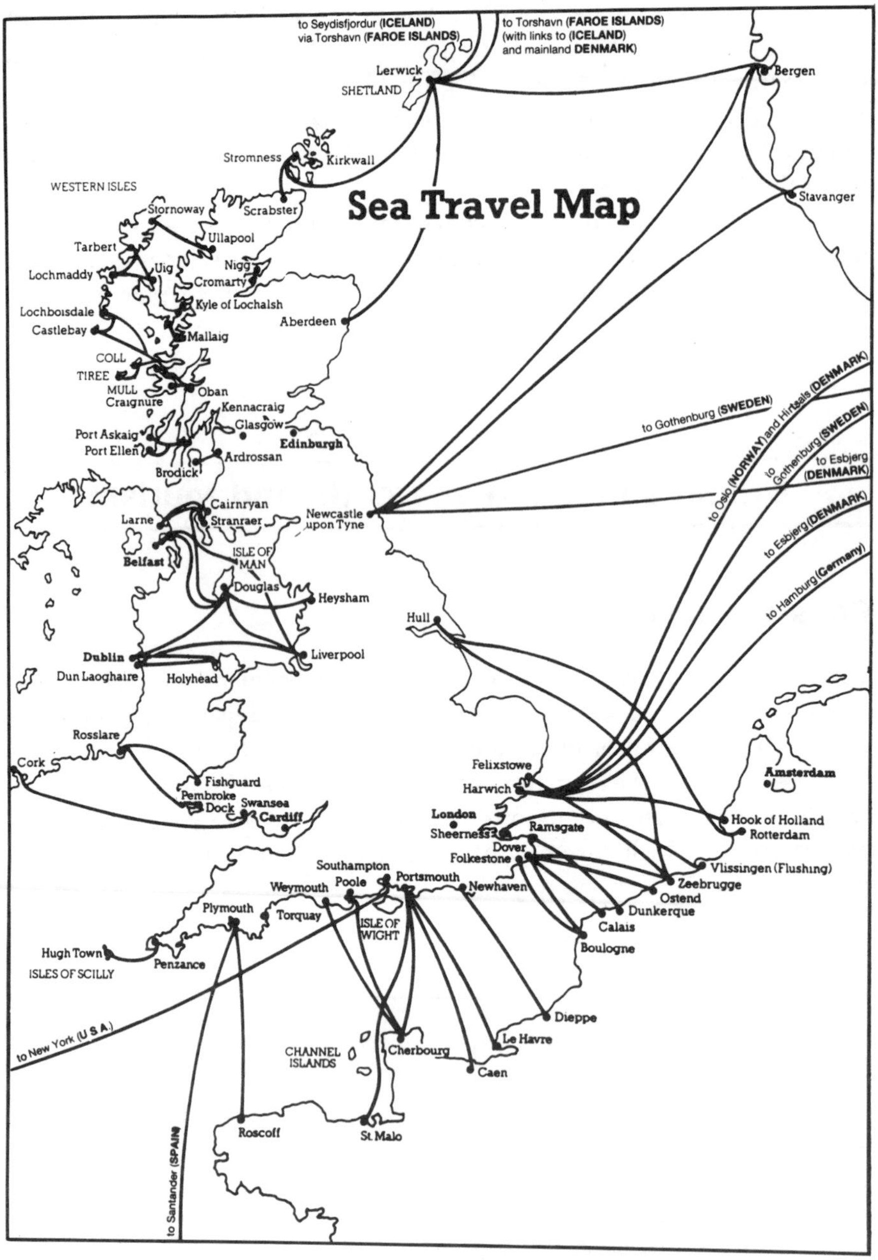

Fig. 2.1 Ports of entry and departure in Britain

Destinations of British outbound tourists

A knowledge of the locations of the most common destinations of outbound British tourists is essential for many of the people employed in the tourism industry. People working in travel agencies, for example, need to have a good idea of where places are located, before they are able to give customers some idea of what the weather will be like and how long it will take to get there.

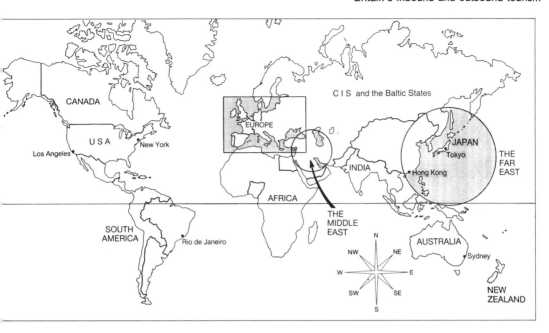

g. 2.2 *Overseas*
estinations of British
urists

Figure 2.2 shows the main overseas destinations of British tourists. Some of these are leisure destinations and some are major centres for business tourism. As so many British outbound tourists travel to Europe, the European section has been enlarged to show more detail.

EXERCISE _____

1 Use the maps in Fig. 2.2 to name:

(a) The country lying due west of Spain;

(b) An important business centre on the east coast of the USA;

(c) An island lying to the north of Sardinia;

(d) A popular country for tourism located immediately west of Turkey;

(e) A Commonwealth country situated south east of Australia.

Country of destination	Arrivals of British	% change over previous year	Market share: % of total arrivals in destination countries
Austria	786 300	− 15.9	4.1
France	7 177 000	− 2.3	12.9
Germany	1 303 110	− 14.6	9.1
Greece	1 674 875	1.7	20.8
Ireland	2 355 000(1)	− 1.7	64.3
Italy	1 711 634	− 16.4	3.3
Netherlands	832 300	0.5	14.2
Portugal	1 100 000	3.7	12.5
Spain	6 144 813	− 2.3	17.4
Switzerland	536 230	− 11.3	7.2

Fig. 2.3 Top 10 destinations of British tourists in Europe in 1991

Source: World Tourism Organisation

2 Figure 2.3 shows the figures for the most popular European destinations of outbound British tourists. Using the scale on the European map, draw up a table indicating the approximate distance of the capital city of each destination from London, in kilometres.

Time zones

An American business person who has just arrived by air at Heathrow Airport may want to go straight to bed on arrival at their London hotel, even though it is 9 o'clock in the morning . This is one effect of travelling from one time zone to another. Because the earth spins around the sun, it is day on the side facing the sun and night on the opposite side of the earth at any one time. For this reason, the earth has been divided into 24 time zones, the time in each zone differing by one hour plus or minus the neighbouring time zones. Figure 2.4 shows a diagram of the world divided into time zones with the number of hours difference between Greenwich (London) and the rest of the world.

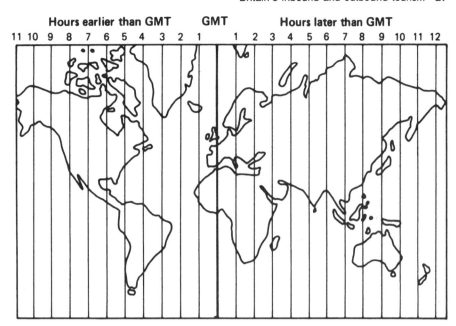

Hours earlier than GMT   **GMT**   **Hours later than GMT**

11 10 9 8 7 6 5 4 3 2 1   1 2 3 4 5 6 7 8 9 10 11 12

Fig. 2.4 World time
zones

The +10 at the head of the time zone which passes through the east coast of Australia means that the time there is always 10 hours ahead of British time: and the −5 at the head of the time zone in which New York lies means that New York time is 5 hours behind the time in Britain.

Moving quickly across several time zones at once can cause tourists to suffer from what is known as 'jet lag'. Changing time zones, by flying from one to another in a short period of time can have the effect of desynchronising the body's natural systems, leading to symptoms of exhaustion in the tourist. The body gets confused because its natural 'internal clock' is saying one thing (such as 'time to eat' or 'time to sleep') while the clocks at the destination are saying something quite different. This is why tourists arriving by air from long distances away often feel tired on arrival and may take several days to recover fully from the effect of the rapid change in time zones.

EXERCISE

1 Explain how a flight from Amsterdam to London can take off at 10am and land at Gatwick Airport at 10am.

2 At what time does someone working in an office in Paris have to telephone in order to speak to someone who starts working in a New York office at 9am?

3 A tourist has breakfast in an airport on the east coast of the USA and then takes a flight to the west coast. Explain why he is ready for lunch on arrival at his destination, while everyone else is having breakfast.

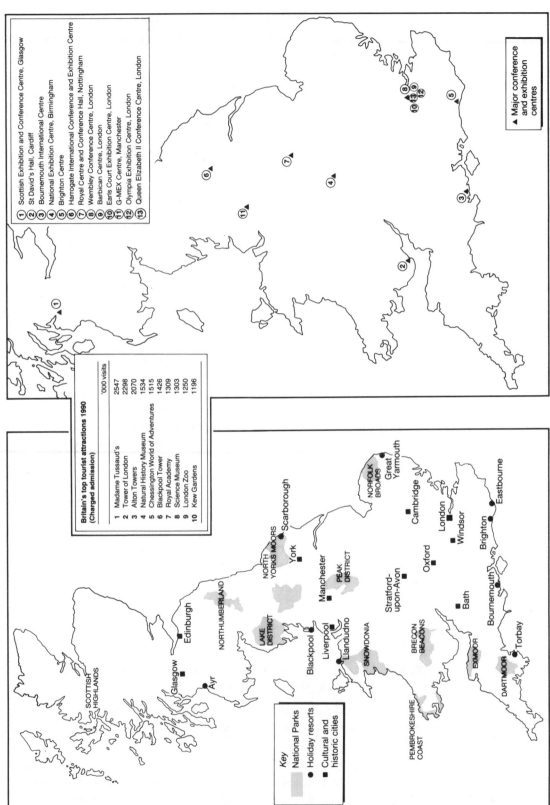

Major conference and exhibition centres

1. Scottish Exhibition and Conference Centre, Glasgow
2. St David's Hall, Cardiff
3. Bournemouth International Centre
4. National Exhibition Centre, Birmingham
5. Brighton Centre
6. Harrogate International Conference and Exhibition Centre
7. Royal Centre and Conference Hall, Nottingham
8. Wembley Conference Centre, London
9. Barbican Centre, London
10. Earls Court Exhibition Centre, London
11. G-MEX Centre, Manchester
12. Olympia Exhibition Centre, London
13. Queen Elizabeth II Conference Centre, London

Britain's top tourist attractions 1990 (Charged admission)

		'000 visits
1	Madame Tussaud's	2547
2	Tower of London	2298
3	Alton Towers	2070
4	Natural History Museum	1534
5	Chessington World of Adventures	1515
6	Blackpool Tower	1426
7	Royal Academy	1309
8	Science Museum	1303
9	London Zoo	1250
10	Kew Gardens	1196

Key
- National Parks
- ● Holiday resorts
- ■ Cultural and historic cities

Fig. 2.5 Britain's features and attractions

4 Explain why someone flying from London to Lagos in West Africa would not suffer from jet lag.

Tourist destinations in Britain

Tourist destinations in Britain are of five main types:
1 A holiday resort or holiday region;
2 A cultural or historic town or city;
3 A natural feature, such as a special part of the countryside;
4 A major tourist attraction such as a zoo;
5 A business facility such as a major conference centre.

Figure 2.5 shows the following features:

● Britain's top 10 tourist attractions where there is an admission charge, for 1990;
● The National Parks of England and Wales – the most beautiful, spectacular and dramatic expanses of countryside which have been set aside for recreation and conservation;
● Britain's principal exhibition and conference centres;
● Britain's major holiday resorts and cultural and historic centres;
● Britain's major cities.

EXERCISE

1 Name the following:
(a) A national park due north of Birmingham.
(b) Two south coast holiday towns, each with a major business facility.
(c) A historic town with a famous cathedral close to the North Yorkshire Moors National Park.
(d) A major holiday resort on the north west coast of England.
(e) A conference and exhibition centre to the west of a historic Scottish city.

2 Describe the locations of the following in relation to their nearest National Parks, using the points of the compass. The first example is done for you:
(a) Bath: a historic town situated north east of Exmoor National Park.
(b) Manchester G-Mex Centre;
(c) Stratford-upon-Avon;
(d) Torbay;
(e) Harrogate.

3 Find out the location of each of the top 10 tourist attractions and plot them on the map of Britain.

4 According to the maps in Fig. 2.5, which of each of the following is the nearest to your home town?
- a major business facility;
- National Park;
- historic or cultural town;
- major tourist attraction.

Route planning in Britain

Planning how to get from one's home to a tourist destination, is something which most people have to do at some time, either for themselves or, if they are employed in the tourism industry, for someone else. Route planning is a useful geographical skill, requiring not only a good idea of where places are but the ability to use a variety of techniques.

The mileage and kilometrage chart in Fig. 2.6 shows, in kilometres and

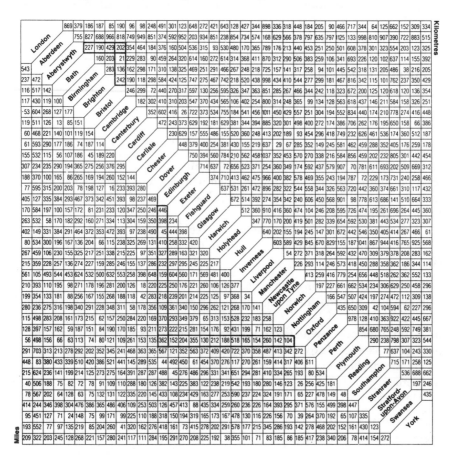

Fig. 2.6 Mileage/kilometrage chart

miles, the distances between major towns and cities in Britain. This is a useful way of presenting such information, and the chart is simple to use. For example, the number of kilometres between Aberystwyth and Bristol, which is 202, is the figure in the box in which the horizontal row leading from the Aberystwyth box meets the vertical column leading from the Bristol box. Below the diagonal line of name boxes, the distances are given in miles, and the example of the number of miles between Edinburgh and Oxford is shown.

EXERCISE

1 Use the chart in Fig. 2.6 to find out:
(*a*) How many miles there are between Aberystwyth and Bristol.
(*b* The distance in kilometres between London and Cambridge.
(*c*) Which city is nearer to Inverness – Edinburgh or Glasgow?

Mileage and kilometrage charts are useful in the initial stages of route planning, because they provide an indication of the distances between places. However, people planning routes need more information and must be familiar with the **transport networks** which enable them to travel to their destinations. This may include finding out whether it is easier and faster to travel from Perth to Inverness by road or by rail.

The main networks which enable inbound and domestic tourists to travel around Britain include road, rail and air.

Road and rail

Figures 2.7 and 2.8 show the two most commonly used networks for travelling around Britain for business or leisure.

Figure 2.7 shows the principal **trunk roads** and **motorways**. Britain has approximately 3000 kilometres of motorways and 12 000 of trunk roads. Although the motorways have been built primarily for the movement of freight (manufactured goods, and raw materials), they are also important for the movement of tourists by public and private transport, for both leisure and business.

Journeys by motorway are easier and faster than by trunk roads and minor roads because they are planned for efficiency and enable drivers to travel at higher speeds. Motorways do not pass through towns, and there are no traffic lights, crossroads or roundabouts to stop the traffic. Although Birmingham and Portsmouth are both approximately the same distance from Bristol, the journey from Bristol to Birmingham will be far easier and quicker than the journey to Portsmouth because of the M5 motorway.

Britain's **rail** network, shown in Fig. 2.8, is made up of approximately

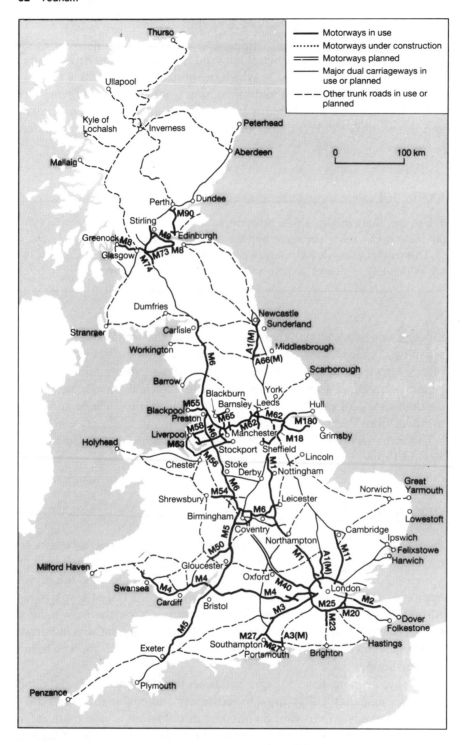

Fig. 2.7 Trunk roads and motorways in Britain

17 000 kilometres of track, most of it covering the InterCity routes which link major towns and cities. Although some trains on InterCity routes reach speeds of 200km/h, the average speed on these routes is closer to 140km/h.

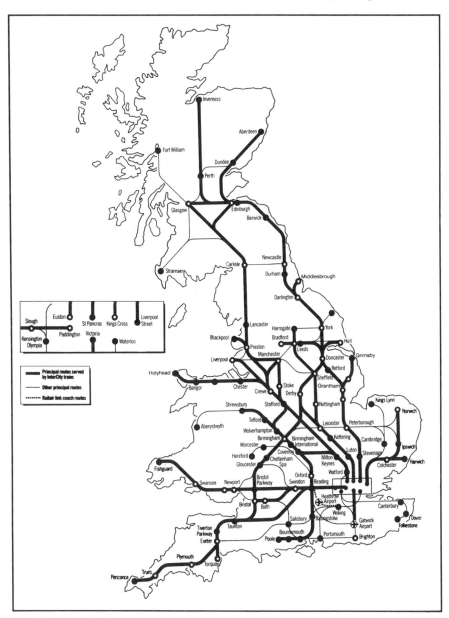

Fig. 2.8 InterCity routes in Britain

On other rail routes, the trains do not reach such high speeds because they stop at more stations.

EXERCISE _____

1 (a) Use the map shown in Fig. 2.7, find out the names of the following motorways:
- the motorway connecting London and Swansea;
- the motorway connecting Nottingham and London;
- the motorway which encircles London;

- the motorway connecting Carlisle and Birmingham.

(*b*) Use the same map to locate the following motorways, and write down the names of the two main towns or cities which each motorway connects:

- the M8;
- the M20;
- the M5.

2 Which of the following pairs of journeys would be easier and faster by road? In each case, both journeys given are of approximate equal distance.

(*a*) Exeter to Gloucester, or Exeter to Southampton?
(*b*) Cambridge to Northampton, or Cambridge to London?
(*c*) Edinburgh to Greenock, or Edinburgh to Dumfries?
(*d*) Leicester to Leeds, or Leicester to Norwich?

3 Name the following:
(*a*) the InterCity station immediately north of York;
(*b*) the London station for travel to Harwich;
(*c*) the London station for travel to the east coast of Scotland;
(*d*) the station furthest west on the south coast of Wales line;
(*e*) the most northerly InterCity station in Britain;
(*f*) the London station for travel to the south west point of England.

4 Explain why a tourist might prefer to travel from Newcastle to Aberdeen by train than by road.

5 Would you recommend to a family wishing to travel from Oxford to Folkestone to travel by car or by train? Give reasons for your answer.

Domestic air routes

Many of our busy airports are important for travel *within* Britain as well as travel out of and into Britain. **Domestic flights** follow routes which are particularly important to people travelling for business purposes, as business tourists are their main customers.

EXERCISE

1 Find out which are the two most frequently used air routes in Britain? Why do you think this is?

2 Which of the important business tourism centres shown in Fig. 2.5 have airports which are used for domestic air routes?

Scenic routes and tourist routes

While people travelling for business purposes usually want to reach their destinations as quickly as possible, leisure tourists often prefer to enjoy the trip by travelling through attractive scenery and stopping off to visit places of interest along the way. For this reason they often prefer to follow scenic routes or tourist routes rather than simply taking the most direct and fastest route. Tourist Information Centre staff are often asked to direct tourists from one place to another along the most attractive and interesting routes.

The map in Fig. 2.9 shows the many ways of travelling by road from Edinburgh to Glasgow.

A businesswoman who has just arrived at Edinburgh Airport and wishes to travel to the Scottish Exhibition and Conference Centre in Glasgow may simply hire a car at the airport and drive along the M8 to her destination. However, a family on a driving tour of Scotland may prefer to travel the same journey by a more leisurely route, avoiding the motorway and stopping at places of interest along the way. In this case, they may drive north west along the A90 to Hopetoun House, an attractive historic house with a fine view over the Firth of Forth, and then continue along the same road to Linlithgow where they might have lunch and spend some time exploring Linlithgow Palace. From there, they may spend the rest of the day travelling south west through the small towns of central Scotland, to arrive in Glasgow by the early evening.

EXERCISE _____

Find a map of the area between and including Bristol and Swindon. Plan two routes from Bristol to Swindon: one for a manufacturer travelling to Swindon for a business meeting, and the other for an American family who are on holiday in Britain and have hired a car. The American family

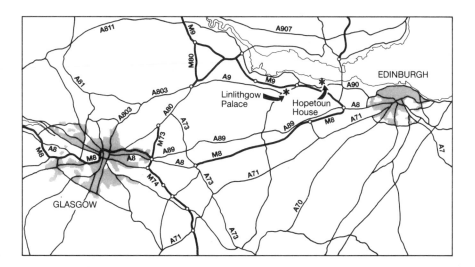

g. 2.9 Routes
etween Edinburgh
nd Glasgow

has all day to complete the journey, but the manufacturer wants to reach Swindon as quickly as possible. Describe both routes as fully as possible, with directions and details of the roads taken, and any stops made along the way.

Weather and tourism

The weather is almost always one of the main factors in leisure tourists' choice of a particular destination. It is also an important reason for making tourists decide to leave their own countries in search of overseas destinations which they hope will have the weather they are seeking. Very few holiday postcards fail to mention the weather which the writer is experiencing away from home.

Holiday brochures and advertisements for particular destinations can give the impression that skies are permanently blue, the sun shines continuously, or the snow is white and crisp all over the world. No one takes photographs for a holiday brochure on a rainy day.

However, there are few places in the world where the weather is perfect for tourism every week of the year. Even exotic destinations such as the Caribbean, Mexico and Asia suffer each year from rain and hurricanes unlike anything experienced in Britain. The sunshine and heat, sought after by so many tourists, can also make places such as Egypt and the tropics unbearable for most visitors at certain times of the year.

The people who produce the package holidays which are sold in glossy brochures and travel agency staff who sell these to the customer must be well aware of the weather at destinations and how this varies from month to month. No one wants to spend 14 wet days in Costa Rica during their rainy season, and many elderly people and babies would find some countries in the Mediterranean too hot during July and August. Similarly, anyone leaving Britain to spend a July or August holiday in Australia should be told that they are heading for the cool, unsettled, weather of an Australian winter.

Weather in Britain

Because of Britain's location, it has a temperate climate, meaning that the weather displays no extremes of heat or cold. Nevertheless, different parts of Britain experience different kinds of weather: the climate of Torbay is quite different from that of Aberdeen, for example. Such varying patterns of weather over Britain have had an impact on leisure tourism development in Britain, and account for the higher concentration of tourism in some areas than others.

Weather variations in Britain can be seen in three aspects: levels of sunshine, levels of temperature, and levels of rainfall.

Sunshine is something which most tourists hope to see while they are on holiday or on a day trip.

Figure 2.10 shows the highest and lowest duration of bright sunshine recorded in each month during the period 1890–1970.

	Jan	Feb	Mar	Apr	May	Jun	Jul	Aug	Sept	Oct	Nov	Dec
Highest (hrs)	115	167	253	302	353	382	384	325	281	207	145	117
	1959	1891	1929	1893	1909	1929	1911	1899	1959	1920	1923	1962
	Bournemouth	Jersey	Aberystwyth	Westbourne	Worthing	Pendennis Castle	Hastings	Guernsey	Jersey	Felixstowe	Falmouth	Eastbourne
	(Hampshire)	(CI)	(Dyfed)	(W Sussex)	(W Sussex)	(Cornwall)	(E Sussex)	(CI)	(CI)	(Suffolk)	(Cornwall)	(E Sussex)
Lowest (hrs)	3.6	4.3	25.0	35.9	59.6	60.9	50.1	43.9	34.3	8.0	4.9	0.0*
	1901	1966	1916	1920	1967	1912	1961	1912	1967	1968	1942	1890
	Morpeth	Gt Dun Fell	Whitworth Park	Whitworth Park	Gt Dun Fell	Crathes	Strathy	Eskdalemuir	Baltasound	Gt Dun Fell	Burnage	London
	(Northumberland)	(Cumbria)	(Manchester)	(Manchester)	(Cumbria)	(Grampian)	(Sutherland)	(Dumfries)	(Zetland)	(Cumbria)	(Manchester)	

*0 at Westminster, 0.1 at Bunhill Row, 0.3 at Kew Observatory

Fig. 2.10 *Extremes of monthly duration of bright sunshine*

Crown copyright. Reproduced by kind permission of HMSO

EXERCISE

1 In which area of Britain are the towns which hold the record for having the highest number of hours of bright sunshine?

2 In which quarter (January to March, April to June, July to September, or October to December) are there the greatest *differences* between the highest and lowest number of bright sunshine hours, and in which quarter are there the least differences?

Temperature is another important consideration for people choosing where to go on holiday. In summer, tourists like to be warm, and in winter, skiers need low temperatures to prevent the snow from melting.

Temperatures will vary, even over as small an island as Britain, changing by four degrees centigrade on average from the north to south coasts. Yet, while the temperature of the north of Scotland may discourage swimmers in August, the cold and longer winters there make the region ideal for winter sports.

The combination of more than a hundred days a year of temperatures less than zero degrees centigrade and high mountains, makes the Cairngorms and Grampians regions natural destinations for those who wish to ski without travelling overseas.

Nevertheless, too much **rain** can spoil a holiday or a day out, however attractive the destination, so most tourists are drawn to places where they hope to avoid the rain if they can. Britain, as an island, has a wet side and a dry side, as shown in Fig. 2.11.

The winds approaching Britain from the sea bring clouds with them. When the clouds come into contact with the mountains, the clouds are lifted up, causing them to drop their rain on to the land below.

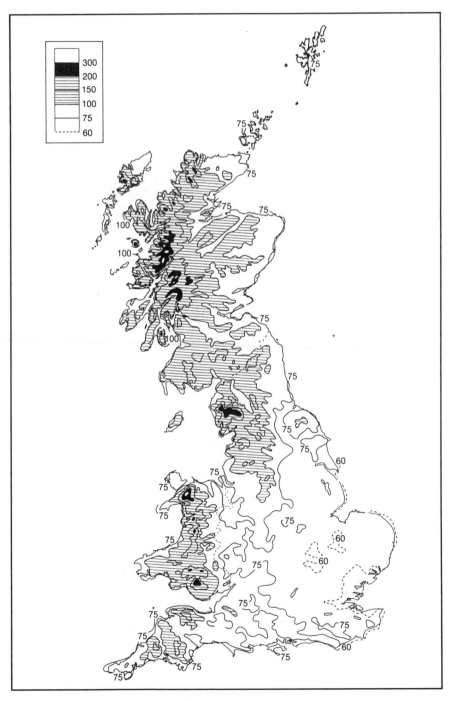

Fig. 2.11 Average rainfall in millimetres for August, 1941–19

Crown copyright. Reproduc by kind permission of HMS

EXERCISE _____

1 From Fig. 2.11, which is the wet side and which is the dry side of Britain?

2 What does this tell us about the direction from which most of the winds come to Britain?

3 Which resort is more likely to experience rain in August:
• Blackpool or Bridlington?
• Ayr or Berwick-upon-Tweed?

4 Give two reasons why Aviemore winter sports centre is located in the Cairngorms.

5 On which coast of Britain would you expect to find the greatest number of successful holiday resorts? Give reasons for your answer.

ASSIGNMENT

A walking tour of your town
Draw a simple street map of your town, a town you know well, or part of the city in which you live. Mark on it places of interest to the day visitor: for example, special buildings, sports or leisure facilities, parks, museums, and art galleries.

Write down instructions for a one-hour walking tour, giving street names, directions of travel, and details of the places of interest to be taken in on the walk.

CASE STUDY

A tour around Northern Ireland

Figure 2.12 gives details of the many places to visit in Northern Ireland.

Using a road atlas, plan a seven-day driving tour of Northern Ireland, beginning and ending in Newry, and travelling around the province in an anti-clockwise direction.

The tour should include six overnight stays in: Newcastle, Newtownards, Belfast, Rathlin Island, Portrush and Enniskillen.

Write out instructions for the tour, giving the numbers of the roads to be taken, the approximate direction of travel, the approximate distances, and (selected from Fig. 2.12) the attractions to be visited along the way.

Places to Visit

Giant's Causeway

One of the world's most celebrated natural phenomena, the Causeway consists of 40,000 many-sided stone columns. A circular walk from the visitor centre passes magnificent rock formations. Gold and silver treasure from the Armada ship *Girona,* recovered here after 400 years under the sea, is on display in the Ulster Museum.

Dunluce Castle

Romantic ruins of a MacDonnell stronghold on a north Antrim crag. Defenders could escape by boat through a huge cave underneath.

Rathlin Island

A hundred hardy people live on Rathlin, six miles from Ballycastle harbour. (Boat trip lasts 50 minutes).

Londonderry, Tyrone & the Sperrins

Derry's Walls

Walk on the massive 17th-century walls, a mile round and 18ft thick, which withstood a siege lasting 105 days.

Ulster-American Folk Park

Preserves Ulster's links with pioneer America, including the actual cottage where Thomas Mellon, founder of the Pittsburgh House of Mellon, was born (1813).

Beaghmore Stone Circles

Seven mysterious Bronze Age ceremonial stone circles and cairns.

Tyrone Crystal, Dungannon

See the blowing and cutting stages of fine glass manufacture (1 hour tours).

Fermanagh Lakes & Clogher Valley

Devenish Island

An abbey and perfect 12th-century round tower on Lower Lough Erne. Other islands with Celtic and early Christian remains in same area. Boats from Enniskillen.

Castle Coole

Neo-classical mansion with Palladian features built 1795 for the Earl of Belmore. Splendid interior, furniture (Nat. Trust).

Enniskillen Keep

The 16th-century castle keep houses two interesting museums – Fermanagh county museum and the museum of the valiant Inniskilling Fusiliers.

Florence Court House

Seat of the Earls of Enniskillen, the house has sumptuous rococo plasterwork (Nat. Trust). In the garden is the progenitor of the famous fastigiate yew tree.

Belleek China

Visit the picturesque pottery to see craftsmen at work on collectors' items.

Ulysses S. Grant Ancestral Home

Restored homestead of the 18th US president's ancestors.

Newry & Armagh area

Newry Museum

Learn something of the historic 'Gap of the North' region of Ulster.

Navan Fort

Capital of the kings of Ulster from 600 BC, stronghold of the Red Branch Knights.

Armagh County Museum

One of Ireland's finest small museums, outstanding library and art gallery.

The Mournes & St Patrick's Country

Annalong Corn Mill

Fully functioning water-powered mill on picturesque site between harbour and river.

Silent Valley

Two artificial lakes in the high Mournes supplying Belfast's water. The reservoir is surrounded by a huge dry stone wall 22 miles long. Mountain viewpoints.

St Patrick's Grave, Downpatrick

The patron saint of Ireland was buried on Cathedral Hill in 461 AD. His grave is a place of pilgrimage on St Patrick's Day (17 March). Heritage centre and museum nearby.

Butterfly House, Seaforde

Tropical landscape with insects and reptiles from four continents.

Castle Ward

Half-classical half-gothic mansion on shore of Strangford Lough, built by the first Lord Bangor in 1765 (Nat. Trust).

Around Lough Neagh

Shane's Castle Railway & Nature Reserve

Narrow-gauge steam railway running through lakeside woods.

Ardboe Cross

Richly carved 10th-century high cross, 18ft high, on the west shore of Lough Neagh (largest lake in the British Isles).

Belfast area and Ards Peninsula

Ulster Folk & Transport Museum

Farmhouses, watermills, a whole small village with shops, terraced houses, school and a parish church, brought from their sites in the Ulster countryside and rebuilt stone by stone in a natural landscape.

Mount Stewart House & Gardens

The National Trust rates its gardens here among the top six in the UK.

Northern Ireland Aquarium

Over 70 species of marine life found in Strangford Lough.

Ulster Museum, Palm House & Tropical Ravine

All in Belfast's botanic gardens. The Palm House (begun 1839) is very early example of a curvilinear glass and cast-iron conservatory.

Belfast Zoo

Mountain zoo with magnificent view over city and lough.

Fig. 2.12 *Places to visit in Northern Ireland*

Courtesy: Northern Ireland Tourist Board

3

TRANSPORT

After reading this chapter, you should have a clear understanding of:
- the importance of transport as part of the tourism industry,
- the different forms of transport used by tourists,
- the difference between carriers and individual travel vehicles,
- the importance of transport networks to tourism.

Forms of transport

As tourism involves people moving out of their normal places of residence, transport is clearly an important factor in tourism. Without transport, travel – except by walking – would be impossible; and there can be no tourism without travel of some kind. Transport is one of the sectors of the tourism industry. It is important to tourism in three different ways:

1 Transport provides the means of **travel to the destination** from the tourist's place of origin, and back again. A flight in an aircraft from Manchester Airport to Canada would be an example of this. Such use of transport is found at the beginning and end of a holiday or business trip only.

2 Transport provides the means of **travelling around the destination**, once tourists have arrived and wish to explore. It includes, for example, a trip in a London bus, from Madame Tussauds' to the Tower of London and is often the kind of transport used by residents living and working at the destination, as well as by tourists. This use of transport is found during the tourist's stay at a destination.

3 Transport can be a **main feature** of a tourist trip when the form of transport itself is one of the main reasons for taking the trip. An example of this would be a Caribbean cruise on an ocean-going cruise ship. The ship is a main feature of the holiday, providing accommodation, food, and entertainment, as well as the means of travel for the tourists. This use of transport is found throughout the holiday – beginning, middle, and end. In some cases, the tourists may never leave the chosen form of transport.

EXERCISE _____

Look through the specific examples below (i–ix) of different uses of transport. For each example, answer the following questions:

(*a*) At which stage or stages of the holiday does the use of transport take place:
- at the beginning and end of the holiday only?
- during the stay at the destination only?
- throughout the holiday?

(*b*) Is the use of transport used by residents at the destination as well as by tourists?

From your answers to (*a*) and (*b*) above, divide the examples into the following three categories:
- transport to and from the destination only
- transport at the destination only
- transport as a main feature.

(i) A ferry crossing from Harwich to the Hook of Holland and back again.

(ii) The Paris Metro.

(iii) A canal barge hired for a week on the Norfolk Broads.

(iv) A steam locomotive restored and running on a private railway line, for train enthusiasts.

(v) A cruise ship sailing around the Mediterranean.

(vi) A flight between Sydney and Singapore and back two weeks later.

(vii) A taxi ride in Rome.

(viii) A hired car driven from home in New York to Washington DC and back.

(ix) A bus journey in Morecambe.

When looking at travel it is useful to think in terms of three different forms of transport: **Land**, **water** and **air**.

Each form of transport has an important place in this sector of the tourism industry.

Land transport

Land transport includes travel by train, by car, and by bus and coach.

It was the advent of the **train and railways** which brought travel for pleasure within the reach of the majority of ordinary working people in the developed world, starting with Britain in the 19th century. When the first commercial railway was opened in Britain in 1830, passengers using it could hardly have imagined how countries all over the world would, one day, have their own railway systems for the transportation of goods and people. Today, with the phenomenal rise in tourism all over the world, trains play an important part in moving people between and within countries. Trains are particularly used for domestic tourism – leisure and business. They are a quick and convenient way of travelling between cities, and in Britain, for example, 36% of all rail travel is for business-related purposes. The majority of people travelling first class on British Rail's trains are people who are travelling around the country on business. Often, their fares have been paid for by their companies or the organisations in which they are employed, not by the passengers themselves. Most trains offer passengers a choice of services and facilities: sleeping accommodation, restaurant cars serving snacks and meals, bars, and even telephones. Most train services offer different classes of travel, varying according to the price paid for the ticket. British Rail has first and standard classes, while some countries have three or more classes of travel on their trains. In India it is even possible to book an entire private carriage in a train.

The most popular era for travel by train throughout the world was the first half of the 20th century. Since the 1950s, many countries, including Britain, have cut back on the frequency of their train services and have closed down some lines. At the same time, advances in technology have made it possible for trains to travel at speeds of 400km/h in some countries. The Deutschebundesbahn, for example, the German railway company, has developed a train called the ICE (Inter-City Experimental), which has already cut the journey time from Hamburg to Munich from 7 hours to 5 hours 30 minutes.

The increase in private ownership of the **motor car** was part of the reason for the decline of the railway system in many countries. Today, the car is the most popular means of transport by far for tourists. In the USA, journeys by car account for 85% of all holiday travel, and although the total cost of travel by car per kilometre works out at more than the equivalent for the train, most people are attracted to the flexibility and convenience of this mode of transport. People using their cars for holidays can use them for travelling to, and around, their destination.

Car hire is also popular, particularly among those people travelling for business purposes. It is often possible to hire a car at one location and return it to an office of the same car hire company at another location. Tourists travelling to their destinations by air can hire a car at the airport and use it to travel to their destination or to explore during their stay. Hiring a car in this way as a pre-paid part of the holiday package is known as a fly-drive holiday.

Taxis provide another important service to leisure and business tourists. Many of the customers of taxi companies in cities are visitors, who use taxis as a fast and convenient way of moving around unfamiliar streets.

Although not popular for business tourism, **coaches** represent a relatively cheap form of transport to and around tourist destinations. In countries where the terrain makes the construction of railways impossible, coaches are the main way of travelling around. Greece and Turkey, for example, depend heavily on coach services for the movement of international tourists as well as their own residents. In the USA, almost 400 million coach trips

a year are made between cities using companies such as the world-famous Greyhound Lines.

Fig. 3.1 A British coach service

In Britain, the rise in ownership of private cars has contributed to the decline of coach services since the peak of their popularity in the 1930s. However, as with trains, coaches are now more luxurious and faster and are capable of providing a wider range of services than ever before. Express services run between most of Britain's cities, and passengers can watch videos, make telephone calls, and be served with a snack by a steward or stewardess, as they travel.

Local **bus** services, too, are used by visitors to a town or city. In London for example, about 20% of all passengers on the famous red London buses are tourists.

EXERCISE

Which form of land transport – taxi, coach, private car, or train – is most likely to be used by the following business and leisure tourists?

(*a*) The Robinsons and their three children want to get to a country village about 30km from their own home.

*g. 3.2 A selection of
ndon transport
~vices*

(b) A businessman who has just arrived by train at Waterloo station has to
get to a meeting about 3km away.

(c) A student on holiday in Crete wishes to travel the 50km from the north
to the south coast of the Island, across the mountains.

(d) Two business colleagues have to travel from Paris to Lyon (370km) and
back in the same day. They want to prepare their papers for the
meeting as they travel.

Water transport

Reaching a destination by **sailing** has been an important method of transport
since the first primitive boat was built. For those living on islands, such as
Britain, travel by sea crossing was, until this century, the only available form
of international transport. For some countries, travel using rivers and canals
has also been important.

Since the early 19th century, tourists have been regularly crossing the
English Channel between Britain and France. Now, Britain is linked by
regular **ferry services** to all European countries with North Sea coasts and
with Ireland. These ferry services are usually used by passengers in
combination with some form of land transport, for example, coach, train

or car, which carries them to the ferry ports from their places of origin, and on to their final destination after the sea crossing. An alternative form of transport now available for short sea crossings is the **hovercraft** which strictly speaking is not a sailing vessel but a flying craft which uses compressed air to hover above the waves. Travel across the English Channel by hovercraft is faster than by ferry, taking approximately only 35 minutes, but hovercraft services are often cancelled when sea conditions are rough or stormy. Like ferries, however, they are capable of transporting cars as well as passengers.

Countries composed of many islands, such as Greece, rely heavily on vast fleets of ferry boats to carry passengers between islands. For Greeks, travel by ferry is a common experience in the same way that travelling between cities by bus or train is for a British person. For international visitors to Greece the journey can be an exciting and memorable experience, and an important part of the holiday, including the opportunity to sunbathe on the deck and watch picturesque islands appear on the horizon.

For tourists on ocean-going **cruise ships**, it is the ship that is the main feature of the holiday. The cruise ship is not only important as a means of getting from one place to another, but also comprises the tourists' accommodation and the source of their meals and entertainment. The tourists may disembark at various points along the route to explore the ports at which the ship calls, but they always return to the ship to spend the night.

Not all cruises last as long as the estimated seventy days it takes to cruise the world. There are many shorter and less expensive trips which can be made using this form of transport. Cruises around the countries of the Mediterranean Sea, or the Caribbean, or along the River Nile provide a variety of destinations and scenery for the passengers, each taking different lengths of time. Ocean-going cruise ships are possibly the most luxurious form of transport, costing many hundreds of millions of pounds to build. An example is the *Queen Elizabeth II* owned by Cunard and one of the world's largest and most luxurious passenger ships (longer than three football pitches). It is described in the brochure as follows:

For years, the *Queen Elizabeth II* has been internationally acclaimed as the world's most prestigious ocean liner. She is beautiful beyond words. She is as comfortable as the most elegant deluxe hotel. And she cruises like a dream.

Each of her four dining rooms carries a coveted five-star rating. Her 900 suites and state rooms are without peer. Her four pools, health club, bars, nightclubs, lounges, and theatre rival the finest resorts. Her service, with more than one crew member for every two guests is outstanding. And with nearly 40 000 sq feet of deck open to the sea, QE2 is truly a destination unto herself, as she cruises to some of the world's most exciting ports of call.

For some she is a once in a lifetime experience. For others she has become a holiday addiction to be enjoyed one or more times a year.

Between ports of call, travellers on the *QE2* can use the putting green, the gymnasium, health club or the four swimming pools. They can learn computing, go shopping in the arcade, or simply relax on deck. In the evenings, they can choose from seven different bars, the theatre, the casino or the disco. The lavish accommodation comes in 23 different categories, ranging from luxurious suites to 'inside' (no sea view) two-berth cabins. More people in the richer, developed countries are trying this form of holiday. Cruises are particularly popular with Americans, but Europeans are increasingly getting used to this form of tourism.

For those who like the idea of a holiday afloat, but who cannot afford the luxury of an ocean liner, river and canal cruising is a more modestly-priced alternative.

Many countries, including Britain have a system of rivers and canals, or **inland waterways**, along which tourists travel at a leisurely pace on various types of boats. Although the boats are not as huge and luxurious as the *QE2*, cruising holidays on inland waterways are based on the same idea of moving from place to place in a floating home, and disembarking to explore a village or town.

The canals of Britain have their own style of boats, narrowboats, which are long and narrow, and often painted in bright colours. Figure 3.3 shows a narrow boat in action. Cabin cruisers, shorter and wider boats, are more often found on rivers. Inland waterway boats of these types usually come equipped with all the comforts of home and are capable of carrying up to 12 people. Some of the larger narrow boats are called hotel boats because they come with a crew who do all the work – cooking, cleaning, washing up, and steering the boat – leaving the passengers free to relax and enjoy the trip.

The boats used for canal or river travel are usually rented by the week and can be handled by people who have no previous experience of sailing. The most popular cruising areas of Britain are the Norfolk Broads, central England and Wales, the River Thames, the Caledonian Canal, and the Rivers Ouse, Cam and Nene in Cambridgeshire. These are shown in Fig. 3.4.

EXERCISE

1 Cruise ships have been called 'floating resorts'. Explain the reason for this name.

2 What is the main advantage of crossing the sea by hovercraft rather than by sea ferry? V·hat is the main disadvantage?

Air transport

The invention of travel by **air** had the greatest impact on tourism. The possibility of rapid travel in comfort over long distances opened up

Fig. 3.3 A narrowboat on the river

Courtesy: UK Waterway Holidays Limited

previously remote and inaccessible destinations to those travelling for business and pleasure. With the invention of the jet-propelled engine during World War II, air transport entered the 'jet age'. For the first time, passengers were able to cross a country as large as the USA in five hours from coast to coast. Faster and bigger jet planes were built, including the famous Jumbo Jet, the Boeing 747, capable of carrying almost 500 passengers while travelling at speeds of over 1000km/h. The Jumbo Jet is still the major long-distance plane, and the majority of aircraft in our skies are jet-propelled.

Jet aircraft are called 'subsonic' because they fly at less than the speed of sound. On 2 March 1969, a new supersonic aircraft, flying faster than the speed of sound, took off from Toulouse airport in France. This was a prototype of the famous Concorde, whose distinctive shape is instantly

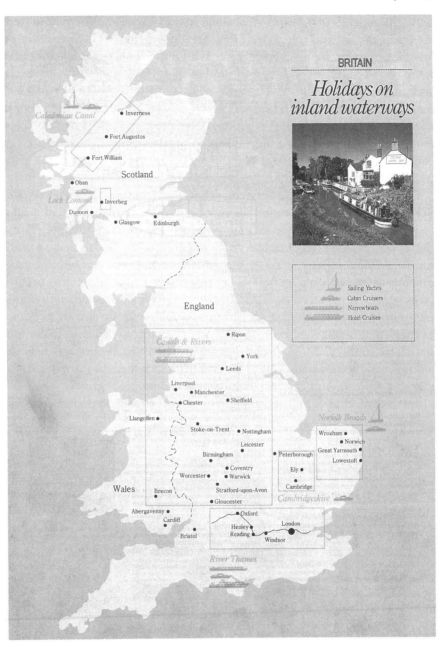

BRITAIN

*Holidays on
inland waterways*

Caledonian Canal

● Inverness

● Fort Augustus

● Fort William

Scotland

● Oban

Loch Lomond

● Inverbeg

Dunoon ●

● Glasgow   Edinburgh

England

Sailing Yachts
Cabin Cruisers
Narrowboats
Hotel Cruises

Canals & Rivers

● Ripon

● York

● Leeds

Liverpool
●
● Manchester
● Chester   ● Sheffield

Llangollen ●

Stoke-on-Trent   ● Nottingham

Leicester

Birmingham   ● Peterborough

Norfolk Broads

Wroxham ●
● Norwich
Great Yarmouth ●
Lowestoft ●

● Coventry

Ely ●

Worcester ●   ● Warwick

Wales   Brecon

Stratford-upon-Avon

● Gloucester

Cambridge

Cambridgeshire

Abergavenny ●

Cardiff

● Oxford

London

Henley ●
Reading
Windsor

Bristol

River Thames

g. 3.4 Holidays on
and waterways

recognisable from the ground as it roars overhead. Capable of travelling at twice the speed of sound, Concorde takes only three hours to fly the 5850km between London and New York, which is only slightly longer than the time taken to travel from London to Newcastle by train. However, even the lowest fare for a journey between London and New York on Concorde, means that supersonic air travel is still a luxury for a small fraction of travellers. Both British Airways and Air France have seven Concordes to carry the very wealthy, and business travellers.

In the early days of air transport, all travel by this means was for the rich only. After the Second World War, when many new airline companies were set up in Britain and other countries, they competed with each other by lowering their fares and air travel came within the spending power of many more people. Despite widespread doubts that 'these aircraft' really could stay 'in the sky', by the 1970s many people in the developed world had had their first taste of air travel and airline meals. For many British people their first flight was to Spain on holiday. Cheaper air travel opened up Spain and other parts of the Mediterranean to tourists from Britain and other countries of northern Europe. Without such affordable air travel, the great package holiday boom of the 1960s and 1970s could not have taken place.

There are two types of air services: **scheduled flights** and **charter flights**. Scheduled flights are so-called because they operate regularly, according to published 'schedules' or timetables which are fixed in advance. These flights operate whether or not there are enough passengers to make a profit for the airline company, in much the same way that local bus services must operate as stated on the timetable, regardless of whether one or fifty passengers wish to travel on a particular route. Airlines operating scheduled flights, for example from Aberdeen to Amsterdam, must fly aircraft according to their own timetables, even if only one passenger wishes to make that particular journey. Most airlines offering scheduled flights are national airlines, taking their names from the countries in which they are based; for example, British Airways, Air France, and Singapore Airlines.

By contrast, charter flights companies operate more like private coach hire

Fig. 3.5 A British Airways aircraft

companies. For example, in the same way that a youth club can hire or 'charter' a private coach for a special occasion, charter flight companies operate by offering aircraft flights to and from destinations for particular purposes, for example to carry holidaymakers from Birmingham to Barcelona and back. The main people who charter such flights are the holiday companies who sell package holidays and need charter flights to provide the transport for their customers. In other words, charter flights only operate when they have been hired for a particular specific purpose – usually to transport holidaymakers. For this reason, there are many more charter flights out of Britain and back in the summer than in the winter. Most charter flights are to holiday destinations such as the Mediterranean and the cost of a charter flight is usually less than the cost of a scheduled flight to the same destination because charter flights have fewer empty places on them than scheduled flights. If a charter company cannot sell enough seats on a particular flight, it can either cancel the flight or combine those passengers with passengers on another flight to the same destination.

Most advertisements for airline companies on television and in newspapers are for scheduled airline companies. This is because charter flights are booked by the travel companies who then sell the seats on the flight to the public as part of a holiday package. The public, however, buys seats directly from the scheduled airline companies. It is these companies, therefore, that compete by advertising directly to the public, claiming that their flights are cheaper, faster, or offer better facilities such as meals, wider seats, more leg room or free drinks.

EXERCISE

1 Why was there a great growth in the number of charter flights in Europe in the 1960s and 1970s? What effect did this have on tourism in Spain?

2 The vast majority of business travellers use scheduled flights, when flying to their destinations. Explain why this is.

3 Why are most charter flights international flights, rather than domestic flights?

Carriers

In tourism, the companies which own and operate the various forms of transport are known as **carriers**, because they carry passengers. Many have already been mentioned in this chapter, such as British Rail, Air France, Cunard and Greyhound Lines. It is important not to confuse the carriers with the names of individual aircraft, ships or trains, such as Concorde.

EXERCISE _____

1 Divide the names from the following list into those which are carriers and those which are names of individual craft or vehicles:

- Deutschebundesbahn;
- British Airways;
- The Boeing 747;
- The Flying Scotsman;
- Hoverspeed;
- London Regional Transport;
- United Airlines;
- The QE2.

2 Name as many different carriers as you can for each of the following forms of transport:

- coaches;
- aircraft;
- ferry boats.

Transport networks

As well as the many vehicles, vessels, and craft which transport tourists by land, water and air, **transport networks** are important for tourism too. Transport networks are the land, water and air routes along which the various forms of transport travel, as well as the bus and rail stations, ports and airports which passengers need at the beginning and end of their journeys. No country, or region within a country, can hope to receive tourists in large numbers unless it has excellent transport networks. Airport runways must be long enough for the jets to be able to land and take off, and the airport buildings must be spacious enough for the passengers to check in and wait comfortably for their flights; docks must be deep to accommodate cruise ships; and above all, the roads into and around a destination must be capable of carrying the great volume of traffic created by tourism. Coaches need wide, fast roads to be able to transport holidaymakers quickly from airports to their hotels. Tourists driving to their destination need good roads, clear signposting, and they need to be able to find a car park easily when they arrive.

Although passengers may not be aware of it, ships and aircraft travel along carefully specified routes too, and do not simply sail or fly at random between two places. Ships follow shipping lanes and aircraft fly along airways or air corridors and rules are carefully laid down to keep ships and aircraft within these 'invisible' paths, in order to prevent collision. Travel by air often makes the news after a collision or near-collision, and many of the problems of lengthy delays and long waits in airports for tourists at the height of the holiday season each year are created by overcrowding in the sky. The airways over Europe in particular, have become so overcrowded that, for safety's sake, aircraft must wait until a space in their air corridor becomes available to them. The main problem is to be found at busy holiday airports such as Barcelona in Spain, where only a few minutes separate the landings of aircraft from all over Europe. Britain's Heathrow airport is among the busiest in the world. Its peak period is during July and August each year, when a flight either takes off or lands every two minutes of the day, on average. In 1990, approximately 40 000 passengers used Heathrow airport – about 40% of passengers of all Britain's airports.

Roads, railways, inland waterways, shipping lanes and airways form the transport networks which help determine how many visitors can reach a destination and travel around it. The bus and rail stations and ports and airports which travellers use at the beginning and end of their journeys are known as **termini** (singular – terminus), from the Latin word for 'end'. Conditions and facilities at the termini of a destination are important in determining how many tourists can pass through them and at what speed. The frequency of public transport services to a destination is also an important factor, whether it is reached by bus, train, aircraft or ferry.

The Director of the West Country Tourist Board which is responsible for the promotion and development of tourism in Devon, Cornwall, Somerset, Avon, Wiltshire, Western Dorset and the Isles of Scilly, describes the transport network of that region as follows:

Efficient transportation systems and good signposting are imperative to the success of the tourism industry, which is worth £1.5 billion to the economy of the West Country. The West Country is fairly well-served by road, rail, sea and air, but there is still no room for complacency. We still need the A30 to be made up to dual-carriageway standard all the way to Penzance. While the 10 and 12 mile traffic jams of the 1960s and 1970s are a thing of the past, there are still a number of bottle-necks in our road network: the approach to Torbay, the Tamar Bridge, Okehampton (now bypassed after some considerable delay) and the approaches to Newquay, Falmouth, Minehead, etc.

An international airport capable of handling Jumbo Jets with regular transatlantic flights is a dream which will eventually come to fruition. But the main obstacle to that at present is the lack of a large centre of population, which could be overcome by greatly improved communication within the region and to other major centres of population. The rail service is patchy at best, west of Exeter.

EXERCISE

Look at a map of the West Country to locate the major routes in the area.

CASE STUDY

The island of Mallorca – transport networks

Mallorca, or Majorca as it is sometimes spelt, is well known as a centre for sunny, enjoyable holidays, and has been popular with vast numbers of tourists since the 1960s. Mallorca is the largest of the Balearic Islands, which belong to Spain and are situated in the Mediterranean Sea, approximately 150km off the east coast of mainland Spain.

The following map of Mallorca shows the main transport network of routes to and around the island.

Mallorca's airport in Palma is one of Europe's busiest, with frequent flights all year round from northern European cities and from Spain itself. It is situated close to Mallorca's capital, Palma, and connected by motorway and dual carriageway to the largest and liveliest resorts, such as Magaluf, Palma Nova and El Arenal.

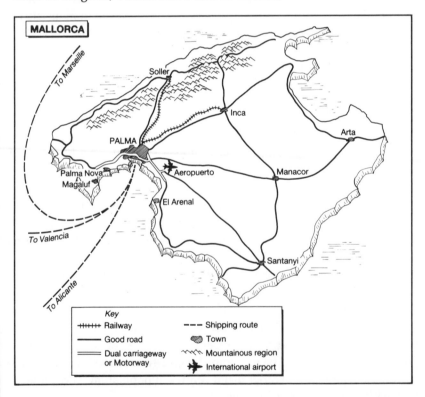

Fig. 3.6 Mallorca

Most of the island's roads are in very good condition, and many have been resurfaced in recent years. The island has excellent coach services to approximately forty of the main inland and coastal towns on the island, and car rental is good value, and plentiful.

As well as by road, the mountainous region in the north may be reached by two train lines branching out of Palma. Public transport of all kinds is cheap, by northern European standards.

Palma is a major Mediterranean port. Car ferries to the island operate from Marseilles and from Alicante, Valencia and Barcelona on the Spanish mainland. Package tourists usually restrict their travelling while on the island to organised sightseeing excursions, arranged by their tour operators. Tourists who have made their own way to the island and their own accommodation arrangements are more likely to travel around and to use public transport.

TASKS

1 From the map of Mallorca, find out where the motorways and dual carriageways are located and explain the reason for their location.

2 Describe the transport network and forms of transport which might be used by the following tourists. Suggest their mode of transport to the island as well as around it.

(*a*) The Dupont family who live near Marseilles wish to spend two weeks touring around the island.

(*b*) Roberto, a Spanish student living in Madrid, wishes to visit Mallorca for a month to do some hill walking and some sunbathing.

(*c*) Señor Fernandez, a businessman from Alicante, wishes to travel to the town of Inca to discuss the purchase of some leather goods for sale in his chain of souvenir shops.

(*d*) Mr and Mrs Jansen from Amsterdam want a two-week package holiday on Mallorca in a large, lively resort. They have heard that Palma Cathedral is worth seeing too.

CASE STUDY

High-speed trains and the Channel Tunnel

A major transport trend of the 1990s will be the development of a high-speed railway network in Europe, capable of carrying trains at speeds of up to 400km/h.

Fourteen different countries in Europe are currently planning high-speed rail systems linking their major cities, and to link up to each other across national borders.

This network will lead to major reductions in train journey times. The first such high-speed train, TGV (Train à Grande Vitesse) between Paris and Lyon has already been built, halving the journey time to two hours, using trains travelling at 270km/h. Since its completion in 1983, 16 million passengers per year have travelled on the TGV. Germany is also constructing two fast railway lines to connect Mannheim with Stuttgart and Hannover with Wurzburg, using trains travelling at 400km/h.

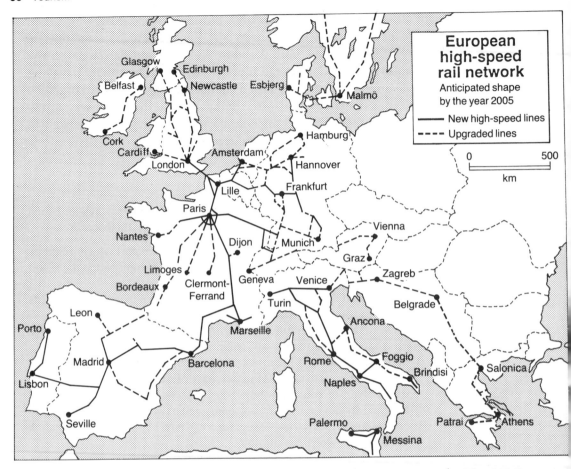

Fig. 3.7 European high-speed rail network

Source: Community of European Railways

Figure 3.7 shows the European high speed train network that is anticipated for the year 2005.

Britain's link to this network will be the Channel Tunnel, which will connect British Rail with the French railway company, SNCF (Société Nationale des Chemins de Fer). By completion of the Channel Tunnel in 1993, a TGV line will connect Paris to the Tunnel via the city of Lille in the north of France. This will enable passengers to travel between London and Paris in three hours.

Shown in Fig. 3.8 is an extract from a leaflet called 'British Rail and the Channel Link'

TASKS

1 Name a form of transport which will face increased competition from the new high-speed railway network in Europe.

2 In terms of termini, what advantage do train services have over travel by air?

3 In addition to train passengers, the Channel Tunnel will carry cars and coaches. What consequences will this have for road networks in Britain and France?

PASSENGER SERVICES

At present 3.1 million rail passengers use the Channel ferry services each year. At least 12 million people a year will use international trains through the tunnel after it opens in 1993. Ten years later that traffic could reach 21 million passengers.

The ease of international access to all regions is expected to treble tourist journeys.

The French government gave consent in 1987 for a new high speed (300 km/h) line between Paris, Lille and the tunnel, which will make the rail link between the French capital and London even more attractive. The Belgian government is studying a similar link between Brussels and the Franco-Belgian frontier near Lille.

Day trains will run hourly between London and Paris and Brussels. They will bring the centre of Paris within three hours' ride of the Waterloo terminal. The journey to Brussels will be even shorter, about 2 hours 45 minutes.

In addition, the possibility of a range of through services to and from the Midlands, north of England and Scotland to serve Paris and Brussels is being examined, as are trains from London to the further reaches of western Europe.

Night trains: a range of night passenger trains is being considered, serving, for example, places in Germany, Switzerland and southern France from London, and Paris or Brussels from points beyond the UK capital.

Motorail services are also being considered between British and continental destinations.

PROPOSED JOURNEY TIMES TO PARIS IN 1993 (TIMES IN HOURS)
Times to Brussels around 15 mins less

South East	London – Waterloo	3 h
	– Kensington Olympia	3 h
	Ashford (Kent)	2 h
Scotland	Glasgow	9¼ h
	Edinburgh	8¾ h
North East	Newcastle	7 h
	Darlington	6½ h
Yorkshire & Humberside	York	6 h
	Leeds	6½ h
	Hull	* 6¾ h
	Sheffield	* 6½ h
	Doncaster	5¾ h
North West & North Wales	Carlisle	△ 8 h
	Preston	△ 6½ h
	Liverpool	6¼ h
	Holyhead	△ 8¼ h
	Manchester	6¼ h
	Crewe	5½ h
East Anglia	Peterborough	4¾ h
	Norwich	# 6¾ h
	Cambridge	⊡ 5¼ h
	Ipswich	** 5½ h
	Colchester	** 5¼ h
	Stevenage	4¼ h
East Midlands	Nottingham	▽ 6¼ h
	Leicester	▽ 5¾ h
West Midlands	Wolverhampton	5¾ h
	Birmingham	5¼ h
	Coventry	5 h
South Coast	Brighton	○ 3¾ h
	Southampton	◆ 4½ h
Mid & South Wales	Swansea	● 7½ h
	Cardiff	● 6½ h
South West	Bristol	● 6¼ h
	Exeter	● 7¼ h
	Plymouth	● 8¼ h

Change Peterborough or Liverpool Street/Waterloo #
Change Stevenage ⊡
Change Liverpool Street/Waterloo **
Change at Doncaster *
Change at Crewe △
Change at St. Pancras/Waterloo ▽
Change at Ashford Kent ○
Change at Waterloo ◆
Change at Paddington/Waterloo ●

COMPARISON WITH PRESENT FASTEST LONDON–PARIS

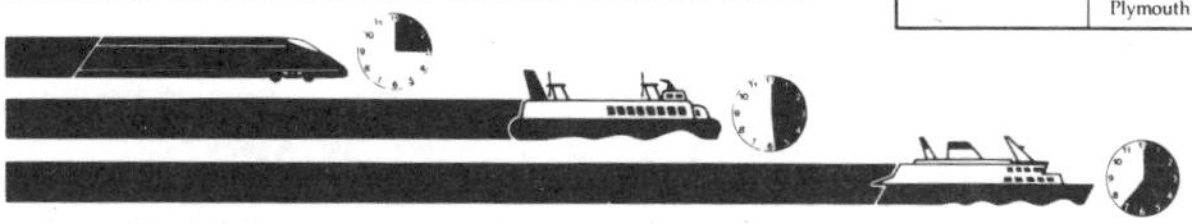

COMPARISON WITH PRESENT FASTEST LONDON–BRUSSELS

. 3.8 Rail travel
es

rtesy: British Rail

4 At present, the majority of passengers crossing the English Channel by ferry and hovercraft are doing so for leisure tourism purposes. From the Passenger Services detailed in Fig. 3.8, describe how British Rail might attract more people travelling for business purposes.

5 Using the information in Fig. 3.8, calculate how long it will take to travel from your home town to Paris by train after 1993.

ASSIGNMENT

Comparing different forms of transport.

Working in small groups agree on a city at a distance of, say, 200km from your own town. Give each person in the group a different form of transport to investigate, to find out the different ways of getting from your town to the city you have chosen: by rail, by air, by coach and by hired car, for example. Find out: the frequency of service (for public transport), the length of time the journey would take, and the total cost per km (maximum and minimum).

4

THE RETAIL
TRAVEL TRADE

After reading this chapter, you should have a clear understanding of:
- how the retail travel trade operates,
- the difference between travel agencies and tour operators,
- how travel and holidays are sold to the public,
- current issues and trends in travel and transport.

Travel agents and tour operators

This chapter looks at how travel is sold to the public and how travel is packaged in the form of package holidays.

The most visible part of the retail travel trade is the travel agency. This is the place the customer of the travel and tourism industry would normally think of visiting first, in order to buy travel tickets or holidays.

It is estimated that a total of 30 000 travel agencies exist around the world, with 70% of these in Europe, and 14% in North America.

Almost every high street in Britain has at least one **travel agency**. All year round, the displays in the travel agency windows tempt us with offers of sunny holidays in far away places, skiing trips in the Alps, or perhaps a long weekend at a country hotel in the Lake District. Most countries in the developed world have similar 'travel shops' in their towns and cities. Because travel agents (the people who run the travel agencies) sell travel to the public, they are said to be part of the retail travel trade. Travel agencies are, therefore, the shop window of the travel sector of the tourism industry, the places where customers go for advice and information, and to purchase travel.

There is, however, an important difference between travel agencies and other high street shops. To illustrate this, suppose that next door to the travel agency, there is a shoe shop. All the shoes in that shop have been already purchased by the shop owner at one price, and the shop owner hopes to sell them all at a higher price in order to make a profit. The shoes in the shop make up the shoeshop owner's *stock*. Until the shoes are sold, they remain on the shelves or in the stockroom. Travel agencies, by contrast, have no stock, because the travel agent does not buy the travel or holidays in advance. He or she only sells *on behalf of* the company which provides the travel or holidays for the customer.

For example, Mr and Mrs McKay wish to fly on a scheduled flight from Shannon Airport in Ireland to Toronto in Canada to visit their daughter and son-in-law. They go into their local travel agency in a suburb of Dublin. The travel agency counter clerk gives them advice on prices and different carriers, as well as the times of various flights. When the McKays have decided on a particular flight, the travel agency counter clerk uses a computer screen to call up the carrier (e.g., British Airways), and checks availability. If there are seats available, the clerk, using the computer terminal, books the two seats in the name of the McKays. The airline tickets are then written and presented to the McKays who pay and leave.

The travel agency had not already purchased the seats which the McKays bought. The unsold seats still belonged to the carrier until the McKays agreed to buy them. If another travel agency in Belfast had contacted the carrier by computerlink just before the Dublin travel agency, then British Airways would have sold the tickets through the Belfast travel agency.

But if travel agencies have no stock, how can they make a profit? The answer to this is that they make their living through **commission** so that the more they sell, the more commission they earn. Commission can vary, depending on the carrier paying it, but it is usually around 10%.

Therefore, if Mr and Mrs McKay paid £1000 for their tickets, the travel agency would be allowed to keep 10% of the total sum – £100 – for selling the tickets. The other £900 would be sent to British Airways.

The previous example used airline tickets as an illustration of how travel agencies work, but they also offer a number of other services including:

- coach, train, and airline tickets: domestic and international
- cruise trips
- package holidays and short break packages
- hotel rooms and other forms of accommodation
- travel insurance
- foreign currency and travellers cheques
- car hire

All these items earn the travel agent the commission which keeps the business running. In the case of airline, coach or rail tickets sold by a travel agency, it is clear that the company which pays the commission to the travel agent is the carrier. But a high proportion of travel agents' income comes through selling the **package holidays** which are advertised in the bright glossy brochures which catch the customer's eye as soon as they walk into a travel agency. An important role of the travel agent is to advise customers on a wide range of matters relating to travel. This can be very time-consuming, but it is worth the time if the customer eventually makes a booking.

For example, Mr and Mrs Smart pay a visit to their local travel agency.

All they know is that they want a winter holiday somewhere warm, and that they have £1200 maximum to spend. They will need advice from their travel agent on:

- the best place to go
- the best time to go
- what their hotel is like
- how far it is from the beach
- what there is to do in the way of entertainment and sightseeing
- whether or not they will need to have special injections to protect them against illness

A good travel agent will be able to answer these questions professionally, using his or her own experience and the information available in brochures. No travel agency counter clerk can be expected to know every single destination in the world, but they can build up their own knowledge of destinations and carriers through reading, and through what are called **familiarisation trips**.

A familiarisation trip is a trip, usually for a few days, organised specially for travel agency staff. For example, a group of travel agents may be invited by the owner of a hotel in York to spend one or two evenings there, sampling the accommodation and learning about the facilities on offer. The hotelkeeper hopes that the travel agents will be impressed, and will remember the hotel and recommend it to their customers. Such familiarisation trips are an important way in which the staff of travel agencies can update their knowledge of what they are selling.

Britain saw a huge increase in the number of travel agencies during the 1960s and 1970s, with the great growth in overseas tourism during those decades.

In Britain, travel agencies are situated mostly in high streets, but sometimes in large shops and department stores. Some are small, family businesses, with only one branch, while others are vast companies with many branches around the country. Pickfords, Hogg Robinson, Lunn Poly and Thomas Cook are names which can be seen in most high streets in Britain, while American Express, based in the USA, is the biggest foreign travel agency company with branches in Britain.

Some travel agencies make their living by selling travel only to businesses, rather than members of the general public. These are known as **business house agencies**. Any large company or organisation will have business travel needs: the manager of an insurance company, for example, may wish to fly from London to Paris for a meeting; the following week some of her colleagues may need rail tickets to take them to a conference in Manchester; the week after that, one of her sales staff may need to hire a car for a few days. To save her and her staff from making all of these travel arrangements on their own, she may decide to use a local business house agency to buy all the tickets on her behalf, and advise her and her staff on travel insurance, foreign currency, and all the other items that are available from a travel agency. Staff of business house agencies often visit large companies to try to persuade the manager to make all their travel arrangements through their company.

Most travel agencies, however, sell both to companies and the general public.

To understand fully how travel and holidays are sold to the public, it is important to learn what lies behind the production of holiday brochures.

Package holidays are also known as package tours, because they include a whole holiday package: transport to the destination; food and accommodation at the destination; the services of a guide or a holiday 'rep' to help with any problems and advise on excursions or sightseeing tours. Most holidays advertised in holiday brochures contain all these elements in one package. The people who put together these elements are called **tour operators**.

The names which appear on the front of the holiday brochures are usually (but not always) the names of the tour operators who have planned the holidays featured and had the brochures printed.

In Europe, Britain, Germany and the Scandinavian countries in particular are where some of the continent's biggest and most powerful tour operators are to be found. Many of these are household names in their own countries and abroad. In Britain, the tour operating scene is dominated by the mighty Thomson, which sold over three million package holidays between March 1991 and March 1992. Its nearest rival, Owners Abroad, sold just over half that number, while in third place, Airtours sold about 800 000. Between them, these three tour operators controlled over half the British market for package holidays in 1991. Similarly, in Germany, the two leading tour operators, TUI (Touristik Union International) and NUR (Neckermann und Reisen) are responsible for over half the sales of package holidays in that country.

However, not all tour operators resemble these giant businesses, catering for the mass market. A vast number of small, specialist tour operators exist in many countries, providing packages for those seeking destinations slightly off the beaten track or some special interest holiday, for example. An example of a small British tour operator would be Cycling for Softies, who specialise in organising cycling tours in France. Although they may only sell 3000–4000 such holidays a year, they have been very successful in attracting a loyal clientele, who appreciate their product and the personal touch which often comes from dealing with a small company.

How do tour operators construct a new holiday product, for sale to the public?

The following example is typical of the way in which tour operators work. After carrying out his market research, a tour operator decides to expand the package holidays it offers in its brochure by adding a new destination, the Greek island of Skiathos. A representative from the company travels to Skiathos on a fact-finding mission and discovers that a new hotel is being built on a pleasant location close to both the beach and the main town on the island. He discusses the plans for the hotel with the owner and is satisfied that it will provide suitable facilities such as a swimming pool and rooms with balconies. He then finds a local coach operator and discusses the journey from Skiathos Airport to the hotel in terms of how long it would take and how much the coach operator would charge. While on the island, he also looks around to see whether there is enough for tourists to do in the evening, and sufficient sightseeing and possible excursions for the daytime. If he is satisfied, he will book a number of hotel bedrooms from the hotelkeeper for the summer season two years from then – the first year his company will offer this new destination in its brochure. The following year, he returns to Skiathos to finalise arrangements with the hotelkeeper, the coach operator, and to arrange sightseeing tours and to ensure that the hotel building is to be completed in time. On returning to his company, he reserves the necessary number of seats on charter flights throughout the following summer season, and agrees a certain price for the entire package. The package is then included in the tour operator's brochure for the following summer's holidays.

From this it can be seen that the role of the tour operator is to plan and put together all the elements of the package holiday and to produce attractive brochures containing details of these holidays, with prices. Because tour operators reserve hotel rooms and aircraft seats in advance and in bulk, they are able to get them more cheaply than a member of the public who only wants one or two seats and one hotel bedroom for two weeks. Tour operators reserve blocks of seats and accommodation for whole seasons at a time, so they can often negotiate with the carrier or hotelkeeper for discounts.

The main problem for tour operators begins at the next stage. After the brochures have been printed, they must get them to the general public in order to sell the holidays advertised in the brochures. This takes us back to the role of travel agents, as discussed earlier in the chapter.

Sometimes, a company can fulfil the roles of both travel agency and tour operator. Thomas Cook, for example, organise package holidays as well as running travel agencies, but their travel agencies sell a whole range of travel and holidays, not only Thomas Cook's own packages.

Tour operators need to plan one or two years ahead, to ensure that all elements of a holiday are packaged and the brochures printed in time. This means that they have to estimate the number of customers they are likely to attract a year or two later. This can be very difficult and often, tour operators over-estimate this number with the result that more holidays are offered than there are customers wishing to take them. When this happens, the tour operators have no choice but to cut the prices from those appearing in the brochures. This is good news for last-minute holiday seekers, but bad news for the tour operators (and for travel agents, who earn less commission).

Price-cutting is less common in the brochures of the more specialist tour operators. If customers have set their hearts on travelling to a holiday in

Iceland, for example, they will probably pay the brochure price, as long as this seems reasonable. Also, they will not have the wide choice of tour operators competing and trying to undercut each others' prices, as is the case for the more popular destinations.

A problem exists, however, when a tour operator goes out of business after the customers have paid for holidays or when customers are overseas on holiday. In the early days of package holidays, there were several cases of British tourists who became trapped overseas because their tour operator went out of business and was unable to pay the carrier to bring them back. In Britain, to protect the public against this, a special emergency fund was set up by **ABTA**, the Association of British Travel Agents. Travel agents and tour operators who are members of ABTA are now entitled to display the ABTA logo.

When a member of the public purchases a holiday through a travel agency showing this sign, they know that the tour operator whose holiday they have bought is also a member of ABTA, because ABTA travel agents only sell holidays organised by tour operators who are members of ABTA. This gives them a firm guarantee that should the travel agent or tour operator go out of business before customers go on holiday, or while they are overseas, the special emergency fund (created from travel agents' and tour operators' subscriptions to ABTA) is used to refund their money, or to bring them back to Britain at the end of their holiday.

Similarly, travel agents who wish to earn commission from sales of international airline tickets must obtain a licence from **IATA**, the International Air Transport Association. As commission from international airline tickets is important to travel agents, it is important to gain IATA approval. Similar arrangements exist for travel agents all over the world who can only sell and earn commission on carriers' and tour operators' products if they have been approved to do so.

In Britain, there are about 2000 non-ABTA travel agencies. Some of these are known as **bucket shops**, where the public can buy cheap, last minute flights which the airlines have been unable to sell and which they sell through the bucket shops at a greatly-reduced price. Airlines would rather make some money on a seat for a flight than nothing at all, and bucket shops are a convenient way of selling these at low prices, if they have not already been sold at the standard price.

g. 4.1 The ABTA
ɔo

Some tour operators choose to sell directly to the public, bypassing the travel agent altogether. The main advantage of this to the tour operator is that it cuts out the agent's commission, and so the tour operator gets 100% of the brochure price of the holiday. This can mean cheaper holidays for the public too, if the tour operator passes on some of the savings on commission, to its customers. These tour operators are known as **direct sellers** and operate in several ways. This may involve buying lists of names and addresses and sending their brochures out by post to households who, they think, may be potential customers. This is known as direct mail but can be expensive, and so is most often used by smaller, more specialist tour operators. For example, a tour operator offering sailing holidays could send their brochures out to members of sailing clubs, and expect that enough people would be interested to make this worthwhile. More often, direct sellers simply advertise in magazines and newspapers and invite readers to write in or telephone, for the brochure. The Scandinavian tour operators Vingressor and Tjaerborg are examples of direct sellers who operate successfully in Britain. Some direct sellers have high street shops where the public can call in to buy their holidays. These may look like travel agents but they only sell the products of one tour operator – themselves.

ASSIGNMENT

The Mediterranean island of Menorca, off the coast of Spain, offers excellent opportunities for bird-watching, with a wide variety of species, some extremely rare.

A Scottish tour operator with a personal interest in ornithology (bird-watching) decides to organise a number of two-week specialist bird-watching package holidays to Menorca. These will take place in springtime when the greatest number of birds are to be seen. The package will include the return seat on a charter flight between Glasgow and Menorca, hotel accommodation, and coach excursions to the best spots on the island for bird-watching.

The tour operator decides to sell these holidays using the direct sell method. In order to carry out a direct mail shot to his potential customers, he obtains a list of the names and addresses of 4000 members of Scottish ornithological clubs.

The cost of sending out a brochure to each member will be £1, including the postage, the brochure itself and the cost of paying someone to stuff and label the envelopes. Direct mail has, on average, a successful return rate of 2%; i.e. for every 100 letters sent out, two people book a holiday.

1 How much will the mail shot cost?

2 How many holidays is the tour operator likely to sell?

3 How much will have to be added to the cost of each holiday to pay for the cost of the direct mailshot?

CASE STUDY

Time Off Ltd – tour operator

Time Off is a small but successful company based in London. It has been operating for 25 years, specialising in short breaks to European cities. Time Off destinations include Paris, Amsterdam, the Hague, Geneva, Brussels, and Zurich. In 1992, Istanbul and New York were added to their list.

Time Off short breaks are very flexible. In addition to a wide range of destinations, tourists can choose which type of transport they wish to use to get there, how long they wish to stay there (minimum of two nights), and which grade of hotel they want, from very simple to luxury standard. This tour operator does not book large numbers of seats on transport or hotel rooms, in advance but instead arranges each individual holiday at the time of booking, using scheduled services and by contacting hotels to check the availability of rooms. The tour operator has a range of hotels in European cities which it uses, and the directors of the company check every hotel personally, to ensure that it is of a high enough standard for its customers. Transport is arranged using carriers who operate *scheduled* services.

Time Off use between 60 and 70 hotels in Paris for short break holidays, according to demand. Figure 4.2 shows the prices per person in £ for accommodation in a 2-star Paris hotel during the high season 1/4/92–31/10/92. The Time Off City Selection brochure is shown in Fig. 4.3.

Method of transport	Number of nights			
	2	3	4	5
Travel on scheduled flights of Dan Air from Gatwick to Charles de Gaulle Airport. Daily departures.	176	203	235	262
Travel on selected British Airways flights from Gatwick to Charles de Gaulle Airport most days of the week.	167	194	220	247
Travel by scheduled flights of British Midland from Heathrow to Paris Charles de Gaulle Airport. Daily departures.	186	213	245	272
Travel by Citysprint coach and hovercraft from London to Paris. Daily departures.	117	144	178	205
Travel by Hoverspeed seacat and catamaran from London via Folkestone to Paris, Gare du Nord. Or travel by Sealink train and ship.	123	150	184	211

Fig 4.2 *Time Off prices per person (£) in Paris during the high season*

TIME OFF

CITY SELECTION

PARIS
AMSTERDAM
THE HAGUE
BRUSSELS
BRUGES
LUXEMBOURG
ROME
VENICE
FLORENCE
MADRID
LISBON
BARCELONA
GENEVA
LAUSANNE
ZURICH
LUCERNE
BERNE
VIENNA
PRAGUE
BUDAPEST
ISTANBUL
DUBLIN
CORK
NEW YORK

1992/93

Fig. 4.3 *Time Off brochure*

TASKS

1 Unlike large tour operators offering two-week holidays, on the Mediterranean for example, Time Off do not pre-book large numbers of hotel rooms or places with carriers. Explain the advantage to Time Off of this system of booking places only when customers book with them. Can you think of any disadvantages of the system?

2 From the table of prices, find out what is the cheapest method of transport for travel to Paris?

3 List the different carriers mentioned in the table.

4 List the different termini mentioned in the table.

5 Explain how some of Time Off's customers could find themselves travelling to Paris with business travellers on the same aircraft. Why does this not happen with most package holidays?

6 Looking at the top row of figures, calculate the cost of each additional night in the hotel. Using this figure, calculate the approximate cost of the transport element of each different method of travelling to Paris.

ASSIGNMENTS

1 Travel agency

In pairs, role play the following situation: A customer with £1000 to spend on a summer holiday for two comes into a travel agency for advice and ideas on where to go. The travel agent wants to make sure that the customer makes a firm booking before he or she leaves the shop, but the customer is very choosy about such details as having enough entertainment in the evenings and being in a lively atmosphere with other young tourists. Since the travel agent is about 50 years of age and the customer is aged 20, the latter is not at first convinced that the travel agent understands what is required on the holiday.

2 Travel agency

Ask the travel agent's permission before doing this project. In groups of a maximum of three, visit a local travel agency to investigate what is being advertised in the window. Make rough sketches of the window, highlighting the displays and any stickers on the window itself. Which countries are being advertised? Are there any special offers on sale? Is the travel agency an agent for British Rail or any other carrier? Is the travel agency a member of ABTA or any other association? Each group should make a presentation to the class on its findings.

3 Tour operators and carriers

Collect a variety of newspapers and magazines over several weeks. Divide them between the class, and working individually, cut out any travel or transport-related advertisements. Divide these into advertisements paid for by tour operators, by tourist promotion offices, and those paid for by carriers. Label each one according to the company or organisation whose advertisement it is, and use these to make a classroom display.

5

ACCOMMODATION AND CATERING

After reading this chapter, you should have a clear understanding of:
- the different forms of accommodation used by tourists,
- the different forms of catering used by tourists,
- the different jobs done by people working in accommodation and catering,
- current issues and trends in accommodation and catering.

Basic tourist requirements

'What was the hotel like?'
'What was the food like?'

These are often the first two questions asked by friends of people returning from their holidays, as a way of finding out whether the holiday went well.

When people are staying away from home, whether for leisure or on business, they need somewhere that provides all the comforts of home. They need a roof over their head – **accommodation**, and they need food and drink – **catering**.

The accommodation and catering which people have – on holiday, for example – are so important to them that if these two elements of the holiday are not satisfactory, the entire trip can be ruined.

The accommodation and catering sector of the tourism industry, therefore, is an important one. No country, and no region within a country, can expect to attract large numbers of tourists unless it has an adequate range of places providing accommodation and catering. Tourists, once they arrive at their destination, need to be able to find somewhere to stay and somewhere to eat and drink. The only exception to this is the day-tripper, who, while not requiring accommodation, may still need to buy food and drink.

The importance of the accommodation and catering sector to tourism is shown by the number of people it employs. Of the 1.5 million people working in the tourism industry in Britain, for example, over 1 million are employed in the accommodation and catering sector, making it by far the largest of the sectors. This applies to any country in which a tourism industry exists: most of the jobs created by tourism are in accommodation and catering. In addition, this is not only the largest sector of Britain's tourist industry, but also the fastest growing, in terms of new jobs.

Tourists, away from home, stay in a huge variety of places, not only in hotels. Figure 5.1 shows the different types of accommodation as defined by Eurostat, the statistical office of the European Communities.

---

1 **Hotels and similar establishments;** which comprise:
- *Hotels*, including hotels, motels, roadside inns, beach hotels, residence clubs and similar establishments providing hotel services.
- *Similar establishments*, including rooming and boarding houses, hostels, tourist residences and similar accommodation arranged in rooms and providing limited hotel services.

2 **Supplementary accommodation establishments,** divided into four groups:
- *Holiday dwellings*, including collective facilities under common management, such as apartment hotels and clusters of houses or bungalows arranged as dwelling-type accommodation and providing limited hotel services.
- *Tourist camping establishments*, including collective facilities – in enclosed areas – for tents, caravans, trailers and mobile homes and boating harbours. All come under common management and provide some hotel services.
- *Social tourism accommodation establishments*, including youth hostels, tourist dormitories, group accommodation, holiday homes for the elderly, holiday accommodation for employees and workers' hotels, halls of residence and school dormitories and other similar facilities which are generally subsidised, under common management and of social interest.
- *Other types*: health establishments, holiday work camps, accommodation in collective means of transport, etc.

3 **Private or special tourist accommodation,** which comprises:
- *Rented rooms in homes*; unlike boarding houses, here the tourist stays with the family that usually lives in the home and to whom he pays rent.
- *Homes rented from private individuals*; apartments, villas and houses rented or leased as entire units between households, on a temporary basis, as tourist accommodation.
- *Accommodation provided without charge by relatives or friends*; tourists allowed by relatives or friends to use all or part of their homes without charge.
- *Own dwellings*: apartments, villas, houses and chalets that are the visitors' second home and are used by them during their tourist trips.
- *Other private accommodation*; includes such accommodation as tents at non-organised sites and vessels at unofficial moorings.

---

*g. 5.1 Different
es of
commodation
rce:* Eurostat

Accommodation can be described as either **serviced** accommodation or **self-catering** accommodation, the difference being whether or not **meals** are included with the accommodation and whether or not **housekeeping** is included. Housekeeping means that guests' rooms are cleaned, beds made, and towels changed, for example. Accommodation which provides meals and housekeeping is known as serviced accommodation. The meals supplied by serviced accommodation can range from simply breakfast only to breakfast plus two main meals per day. Breakfast plus one main meal (lunch or dinner) is known as **half-board**, and breakfast plus two main meals is known as **full-board**. Without any meals or housekeeping, accommodation is known as self-catering, or unserviced. In self-catering accommodation, guests are responsible for getting their own meals, either by making them themselves or by going out to eat.

EXERCISE

Look back to Fig. 5.1 and divide the different forms of accommodation into (a) serviced and (b) self-catering. Are there any examples which could fit into *either* category?

Serviced accommodation

Hotels, and hotel facilities

Even people who have never been inside a hotel have gained some idea of what they look like from films, magazines, and TV programmes. Hotels may be generally defined as places which provide overnight, **furnished**, and **serviced** accommodation in return for payment.

'Furnished' means that the rooms contain the furniture and equipment essential to someone who wishes to spend the night in comfort – a bed, a wardrobe, a table and a chair being the basic minimum.

A wide variety of hotel establishments, even within one country provide 'serviced' accommodation, ranging from luxury to basic and from places with many hundreds of bedrooms to those with only six or seven. A small hotel, guest house or bed and breakfast may be run by only one or two people – often the owners, while larger hotels employ many hundreds of staff. For example, in the latter category, London's famous Dorchester Hotel on Park Lane, overlooking Hyde Park has a staff of 600. The standards of facilities provided by these forms of accommodation vary widely too. Depending on how much tourists wish to spend, most developed countries offer a range of establishments, from grand hotels which seem more like royal palaces to those providing only the most basic facilities.

Tourists need an easy way of knowing the standards of facilities they can expect in a hotel. For this reason, most countries operate a **classification scheme** which groups hotels into classes, according to the facilities they offer, so that the more facilities a hotel offers, the higher its class. In some countries,

. 5.2 *A well-
uipped hotel
droom*

it is *compulsory* for accommodation establishments to obtain such classification. This is often done in the form of an inspection by a representative from the country's Ministry of Tourism, who visits the hotel in question, and gives it a classification grading.

In Britain classification is *voluntary* – accommodation establishments can choose whether or not they wish to become classified. Several schemes exist to do this: the motoring organisations, the AA and the RAC, classify hotels and list them in their handbooks which are purchased by the public. The national Tourist Boards also operate classification schemes.

Figure 5.3 shows details of the classification scheme operated for serviced accommodation by the Scottish Tourist Board, whose classifications run from simply 'listed' to '5 crown'. In parallel to this classification system, establishments are graded according to the *quality* of the facilities and services on offer: from 'approved' to 'deluxe'.

Forms of accommodation which participate in a classification scheme are entitled to display the classification which they have been given on a badge or plaque on a wall near the entrance, and to use the classification in any of their advertising material.

Classification Criteria

Classification simply checks the *facilities* offered in accommodation – it gives no indication of their quality. Some of the requirements within each classification category are detailed below.

'Listed'

For this minimum classification, an establishment must firstly comply with all legal requirements, including fire regulations. In addition, other specific requirements such as general cleanliness, lighting, heating and ventilation will have been met. Further examples of items checked under this category include: bedding in sound condition, provision of clothes hanging and drawer space, hot water at all reasonable times and provision of breakfast.

Please note that all classifications above 'Listed' must also meet all the requirements of classifications below the classification actually advertised. For example, a three crown guest house will also include all facilities found within 'Listed', one and two crown classifications.

1 Crown

Additional items within this classification include: your own bedroom key, private washbasin, heating without extra charge and provision of a lounge area.

2 Crown

Facilities include hot beverages in the morning and evening, a television in the lounge or in bedrooms, assistance with luggage on request and an electric razor point in bedrooms.

3 Crown

The range of facilities continue to increase with, for example, private bath or shower and WC en suite in at least a third of all bedrooms, individually controlled fixed heating in bedrooms, hair dryer on request and the use of a public telephone.

4 Crown

Additional facilities include bedrooms with radio and colour television and telephone and at least three-quarters with a private bath or shower and WC en suite. You will find lounge service available to 2400 hours and will be able to request items such as toiletries, message taking, newspapers etc.

5 Crown

As well as having all the facilities in lower classifications, every bedroom will have a private bath with shower and WC en suite, direct dial telephone and trouser press (or valet service). The establishment will also offer room service of hot meals to 2400 hours, an all-night lounge service and the facility to call a night porter.

Fig. 5.3 The Scottish Tourist Board classification scheme

Courtesy: Scottish Tourist Board

Establishments calling themselves hotels, guest houses and bed and breakfasts, can be divided roughly into 'small' (10 rooms or less), 'medium-sized' (11–50 rooms) and 'large' (more than 50 rooms). In Britain, there are about 50 000 such establishments, of which approximately 40 000 belong to the small category of ten rooms or less. The majority of these are independent hotels, that is, run by the one or two owners, who usually live on the premises too. The landlord and landlady who offer seaside bed and breakfast would be a typical example of this. Large hotels, by contrast, only number about 1500 in Britain. The majority of these are operated by **hotel groups** rather than by owner-proprietors. A hotel group is a company which owns several hotels and Forte, Hilton International and Holiday Inn, for example are companies which own a number of different hotels and run them as a recognisable group or chain.

However, just because hotels belong to a hotel group does not mean that they are all necessarily identical to each other. Often, they fall into many different categories, as is the case with Forte hotels, for example, whose establishments range from traditional country inns to modern city-centre hotels with full business facilities. Similarly, in the Savoy Group of Hotels and Restaurants, which includes six of the world's most celebrated hotels – The Savoy, The Berkeley, Claridge's and The Connaught in London, The Lygon Arms in Broadway, Worcester, and The Lancaster in Paris – no two properties are alike, and nor do they offer identical facilities.

CASE STUDY

Mount Charlotte Thistle Hotels

Mount Charlotte Thistle Hotels is a leading British hotel group, with over 100 properties ranging from 3-star to 5-star hotels all over Britain. While the group emphasises the individuality of each of its hotels, the majority of its establishments offer a range of facilities to meet the needs of different categories of clients. These facilities are described in the extract from the Mount Charlotte Thistle Hotels' brochure shown overleaf on page 74 in Fig. 5.4.

TASKS ─────────────────────────────────────

1 Make a list of the special facilities offered for the group's different client categories.

2 Discuss the advantages of a hotel belonging to a chain, rather than operating independently. Are there any disadvantages?

Hotels, of whatever size, can be **purpose-built** or **converted**. Purpose-built hotels are those which have been specifically built with that use in mind – to be used as hotels. By way of contrast, converted hotels are those using buildings which were originally built for a different purpose – as a castle or a palace, for example. Many historic buildings around the world have been converted into beautiful hotels, including churches, stately homes and even rows of private houses.

Hotels, large and small, use **new technology** to improve the efficiency of their operations. Often, computers are used by hotel staff from the moment a guest rings up to make a reservation to the final paying of the bill as the guest departs. Special computer software has been produced for hotels and hotel chains, which make possible great savings in staff time and paperwork.

From Brighton to Wick in Scotland's far north, Mount Charlotte Thistle Hotels give you one of the widest choices of hotels in key business and leisure destinations throughout Britain. In central London alone we offer a selection of 24 properties.

Ranging from large city centre to quiet country house hotels, we can meet your accommodation requirements perfectly. Whether the hotel you choose offers de luxe, executive or standard facilities, each has its own special way of looking after guests.

From three-star comfort to five-star luxury, we have the hotel – the choice is yours.

Bedroom Selection. In every one of our hotels, each bedroom is well appointed and comfortably furnished with private bathroom, colour television, radio and telephone. In most hotels, bedrooms also have hairdryer, trouser press, tea and coffee making facilities.

Executive Bedrooms. Designed to an exceptionally high standard and available in the majority of hotels, these rooms, with many additional features, will particularly appeal to the business executive.

De Luxe Bedrooms. This category of bedroom offers de luxe accommodation for the discerning traveller and is available at seven hotels chosen for their overall superior quality and standard of service.

Studios and Suites. The majority of hotels offer a selection of studio bedrooms and suites.

Bedrooms for Lady Executives. A number of bedrooms in every hotel are specially equipped with additional toiletries for our lady guests.

Bedrooms for Non-Smokers. Twenty per cent of bedrooms in every hotel have been designated as no-smoking rooms. Please request this facility at the time of booking.

Facilities for the Disabled. The majority of hotels have purpose-built facilities for disabled guests. Please check with the hotels direct for further details.

CONFERENCES

Many of our hotels are ideally suited for conferences, being located in prime business centres. Each has a main meeting room with capacity for at least 100 delegates, along with a separate dining area, and full back-up services.

BUSINESS CENTRES

Our hotels provide services that enable executives on the move to conduct their business away from the office. Four London hotels, The Selfridge, Royal Horseguards, The Tower and Heathrow Park, along with The Haydock in Merseyside and the Hospitality Inn Glasgow have business services centres. The majority of hotels provide facsimile, telex, photocopying and secretarial services on request.

RESERVATIONS – UK AND WORLDWIDE

Part of our commitment to the business traveller is a fast and efficient reservations service – not only for our hotels in the UK but also for over 600 associate hotels worldwide, members of the Supranational Hotels reservation network.

This fully computerised reservation system is directly linked to the major airline CRS to provide instant confirmation 24 hours per day, along with a full information service on hotel facilities and locations.

For example, through the use of new technology, many hotel groups have set up centralised advanced reservations systems through which a potential guest can telephone one number – usually at the group's head office – and book any available night in any hotel in the group.

Having made the reservation, the guest's next encounter with new technology is likely to be on arrival at the hotel's reception desk. Reception staff will use the computer to register the guest – to check the reservation, take the guest's details, and allocate a room. For guests who are frequent customers of the same hotel group it is possible that his or her details (name, home address, car registration number, etc.,) may be stored in the computer's memory to speed up the registration process. Finally, on departure, the guest's bill is compiled by the reception desk computer. The cost of the room, meals taken, telephone calls made, newspapers provided etc., are stored on the computer and printed out as a bill.

Behind the scenes, too, computers are used by hotels in the same ways as they are used by most businesses, which include accounting, payroll, stock control, and staff personnel records. The following extract from an article on innovations in hotel facilities gives further examples of how new technology can be used to make guests' lives easier:

Fig. 5.5 *(b) The Pla*
Athenee Hotel, Paris

More technology is to be found at London's latest luxury landmark, The Lanesborough, which is the distinctive name given to a hotel which has risen Phoenix-like from what was formerly the St George's Hospital at Hyde Park Corner.

Although the Lanesborough is intended to recreate the ambience of a 19th-century town house, it is technologically ahead of its time. It has more than ten computer systems, which include:

- the Mitel dialling-in system which assigns each guest an individual direct phone and fax number to be used on every visit;
- the Encore property management system which gives quick and easy updates of guest information; and

- the Systemteq butler call and room management technology which allows the butler to know whether guests are in or out of their rooms. When a guest goes out of the room, the temperature automatically drops ten degrees.

The Rosewood Hotel Group, which owns the Lanesborough, says its first London hotel will also be the most secure in the capital, with hidden cameras on every floor, scanning devices and panic buttons. Yet, despite all these glimpses of tomorrow, the property is a Grade Two listed building.

Horizons, BTA, December 1991

Staff and service

The main difference between serviced and self-catering accommodation is that in serviced accommodation, tourists (the guests) come into direct contact with the **staff** of the establishment, who provide them with the services they need; mainly meals, and housekeeping.

There are many jobs to be carried out by the staff in serviced accommodation. Some are **behind the scenes**: in a large hotel there may be catering staff preparing meals in the kitchen, accountants looking after the hotel's finances, laundry staff, maintenance staff responsible for the upkeep of the building, personnel staff to recruit and look after the hotel's employees, computing staff, sales and marketing staff responsible for attracting customers to the hotel, and a whole team of managers to supervise the work of all members of staff. All of these people have an important job to do to keep the hotel running smoothly.

Yet, equally important, are the employees who have direct contact with the guests visiting the hotel. They are often called **front-of-house** staff, because they have face-to-face dealings with guests.

Imagine that a business tourist, Sandy, arrives one evening at a large hotel in Hull. He has travelled to Hull by train from Scotland for an important business meeting in that town, timed for 9.00 am the following day. He arrives at the hotel at 6.30 pm and is first greeted by the *doorman* who welcomes him and opens the front door for him. The first member of staff he meets inside the hotel is the *hotel receptionist*, at the reception desk in the entrance hall. She welcomes him, registers him, and issues him with a key to his room. Before going to his room, Sandy speaks to the *hall porter* who finds a *luggage porter* to help him with his bag. Sandy changes in his room and then decides to use the health and leisure facilities of the hotel. He goes to the health club where an *instructor* shows him how to use the weights machines, and the jogging machine. Having worked up an appetite, Sandy goes to the hotel restaurant, where he is greeted by the *head waiter* who shows him to a table and takes his order. The meal is served by a *waitress* and a *wine waiter*. To finish off the day with a night cap, Sandy takes himself off to the hotel bar, where he has a drink and a chat with the *bar staff*. The following morning, on the way to the restaurant for breakfast, he meets the *chambermaid*, who wishes him 'good morning'.

The photograph shown below shows some hotel staff at work.

The tasks performed by staff behind the scenes, and at front-of-house in a large hotel must be done by staff in any size of serviced accommodation establishment, whether it is a hotel, guest house, bed and breakfast or holiday centre. In a very small guest house or bed and breakfast, all of the tasks may be done by only two or three people. The way in which the front-of-house jobs are done, in particular, directly affects the guests' experience. To make a guest's stay enjoyable and memorable, the attitudes and skills of the staff in any accommodation establishment are of equal importance to the standard of facilities that are provided. Chapter 11 looks at this question in more detail.

Self-catering accommodation

Tourists who choose self-catering forms of accommodation have to work a little harder than those in serviced accommodation. They usually have to do their own housekeeping – keeping the place clean and tidy – and have to either cook and wash up for themselves or go out to eat in local restaurants and cafés.

Fig. 5.6 A hotel reception area

This type of accommodation can often be less expensive than serviced accommodation because less is provided in the way of services. It therefore appeals to tourists who are prepared to be a little more independent in order to have more control over their holiday finances as well as over what they eat – and when.

There are as many types of self-catering accommodation as there are of serviced accommodation.

Rented accommodation and time share

One of the simplest ways in which tourists obtain self-catering accommodation is by **renting** a house or apartment. There is almost no limit to the type of accommodation which can be rented by tourists. Apartments in Spain, villas in Italy, chalets in Switzerland, log-cabins in Canada, farmhouses in France, and country cottages all over Britain are all important elements in the accommodation sector of the tourism industry of these countries and others like them. Rented accommodation of this kind often appeals to tourists who prefer to live in a 'real' home similar to those of the inhabitants of the country or region they are visiting, rather than specially-built tourist accommodation. This enables them to experience a little of the life of the people living at their holiday destination. They shop in the food shops, they use the restaurants, and generally have more opportunities to mix with the 'locals'. Much rented self-catering accommodation is owned by people who already have a home of their own elsewhere, but who want to own a **second home** to be used by themselves and let out to others, in return for payment. Sometimes the owner of the second home may live in another country, far away from where the home is located. For example, many British people have bought second homes overseas which they use themselves and let out to other British people as holiday accommodation.

Over the last 20 years, self-catering accommodation has grown in importance in Britain and in other countries, as more and more places have been converted for use as tourist accommodation. As countryside areas have become more popular for weekend breaks and longer holidays, many farm buildings and village dwellings have been used as accommodation for tourists. In many tourist destinations, new accommodation has been built, to be sold to people who live in other countries or in different parts of the same country. Many Mediterranean countries, for example, have constructed blocks of holiday apartments and holiday villages which are sold to overseas residents.

Timesharing is a variation on this arrangement. Timesharing is the name given to the arrangement by which someone buys a share in an apartment (for example) which entitles them to use the apartment as their own during a specific set time every year. Timeshare accommodation is sold in units of time – usually one week – and people buy as many units as they can afford.

The units vary in price according to which week in the year they cover. Naturally a week in August will cost much more than a week in February. Owners of units of timeshare accommodation can either use the time to have holidays there themselves, or let out the accommodation to others in exchange for rent. Most timeshare accommodation is sold in Mediterranean countries in the form of purpose-built apartments or villas but it is also becoming more popular in Britain, where some large country houses have been divided into flats and sold on a timeshare basis. Areas such as the Lake District contain purpose-built holiday accommodation which is also sold as timeshares.

Holiday centres and holiday parks

Holiday centres and parks are a special form of accommodation, where, in addition to the accommodation itself, entertainment and leisure facilities are provided. In Britain, holiday centres used to be called 'holiday camps' in the days when they looked something like the camp in the television programme 'Hi-di-Hi'. Now, not only the name has changed: holiday centres such as Butlins Holiday Worlds and Pontins, the best-known British examples, are exciting places with comfortable accommodation and the very latest in sports, leisure and entertainment facilities. Since the mid-1980s, Butlins have invested £100 million in updating their five holiday centres, which between them now welcome over 1.5 million tourists every year. Accommodation in holiday centres such as these is in bungalow-type chalets arranged in 'streets' as in a small village. Guests may cater for themselves or choose to eat in many of the restaurants and cafés available.

A Dutch company, Center Parcs runs 14 holiday centres in Europe, including one in Sherwood Forest, Nottinghamshire and one at Thetford on the Norfolk/Suffolk border. The accommodation in these comprises comfortably-furnished villas, each with a small patio. A range of outdoor sports is available including archery, canoeing and pony trekking, but the most popular facility, regardless of the weather, is the covered sub-tropical swimming paradise at the centre of the park. A huge domed roof ensures that the pool is usable all year round and maintains a sub-tropical climate inside.

Holiday parks developed from the **camping and caravanning** tradition. Since the 1930s, camping and caravanning have been popular holiday activities among tourists who enjoy the countryside and who are prepared to provide their own meals and home comforts in the limited space of tents or caravans. British tourists in particular have always been enthusiastic about this form of self-catering accommodation, even in their own country with its often unpredictable weather.

Some of the major changes in the accommodation sector in the past 20 years or so have taken place in this part of the industry. Camping and caravanning parks in Britain and in other countries have developed considerably from being no more than a field with a concrete toilet block in the middle. The parks themselves have become much more luxurious, providing a whole range of facilities such as restaurants, pubs, sports and leisure centres, shops, and all kinds of entertainment, from play leaders for children to night clubs and discos for older customers. British camping and caravanning parks offering these facilities often call themselves holiday parks, to emphasise that they offer much more than simply a place to eat and sleep while on holiday.

Tents and caravans have also changed considerably in recent years. Most caravans now being used by holiday makers are similar to small apartments, with separate bedroom, toilet and bathroom and all the comforts of home, including colour television. Even tents are now sold with room divisions, and built-in groundsheets and linings make them easy to erect as well as being light and strong.

Holidays using this form of accommodation are not limited to those people who own tents or caravans. Many holiday companies provide these, together with all the necessary furniture and equipment, and their customers simply arrive at the holiday park and move in.

EXERCISE

1 Self-catering accommodation is very rarely used by tourists travelling for business purposes. Why do you think this is?

2 Which type of accommodation provides most employment for local people: serviced or self-catering? Why is this?

3 Imagine that you are spending a week on a modern caravan holiday park with a range of facilities for eating out and entertainment. List as many jobs as you can think of which will be done by the people you see working there.

4 Sometimes local populations living at tourist destinations resent people from other regions or other countries buying second homes in their area. Why do you think this is?

Catering for tourists

The food and drink that are available to tourists when they are away from home is very important to them. Tourists usually have high expectations of eating well, whether this includes trying new and unfamiliar dishes of the destination, or simply looking for their favourite food, well cooked and well presented. Some places have earned such a high reputation for the food they serve that tourists may choose to visit such a place partly because of the food they know they will find there. The high standard of French cooking is well known all over the world, and is no doubt one of the reasons why France is so high in the league of the world's most popular tourist destinations. In Britain there are many regional foods and drinks to tempt the visitor, from Devon's scrumpy cider to Scottish haggis. The food of Britain's various ethnic population groups is important too, in providing variety and choice for visitors. Bradford in West Yorkshire is able to attract tourists on the strength of its many Indian restaurants which enjoy the reputation of being among the best in Britain. Special 'Taste of India' weekends are available to visitors who wish to sample the delights of Bradford's popular Indian restaurants.

The **catering** sector of the tourism industry has grown rapidly in Britain and in other countries over the past 20 years. Between 1980 and 1990, eating out in Britain increased by 25% to the 4,000 million meals eaten every year in restaurants and other establishments by the end of the decade. Part of this phenomenal growth is due to social changes and the fact that more and more British people eat out on a regular basis; but a major factor has been the increases in domestic and international tourism in Britain.

Only a minority of tourists in most countries take accommodation with full board. The majority take at least one meal a day away from their accommodation. For this reason, any popular holiday destination will have a wide range of catering establishments serving food and drink to suit the taste and budget of each individual visitor.

Restaurants, cafés and fast food establishments

Restaurants and cafés are places where tourists have an opportunity to mix with the local population while having a meal. For self-catering tourists, the waiter or waitress may be their first or only personal contact with the people living in the destination. Those who are not in their own country may need help in order to understand the menu, although in popular international destinations the menu is often printed in the languages of the main tourist groups. In such places, special 'tourist menus' are sometimes available in which a set meal, clearly described in several languages, makes life as simple as possible for the visitor.

Tourists' needs vary greatly. Some may wish to try the local dishes; some may prefer something already familiar to them; and some may have special requirements, such as vegetarian food. Business tourists may need to eat out with colleagues in quiet surroundings where they can talk business with a minimum of disruptions or distractions. Young tourists, especially in groups, may want to eat in a busy, informal place, with plenty of atmosphere. Any large, popular destination will be able to satisfy all these different types of tourists' needs.

5.7
A hotel restaurant

A high street self-
vice restaurant

EXERCISE

Figure 5.7 shows food being served in two contrasting styles of establishment; one in a hotel restaurant and one in a health food self-service restaurant in a high street.

1 Which is the more formal setting? Give as many reasons as you can for your choice.

2 Who is in more of a hurry – the hotel guests or the businessman?

In Britain there are approximately 15 000 **restaurants**. The majority of these are operated by the owners, who may work in them, either alone, or with the members of their family or staff employed by them to cook and serve the food. About 10% of restaurants in Britain are owned by group companies, in the same way that many hotels are operated by the hotel groups as a chain. Restaurants with group owners usually carry the same name wherever they are located. For example, Beefeater Steak Houses can be found in many towns in Britain: these are owned by the group Whitbread & Company plc. Similarly Britain's Little Chef and Happy Eater roadside restaurants are owned by Forte, the same company which operates the international chain of hotels.

Fast food establishments have revolutionised the eating habits of Britain and many other countries since the late 1970s. Many people have grown so used to the speed and convenience of fast food catering in their home areas that they continue to use these places for eating out when they are away from home, on holiday for example. Many fast food companies have the advantage of being international chains, so tourists looking for familiar food can be tempted by these establishments even when they are outside their own country.

CASE STUDY

Fast food in the USA

In the USA, the birthplace of fast food, the fast food sector accounted for almost half of all food service in 1991 – an industry with a total turnover of $248 billion that year. Figure 5.8 shows the top ten brands for 1991, with their total sales in the USA, the percentage change in sales over the previous year, and the number of units (restaurants) each brand has in America.

Company	Sales	Change (%)	Units
1 McDonald's	19 928	6.2	12 418
2 Burger King	6 200	1.6	6 409
3 KFC*	6 200	7.4	8 480
4 Pizza Hut	5 300	8.2	9 000
5 Hardee's	3 431	N/A	3 727
6 Wendy's	3 224	5.0	3 804
7 ARA Services	2 830	4.8	2 720
8 Taco Bell	2 800	16.7	3 670
9 Marriott MS	2 500	N/A	2 400
10 Domino's	2 400	– 9.4	5 500
*Kentucky Fried Chicken			

Fig. 5.8 Top American brands
Source: Caterer and Hotelkeeper, 30 July 1992

The publication, *Caterer and Hotelkeeper* from its sister magazine *Restaurants and Institutions*, describes the following trends in fast food service in the USA, in its review of 1991:

Against a background of flat or slow-growing sales, the US burger market has shifted the emphasis from new menu items to new customer service ideas.

McDonald's, which once again took number one spot, successfully introduced its 'What you want is what you get' money-back guarantee. In addition to this promise of refunds, the programme includes touches such as free ice-cream for children, drink refills and greeters at all restaurants. Among its menu innovations has been the introduction of pizza and pasta menus, currently being tested in Tennessee and New York. A healthier alternative to the fried pie has also been added in the form of a baked apple pie. Other new projects which are said to be working well include the McDonald's 'Friendly Sky Meals' on United Airlines flights between Chicago and Orlando, and 'Leaps and Bounds' play centres, which are to be introduced at 15 more stores this year.

For its part, Burger King responded by giving its franchisees freedom to develop their own product lines. In Seattle, for example, restaurants are testing espresso coffee, and in Detroit one store is offering low-calorie turkey, chicken salad and tuna salad sandwiches called BK Healthies, costing $1.79. The chain is also testing its 'Lighter way' menu in 350 locations, offering weight watchers' fettuccine and side salads that all contain less than 300 calories.

While burger chains struggled against increasingly sluggish sales, pizza market leaders found the Americans' love for Italian food undiminished. The top brand, Pizza Hut's, growth came about partly as the result of a big push into non-traditional areas such as schools, staff canteens and airport/stadium kiosks. In its bid to corner the entire pizza market, the company also moved into the drive-through sector, with the opening of its first Fastino's by Pizza Hut, which offers both pizza and pasta.

Pubs

People on holiday or on a day out often like to relax with a drink, and the great British **pub** is always a favourite with incoming tourists as well as with the local population. Over the 1980s, two major developments changed pubs dramatically. First, the spectacular growth in the sale of **food** in pubs which now ranges from simple snacks to elaborate meals chosen from a full menu. Sandwiches, ploughmans lunches, basket meals and restaurant-type meals have become so popular in pubs that in some, the income from the sale of food is greater than that from the sale of alcohol. The second development concerns the time when alcoholic drinks can legally be sold. Since the summer of 1988, pubs throughout Britain have been legally allowed to remain open for business all day, instead of closing in the afternoons. Business for pubs, especially those in busy towns, has increased as has the number of people employed in pubs.

Two-thirds of all pubs in Britain are owned by the major brewing companies whose products they sell. The others, known as free houses, are owned independently and may sell any brand of drinks.

CASE STUDY

Youth hostels

The International Youth Hostel Federation (IYHF) represents all national youth hostel associations in the 60 countries worldwide which have youth hostel accommodation.

It produces figures every year to show the development of youth hostels throughout the world.

The level of use of youth hostels is a useful way of measuring trends in 'youth tourism', because many young people use this kind of accommodation when they travel in their own countries or abroad.

The growth in importance of youth hostels for tourism can be measured in several different ways:

(1) By measuring the total number of youth hostels open for business.

(2) By measuring the number of overnights recorded. An overnight is equivalent to one person spending one night in a youth hostel. So a group of four people spending one night in a youth hostel amounts to four overnights and one person spending four nights in a youth hostel amounts to four overnights.

(3) By measuring the total number of individual members of national youth hostel associations. People using youth hostels as accommodation must be members of their national youth hostel association. Therefore, the growth in popularity of youth hostels can be seen by keeping count of the number of individual members.

Information on youth hostels throughout the world is given in Fig. 5.9.

The first two columns show the number of individual members of each country's national member association, for 1990 and 1991.

TASKS_____

1 Using the data given in Fig. 5.9, write a paragraph describing the general trends in Youth Hostel use worldwide, between 1990 and 1991. What

	Total (individuals)		Number of Hostels		Overnights recorded by own members		Overnights recorded by foreigners		Total number of Overnights	
	1990	1991	1990	1991	1990	1991	1990	1991	1990	1991
Algeria	27,614	25,000	34	46	27,137	38,940	7,358	4,166	34,495	43,106
Argentina	7,552	23,358	22	20	29,415	48,321	6,634	4,799	36,049	53,120
Australia	150,156	127,616	152	156	290,397	292,721	608,168	540,080	899,105	832,801
Austria	134,760	118,474	101	107	668,066	689,227	685,612	726,230	1,353,678	1,415,457
Bahrain	802	1,036	2	2	2,370	1,219	11,261	18,220	13,631	19,439
Belgium (Les AJ)	4,873	6,256	9	9	26,551	25,858	79,049	75,105	105,600	100,693
Belgium (VJH)	24,561	28,223	19	20	59,000	60,826	145,302	157,093	204,302	217,919
Brazil	37,006	48,811	73	91	171,060	133,337	19,530	16,886	190,590	150,223
Bulgaria	71,587	33,247	73	73	891,033	290,963	45,155	11,746	936,188	302,709
Canada	43,118	35,279	67	77	143,704	154,973	292,230	285,159	453,934	440,132
Chile	5,803	5,928	18	19	26,340	31,267	1,557	2,210	27,897	33,477
Colombia	5,955	7,707	16	16	17,642	22,935	1,157	1,446	18,799	24,381
Cyprus	1,215	989	6	6	4,320	3,056	7,114	5,602	11,434	8,658
Czechoslovakia	60,094	75,110	46	46	30,007	25,780	28,245	40,780	58,252	66,560
Denmark	39,890	19,080	105	105	521,868	526,428	470,393	525,508	992,261	1,051,936
Egypt	23,906	29,215	15	15	81,993	87,424	21,365	11,515	103,358	98,939
England & Wales	282,676	306,538	256	253	1,471,567	1,369,456	612,860	573,634	2,084,427	1,943,090
Finland	17,976	14,416	154	155	207,643	205,569	128,408	105,801	336,051	311,370
France	170,328	166,766	227	220	552,041	591,523	762,342	657,793	1,314,383	1,249,316
Germany	725,055	793,060	521	643	8,046,090	9,236,972	1,113,672	1,166,129	9,159,762	10,403,101
Greece	2,000	(b)	29	29	65,000	205	84,626	26,853	149,626	27,058
Hong Kong	21,975	20,984	6	6	30,162	27,141	16,721	15,159	46,883	42,300
Hungary	27,942	28,707	36	26	196,495	112,300	207,402	124,450	403,897	236,750
Iceland	1,349	657	17	24	6,343	6,066	25,374	29,930	31,717	35,996
India	41,886	47,709	56	59	144,276	176,573	9,286	9,662	153,562	186,235
Ireland (Northern)	5,627	5,692	7	7	9,232	8,086	19,463	20,986	28,695	29,072
Ireland (Republic of)	24,440	33,048	46	44	69,069	66,987	215,554	233,100	284,623	300,087
Israel	4,310	5,865	31	31	502,599	570,749	181,719	152,143	684,318	722,892
Italy	36,063	40,760	46	44	85,770	80,535	534,514	506,438	620,284	586,973
Japan	191,637	195,172	434	413	1,107,332	1,220,251	132,414	148,474	1,239,746	1,368,725
Kenya	1,230	1,501	7	7	4,387	4,786	17,447	18,963	21,834	23,749
Korea (S)	13,548	18,241	15	15	61,870	118,750	6,840	9,336	68,710	128,086
Libya	18,370	22,770	31	31	50,425	63,350	82,718	93,593	133,143	156,943
Luxembourg	3,882	3,765	12	12	16,709	15,479	94,428	97,934	111,137	113,413
Malaysia	1,469	1,219	10	9	9,532	9,114	9,380	11,172	18,912	20,286
Mexico	(a)	(b)	21	25	156,842	117,000	14,629	10,663	171,471	127,663
Morocco	18,339	10,097	11	11	5,358	8,080	25,636	18,102	30,994	26,182
Netherlands	71,390	61,036	45	42	298,567	292,082	474,709	513,262	773,176	805,344
New Zealand	38,557	31,394	48	34	38,135	41,044	258,376	295,025	296,511	336,069
Norway	10,599	9,124	84	88	132,658	133,154	193,103	198,792	325,761	331,946
Pakistan	2,624	1,386	57	59	43,410	40,605	340	488	43,750	41,093
Peru	5,051	6,964	23	23	25,760	29,230	70,056	55,223	95,816	84,453
Philippines	1,947	3,231	19	20	41,810	80,210	50,559	75,990	92,369	156,200
Poland	410,093	372,485	954	842	1,368,230	1,306,483	42,419	76,883	1,410,649	1,383,366
Portugal	12,101	14,471	17	18	100,219	102,068	65,710	59,912	165,929	161,980
Qatar	1,098	1,054	5	5	3,283	2,963	6,976	7,154	10,259	10,117
Saudi Arabia	38,481	38,798	19	19	99,267	93,937	61,570	28,857	160,837	122,794
Scotland	49,392	52,188	84	84	246,141	257,514	382,868	372,418	629,009	629,932
Spain	65,446	56,517	93	118	843,947	912,547	183,135	137,461	1,027,082	1,050,008
Sri Lanka	957	1,158	18	18	1,208	1,892	2,698	3,186	3,906	5,078
Sudan	4,750	2,708	10	10	12,100	12,774	7,148	4,337	19,248	17,111
Sweden	252,152	342,678	275	273	831,689	790,364	253,207	217,363	1,084,896	1,007,727
Switzerland	57,927	59,336	86	84	367,705	388,684	564,024	556,490	931,729	945,174
Syria (a) (b)	–	–	–	–	–	–	–	–	–	–
Thailand	883	1,492	13	10	254	45	17,421	15,393	17,675	15,438
Tunisia	6,500	6,000	27	27	63,067	71,125	35,207	24,300	98,274	95,425
UAE	659	784	6	6	9,152	11,204	4,200	4,282	13,352	15,486
USA	125,524	111,651	244	242	257,561	265,970	526,544	633,111	784,105	899,081
Uruguay	5,164	6,000	13	13	33,120	34,840	5,054	5,158	38,174	39,998
Yugoslavia	119,031	27,764	32	13	459,382	224,042	37,604	1,397	496,986	225,439
Total	3,529,320	3,510,515	4,903	4,920	21,066,750	21,535,024	9,968,491	9,743,342	31,035,241	31,278,366

Fig. 5.9 *Information on youth hostels worldwide*

evidence is there that youth hostels grew more in importance for domestic tourism than for international tourism?

2 Consider the data concerning Youth Hostel use and membership in Eastern European countries. What evidence is there for an increase in interest in travelling to some Eastern European countries? Give reasons for the dramatic changes in the figures from the former Yugoslavia, between 1990 and 1991.

3 Figure 5.11 gives part of the Youth Hostel Association's (England and Wales) annual report to the IYHF. Give as many examples as you can of the different client groups which English and Welsh Youth Hostels are trying to attract. What kind of facilities and services do Youth Hostels offer these groups?

Fig. 5.10 *An example of a British youth hostel – St Briavels Castle in Lydney, Gloucestershire*

ENGLAND AND WALES

England and Wales continued to invest to improve their youth hostels, installing additional showers, smaller dormitories, better heating etc. The new Rotherhithe Youth Hostel opened in November 1991 amid worldwide publicity of its excellent facilities, including three rooms for wheelchair users and toilets and showers in every bedroom. Both Rotherhithe and City of London Youth Hostels have meeting rooms for conferences and seminars. Sadly Rock Hall closed, but a new hostel was opened at Broadstairs on the coast near Canterbury. The network of camping barns was extended; these are now available in the Forest of Bowland north of Manchester and in the North Pennines, some of the wildest, most remote landscape in England. YHA added more family rooms and facilities for the disabled, and provides comprehensive information on these through new publicity leaflets.

School group usage held up well, benefitted by more targetted marketing. Teachers' needs are being met with greater variety, provision of more privacy for leaders and flexible packaging of transport and activities. The demand for family accommodation continues to outstrip ability to provide more family rooms and is seen as a key area of growth

potential. YHA's new Rent-A-Hostel product is very popular, enabling "closed" hostels out of season to be hired by a group or family for their exclusive use. However, usage by foreign and domestic individuals showed a decline, reflecting the worldwide recession and the effects of the Gulf War. The newly centralized accounting system enabled a much more accurate recording of foreign visitors, and showed that 40,000 overnights were lost in London alone from seven countries which contribute 70% of foreign overnights. Remedial action was taken in March 1991 to counter-balance this unavoidable situation.

Customer service was improved by the development of the fax "Book-a-Bed-Ahead" scheme, linking key hostels in England and Wales, Ireland, Northern Ireland and Scotland. London youth hostels connect with other international city youth hostels to offer a similar service. The use of credit cards is increasing.

A wide range of activities is available, packaged and offered through the Great Escapes brochure. Marketing of these has proved most successful to existing members and is supplemented by short breaks in Triangle, YHA's magazine.

Fig. 5.11 *The Youth Hostel Association's (England and Wales) annual report to the International Youth Hostel Federation.*

ASSIGNMENTS

1 Accommodation and catering in your area

Where do visitors stay when they come to your area or town for business or leisure? Where do they go out to eat or drink?

Conduct a survey of local newspapers, *Yellow Pages* etc., to find out various examples of each kind of accommodation and catering establishment mentioned in this chapter.

Which of the following tourists could find somewhere appropriate to eat or drink in or near your area?

- A family with three young children looking for inexpensive accommodation with leisure and entertainment facilities included.
- A vegetarian looking for somewhere to eat out.
- A group of visiting Italian students looking for the kind of food they eat in their own country.
- A French woman visiting your area for two days on business, and looking for a place to stay.
- A group of school friends on their first holiday without their families in search of suitable accommodation.
- A business person looking for somewhere to take visiting business clients for a meal out.

2 You and a friend have just returned from a two week package holiday in Turkey. You have three specific complaints about your hotel:

- a specific incident concerning the food
- something which was wrong with your room
- the general standard of service of the hotel staff

Write a polite but firm letter of complaint to the hotel manager, describing the incident with the food, and stating why you were not happy with your room or the hotel staff.

Explain in your letter that you did complain at the time, but that you were still not satisfied with the result.

3 Role play the following situation.

If no real restaurant menu is available, invent one with four or five items each for starters, main courses and desserts. Do not forget wines and other drinks.

Two friends are shown to their places at a table in a restaurant. One is buying the other a special meal as a birthday present, so the meal is something of a celebration. The friend whose birthday it is feels determined to have a good time, but, out of politeness does not want to choose the most expensive items on the menu, so decides to wait and see what the other orders.

The waiter or waitress who shows them to their table and gives them the menu is keen to make a good impression, thinking of the tip which the customers may leave. At the same time he or she wants the customers to spend as much as possible on food and drink, and so recommends the most expensive items on the menu. In fact, the customer who is paying wants to keep the bill to a fairly modest amount. The customers ask for explanations of the items on the menu.

Role play the ordering of the meal and hold a class discussion on how it was done, what was good about the way in which it was done, and how it might have been done better.

6

TOURIST ATTRACTIONS AND BUSINESS FACILITIES

After reading this chapter, you should have a clear understanding of:
- the range of tourist attractions available to people travelling for pleasure,
- the kind of facilities required by people travelling for business purposes,
- current trends in tourist attractions.

Once visitors have arrived at their destination, and found accommodation if they need it, their next requirement is entertainment, or (if they are travelling for business) business facilities.

People travelling for pleasure – on holidays, day-trips or short breaks – look for facilities which will provide them with fun, entertainment, or interest. Most people choose their destinations because of the facilities they expect to find there.

Natural features	Rides and transport	Entertainments
beaches and sea	steam railways	cinemas
volcanoes	canals	fairgrounds
parks and gardens	gondolas	nightclubs
spas	hot air ballooning	zoos
lakes	camel rides	racecourses
mountains	coaches	theme parks
rivers		

Sports facilities	Shopping	Artistic and cultural heritage
leisure centres	leisure shopping complexes	historic buildings
ice rinks	oriental bazaars	archaeological sites
golf courses	speciality shopping	arts/music festivals
ski slopes	hypermarkets	tribal customs and crafts
tennis courts	duty-free shopping	museums
swimming pools		

Fig. 6.1 Categories of tourist attractions

Any facility or event which attracts visitors to a particular place can be called an **attraction** or, more specifically, a visitor attraction or tourist attraction. Attractions come in many forms and may be either **natural** or **man-made**. The six main categories of attractions are shown in Fig. 6.1, with some examples.

EXERCISE

Write down three examples of the kind of attractions given under each category, either in Britain or overseas.

CASE STUDY

Attractions in Tyne and Wear

Figure 6.2 shows a list of the attractions of Tyne and Wear, taken from a promotional booklet on the area.

TASKS

1 Divide Tyne and Wear's attractions into six lists following the categories given in Fig. 6.1.

2 Explain who else, apart from visitors to Tyne and Wear, will use the facilities there.

Trends in attractions

Natural attractions such as sandy beaches and beautiful lakes change very little through time. Built attractions, however, do change, in line with public taste and fashion. With each new attraction that is built, the competition to attract visitors increases, so great imagination and creativity is required of designers and managers of such attractions, in order to make their particular place stand out. Over the past 20 years, there has been a marked trend in the tourism industry towards more exciting and sophisticated attractions of all kinds.

Museums have become more interesting and entertaining places to visit, while still maintaining their role of teaching visitors about the past. Some have been converted into 'living museums' where actors and actresses in

SIGHTSEEING

WHAT TO SEE AND DO IN TYNE AND WEAR

Tyne and Wear is an ideal place to visit. There is
a tremendous variety of things to see and do. We
can only suggest a selection of attractions here –
to appreciate the rest you really must come and
find out for yourself. We hope this selection will
whet your appetite.
Where to start? Start at the beginning!

A LONG HISTORY AND A RICH HERITAGE

Tyne and Wear shows evidence of a long history,
from the Roman occupation, when this area was
the northern frontier of the Empire and thus of
strategic military importance, all the way
through to the arrival of the industries which
totally transformed the county – and are still
bringing major changes today.
Hadrian's Wall is the main Roman showpiece, of
course, and the most outstanding stretches are
just a short drive west. The Wall finishes, as you
would expect, at Wallsend. There, and at South
Shields, the Roman forts of Segedunum and
Arbeia are being excavated and put on show.
Northumbria was also the first great Saxon
kingdom, a centre for early Christianity and
culture, as far back as the 7th century. St Paul's
Church in Jarrow, and St Peter's at
Monkwearmouth were both connected with St
Bede; and both still have substantial Saxon work
intact for you to go and admire.

The mediaeval period also produced impressive
remains: The Castle and Priory at Tynemouth,
the Castle Keep, the Black Gate, the town walls
and Blackfriars in Newcastle, as well as many old
churches around the county.
Washington Old Hall is a great attraction for
Americans, being the ancestral home of the first
president. The Hall was built in the 17th century
and has been immaculately restored.
But perhaps Tyne and Wear is most noted for its
industries – great machines and the strong
personalities who designed and built them. We
only have to recite a list of names: George and
Robert Stephenson, Joseph Swan, Lord
Armstrong, Sir Charles Parsons and his ship
Turbinia; the railways and the great shipbuilding
yards on the Tyne and Wear. Much remains to be
seen – Turbinia for instance, and the Bowes
Railway – and more will become available in
years to come as Tyne and Wear continues to
present its heritage to the world.

COAST AND COUNTRY

Though Tyne and Wear is a major conurbation,
open land, coastline and countryside form a large
part of its area. It is a constant surprise to people
who do not know the area.
The long coastline is a splendid asset. The
beaches are sandy and clean, and there are
dramatic coves, headlands, stacks and cliffs.
Lighthouses and fishing villages add variety to
the scene. Inland the valleys and foothills of the
northern Pennines are soon reached, and much
of the western flank of Tyne and Wear offers
good areas for walking and riding.

CULTURE, ENTERTAINMENT, SHOPPING AND SPORT

Tyne and Wear is one of the most vibrant cultural
centres among the regions of England. It has a
great wealth of entertainment available and
shopping facilities to rival any in Europe – or the
USA. It is an area worth visiting on these
grounds alone.
Live theatre flourishes in Tyne and Wear, with
nine theatres offering everything from the Royal
Shakespeare Company – who regard the Theatre
Royal, Newcastle as their third home – to
translations of Moliere into Geordie! The

Gateshead's Metro Centre, modern shopping at its best.

Northern Sinfonia orchestra is based in
Newcastle. Cinema, jazz and folk music are all
strongly represented. In a more popular family
vein, the Spanish City amusement park in
Whitley Bay is a big seaside attraction, and
funfairs and events of all kinds cater for all tastes.
There is a vibrant nightlife, with a host of pubs
and many and varied restaurants to tempt your
palate. The famous nightclubs draw late-night
revellers from a very wide area – offering the
chance to dance on board ship as well as land – a
case, perhaps, of rocking the boat! Rock music
is, incidentally, well catered for in many venues
of the County; and the County has blessed the
industry with the Animals, Dire Straits,
Lindisfarne and Sting, to mention just a few
names.
Shopping, already a major attraction, has been
greatly enhanced by Gateshead's Metro Centre,
soon to be the largest shopping and leisure centre
in Europe. Every major town has its
well-equipped shopping area, where the famous
national retailing chains are represented
alongside local firms. There is also a great
number of speciality shops and markets to attract
the visitor's attention.
It is well known that people in Tyne and Wear
are mad about sport. Newcastle United and
Sunderland are amongst the best supported
football teams in Britain; Brendan Foster and
Steve Cram have made this area into a
stronghold of athletics, whose principal stage is
the Gateshead International Stadium.
Multi-purpose sports and leisure centres, like the
Crowtree Leisure Centre in Sunderland, cater
for every indoor sport. Leisure pools at Whitley
Bay and South Shields offer swimming facilities
all year round. Golf, fishing and sailing are
available in abundance. The Whitley Bay and
Crowtree Ice Rinks are popular facilities.

costumes meet the public and play the roles of characters from the past, in attempts to make the exhibits come alive for visitors. In others, history is made vivid and exciting through the use of realistic waxworks, sounds, and even smells, to conjure up a sense of the past. A good example of this is the Jorvik Viking Centre in York. Visitors to Jorvik enter electrically-powered 'time cars' which transport them back in time to a reconstructed Viking village in 10th-century York. The cars move past a series of realistic, three-dimensional scenes of Viking life of that time, and the clever use of sounds, smells and lighting create the effect for the visitor of actually experiencing the life of the Viking people.

Fig. 6.3 *The Jorvik Viking Centre, York*

Courtesy: York Archaeological Trust

In 1988, The Oxford Story opened on the site of a former children's bookshop, to tell the story of Oxford University through a series of full-size 3D scenes from the past life of the university. Sitting at wooden desks, visitors are transported through the scenes. As with the Jorvik Viking Centre, much use is made of realistic sounds and smells, and the life-size characters in the scenes look very real indeed. Visitors see students' lodgings in mediaeval Oxford, for example, and a selection of the great thinkers who have been associated with the university.

Sports facilities have also changed dramatically, in developed countries. To replace the plain, rectangular, white-tiled swimming pools, possibly with one or two diving boards, new developments in engineering and technology, and changing public taste, have led to the widespread construction of 'leisure pools'. These are exciting, fun places, built more for 'waterplay' than straight swimming. Leisure pools provide a host of features, including fountains, whirlpools, artificial waves, waterfalls, water cannon and, most popular of all, flumes or waterslides – huge tubes down which visitors slide, through various twists and turns, to emerge at the bottom into a splash pool.

CASE STUDY

The Waterfront

Figure 6.4 describes the Waterfront development in Greenwich. (*See* page 96.)

TASKS

1 Why has the London Borough of Greenwich built Waterfront? Give as many reasons as you can.

2 Some swimming pools in Greenwich were built last century. Describe the main differences between those pools, and Waterfront, from the visitor's point of view.

3 What *type* of visitors do you think Waterfront will attract?

4 Find out whether your area has a leisure complex. If it has, find out the costs of setting it up.

Side by side with the current trend of built attractions becoming more sophisticated and exciting places to visit, another trend is being followed. More places are being opened to the public as attractions, although the original purpose for which they were built had nothing to do with tourism.

Some of the earliest examples of this trend are the churches, temples and cathedrals all over the world, which have come to serve a **dual function**, as places of worship and as attractions for visitors.

ON THE WATERFRONT

Waterfront, a £9 million leisure centre, opens in Woolwich, London this Spring Bank Holiday weekend.

Developed by the London Borough of Greenwich, the centre's opening is timed to coincide with 'Woolwich Week' activities. It will also play an important role in ITV's largest ever national fund-raising event, Telethon '88, by organising competitions for sponsored teams.

Waterfront's central features are its pools, which contain nearly 300,000 gallons of water. Described by their developers as 'easily the most exciting in London', they feature waves, fountains, underwater springs, disco music, underwater lighting, vortexes, rapids, and monsoon rains. When users tire of those, they can take a turn on the giant flume, which goes outside the building and incorporates strobe effects, mists and tunnel sections. There is also a lagoon diving pool and a whirlpool hot bath, while more serious swimmers are catered for with a full size 25 m six-lane competition pool. Children can play in the large, gently shelved kiddies/learner pool and there are special lifts to take handicapped swimmers to the top of the flume ride. Tropical plants and rock effects enhance the holiday atmosphere, which is kept warm with heat reclamation and special air-conditioning features.

A huge sports and entertainments hall complements the wet-area activities. It has a sauna and solarium suite, a dance studio, a fitness suite, a projectile hall and conference and function rooms. Four glass-backed squash courts and a newly created riverside promenade complete the sports-based facilities and the centre also has a creche, a luxury lounge, a poolside fruit juice bar, a fully computerised booking and admission system, car parking for two hundred, and an integral mall containing retail units and providing access to the Woolwich foot tunnel.

There will additionally be facilities for sports injury diagnosis and treatment and a wide variety of organised activities for every age range.

The admission prices have yet to be finalised, but disadvantaged persons will be allowed special rates at various times, Borough residents will be charged lower rates than others and families will be entitled to discounts. However, a 'realistic policy', which reflects the range and standard of facilities to be offered, is to be generally enforced. Members of the Centre will be entitled to free admission, telephone credit booking, and reduced rates on some special events.

The Council regards the project as an example of its own commitment to direct investment in the community, and recognises that it has an important part to play in the stimulation of the local economy. It also feels itself responsible for ensuring that leisure facilities are available to all local residents, not just those who can afford to pay full prices.

In all, the Council avers that the project will provide the people of Greenwich with some of the best facilities in the country, create many new jobs for the local population, inject further life into Woolwich town centre, provide a new tourist venue for the Capital and open up the river frontage. The Waterfront Leisure Centre will also indirectly improve the quality of local residents' lifestyle, increase business for all local traders, cut down on vandalism, ease the Woolwich parking problem and put Woolwich on the map, claims Jim Gillman chairman of Greenwich's Leisure Services Committee.

Fig. 6.4 An article on The Waterfront development, prior to its opening.

Courtesy: Leisure Management Dicester Limited, Hitchin, Herts

Another example of places which can be turned into attractions, are people's homes, especially if they are very historic and on a grand scale, such as castles and palaces. Stately homes, particularly those with attractive gardens, are also appealing to visitors. In some cases, part of the building may be out-of-bounds to the public, and used as living quarters for the resident family.

There are many examples of members of the British aristocracy whose homes have been partially or completely opened to the public as tourist attractions. Hatfield House, situated 20 miles north of London is a good example of this. The home of the Cecil family, this house, dating from Jacobean times is popular with the visitors who tour the lavishly decorated state rooms – the drawing room, halls, galleries, library, dining room and chapel. One wing of the house remains the private living accommodation of the current inhabitants of Hatfield House.

But not only members of the aristocracy have their homes open to view. Tourists often have an interest in exploring the homes of famous writers and artists from the past, however humble the buildings themselves may be. Not far from Madrid, in the town of Toledo, tourists flock to the tiny house of the famous painter El Greco, who lived there 400 years ago. Similarly, the parsonage which was the home of the Brontë sisters, whose 19th-century novels include *Jane Eyre* and *Wuthering Heights*, brings many thousands of tourists each year to Haworth in Yorkshire.

More recently, especially in Britain, there has been a growing interest in attractions which show people at work, or familiar objects being manufactured. One example of this is the Edinburgh Crystal factory, which regularly opens its doors to the visiting public. Visitors are shown around the modern factory by a guide and they see the famous Edinburgh Crystal glassware being manufactured in red-hot ovens. After the tour, they have the opportunity to buy crystal decanters and goblets similar to those they have seen being made. The visitors do not interfere with the production process, so the factory serves a dual function of being both a real workplace and an attraction. There seems to be no end to the kinds of places which can be turned into attractions. Visitors can see Mercedes Benz cars being manufactured by robots in a fully-mechanised factory near Düsseldorf, Germany; they can watch cows being milked by hand on farms in Wales. Even the Granada television studios in Manchester where 'Coronation Street' is filmed have been turned into a novel kind of attraction where visitors receive a guided tour of 'the Street', including the Rovers' Return!

EXERCISE

1 Name at least two examples each, one from Britain and one from overseas, of:
(*a*) a place of worship which is also an attraction for visitors.
(*b*) a palace or castle which is also an attraction.

Theme parks

Many attractions appeal to visitors because they are very old and historical. Theme parks are a comparatively new type of attraction, with Disneyland in California, USA, being one of the most famous.

CASE STUDY

Disneyland

Opened in 1955, Disneyland's theme is the collection of characters created and made famous by Walt Disney. Over 12 million people every year pay the admission fee, giving them access to the vast range of rides and shows, which are among the most exciting in the world. Disneyland constantly adds new, even more thrilling attractions to keep the public arriving in their millions. The most popular single attractions recently have been Captain Eo and Star Tours. Captain Eo stars Michael Jackson in a three-dimensional space musical film, which uses advanced technology to give the appearance of laser beams shooting out of the screen. Star Tours is a computer-controlled spaceship cockpit simulation designed by Steven Spielberg. The audience has the illusion of being in the spaceship, which lurches around and goes out of control. The fact that these two attractions are the most popular in Disneyland means, inevitably, that the queues for these are the longest.

On the opposite coast of the USA, in Florida on the east coast, the Walt Disney World Resort covers an area of 43 square miles. Composed of different centres on specific themes, Disneyworld offers visitors such delights as the Magic Kingdom which includes over 40 rides and attractions as well as more than 70 shops and restaurants. Visitors to the Magic Kingdom have the opportunity to shake hands with their favourite Disney characters such as Mickey Mouse, Goofy and Donald Duck.

Connected to the Magic Kingdom by monorail is the EPCOT Center which takes the future as one of its themes. The wonders of science and technology are used to entertain visitors, with robot displays and the latest developments in energy, communications and transport on offer.

Theme parks as attractions have developed from the idea of amusement parks, with thrilling rides such as roller coasters and a range of interesting exhibits to look at. The main difference from the original parks is one of scale. Theme parks stretch over vast areas of land, often the size of small towns (for this reason, most are situated in the countryside). The individual attractions in a theme park are more numerous, often more terrifying, and they use more high-technology than in traditional fairgrounds or amusement parks. A fixed-rate admission is usually charged for the whole day, with the rides then coming free. The biggest theme parks attract millions of visitors every year which can result in long queues for individual attractions at peak times. Some theme parks provide entertainments such as live music to keep the queuing visitors amused, while between rides, there are usually plenty of souvenir shops and fast-food outlets to tempt customers.

EXERCISE

1 What kind of visitors do you think theme parks are designed to attract?

2 Some of the most terrifying rides in theme parks are called 'white knuckle' rides. Why do you think they are so called?

3 Apart from the entrance fees, how else do visitors to theme parks spend their money on their day out?

Because theme parks are expensive attractions to construct, they are likely to be found in the more developed countries of the world. They are also found in locations which make them accessible to large numbers of potential visitors, the customers of theme parks. In the USA, there are about 30 major theme parks, each attracting more than a million visitors per year, in some cases from all over the USA, and even from other countries, including Britain.

Figure 6.5 gives details of the major European theme parks.

Theme park	Country	Year of opening
Alton Towers	Britain	1924
Astérix Park	France	1989
Bellewaerde	Belgium	1969
Bobbejaanland	Belgium	1962
Chessington World of Adventures	Britain	1987
De Efteling	Netherlands	1951
Duinrell	Netherlands	1935
Euro Disneyland	France	1992
Europa Park	Germany	1975
Frontierland	Britain	1985
Futuroscope	France	1987
Hellendoorn	Netherlands	1960
Heide Park	Germany	1978
Meli Park	Belgium	1935
OK Corral	France	1963
Smurfs' Park	France	1989
Thorpe Park	Britain	1979
Walibi Park	Belgium	1975

Fig. 6.5 *European theme parks attracting more than 500 000 visitors per annum*

EXERCISE

Study Figure 6.5 and then answer the following questions:

(*a*) In which part of the continent of Europe are the countries appearing in Figure 6.5 mainly situated?

(*b*) Why do you think major European theme parks are situated in these particular European countries rather than countries with long Mediterranean coastlines? For example, consider:

- the climate
- the concentration of population in large cities
- the months of the year when tourists are present in large numbers

---

CASE STUDY

Euro Disney

On 12 April 1992, Euro Disney opened its doors to the public, at Marne-la-Vallée, 32km to the east of Paris. In almost every way possible, Euro Disney is different from the traditional, established European theme parks. The most obvious difference is one of scale: Euro Disney is almost six times the size of Alton Towers, Britain's biggest theme park. But the Disney park forms only part of the 3500 acre **Euro Disney Resort**, which covers an area about one-fifth of Paris itself. Outside the theme park, the resort provides a whole range of other facilities: six hotels, a campsite, restaurants, shopping and entertainment facilities, housing, and a championship golf course. After 1992, more hotels, sports facilities, and housing will be constructed, as well as 95 000 square metres of shopping development, 700 000 square metres of offices, and 750 000 square metres of industrial development. In other words, people will visit Euro Disney Resort, not only to amuse themselves in the theme park, but to stay in the accommodation, shop, play sports, attend a conference, or to work in the offices or industrial zones.

How are other European theme parks responding to the challenge of Euro Disney? The following article suggests that the new competition created by the arrival of Euro Disney is by no means bad news for Europe's more established theme parks.

THE CHALLENGE OF EURO DISNEY
by Terry Stevens

Since 1985, there has been unprecedented investment in leisure park development in northern Europe, encouraged by the 3500 acre Euro Disneyland at Marne-la-Vallée to the east of Paris.

Much of this new investment has taken place in the densely populated heartlands of northern Europe, in the Nord Pas de Calais and Lorraine in France, in Belgium and Holland, and in the Ruhr region of Germany. These new developments have included the £70 million Parc Astérix, which opened in 1989 at Plailly, north of Paris; the £80 million World of the Smurfs in Lorraine; and Bruparck, the retail-leisure entertainment complex at Heysel in Brussels, which takes the European Community as its theme.

The existing theme parks are upgrading their rides and facilities in preparation for the Disney challenge and to meet the enhanced demands and expectations of the market. They are aware that in future, visitors will travel to Phantasialand, De Efteling, and Walibi fresh from a visit to Euro Disney.

These operators are taking a pragmatic approach to the challenge. Most are devoting their energies to ensuring they retain their current market share.

Euro Disney will handle 11 million visitors in its first year of operation, increasing to 15.2 million by 2001: three times as many visitors as the top 10 attractions in Holland and Germany put together.

Most operators of existing theme parks believe that Euro Disney will have a positive impact on their parks. In particular, it is thought that Euro Disney will increase awareness of theme parks, raise public expectations, develop the market's willingness to pay an economic admission fee, and encourage financial institutions to invest further in this sector.

Paul Beck, Managing Director of De Efteling, believes Euro Disney will cause great changes in the leisure park industry. While De Efteling is bracing itself for a small decline in numbers in 1992–1993, it is predicting stable performances from 1994 to the year 2000. 'We expect Euro Disney will have a positive influence. It is a stimulus to us to further improve the quality of our product. Some of our visitors will look at Euro Disney's American concept but, considering its high entrance charge, we believe they will remain loyal to the European concept'.

Herr Loftellhardt of Phantasialand also refers to the European versus American battle. How do you define the difference? Is it the atmosphere in the themed areas, the food and beverage outlets or maybe the gentler pace? It is also the smaller scale: few European theme parks are able to handle more than a million visitors a year. In addition, European day visitor attractions tend to make more use of environment and heritage attractions than their American counterparts.

The policies adopted by the existing parks appear to be well founded. There is evidence of modest and gradual diversification, and investment in improvements to the quality of existing provision. Most parks have also introduced more rigorous target marketing.

Fig. 6.6

© *Leisure Management*, July 1990. Tel: (0462) 431385

Business facilities

People travelling for business purposes also visit attractions during their free time. Japanese business people in Birmingham for a conference, for example, will take some time off for a tour of the city and its tourist attractions.

Nevertheless, business people need specific facilities to enable them to conduct the business they have to do, whether it is a meeting, a trade exhibition, or a convention.

Many business meetings and conventions take place in hotels which offer special meeting rooms or exhibition areas. However, larger conference and exhibition centres exist to cater for major events such as the Ideal Home Exhibition, or the annual conferences held by the main political parties in Britain, for example.

Whatever the size of the event they are attending, people travelling on business need certain facilities, including appropriate accommodation, ease of access, and the right size of rooms in which to conduct their meetings or hold their exhibition. Brighton, on the south coast of England, is a well-known business tourism destination, as well as being popular with day-trippers and others travelling for leisure purposes. Figure 6.7(a) is an extract from a booklet describing Brighton's assets for the business tourist, and Fig. 6.7(b) shows a conference room in The Brighton Centre, the jewel in the city's crown.

Large companies, who hold a number of meetings, conferences and

Brighton has been successfully hosting major conferences for over a century, and now welcomes over 1,500 gatherings each year. The town's lively, cosmopolitan atmosphere, magnificent Regency architecture, and excellent modern meeting facilities, combine to make it a firm favourite with delegates from all over the world.

Accessibility
Less than an hour from London by fast train, only half an hour from Gatwick airport and ninety minutes from Heathrow, Brighton is easy to get to, particularly for overseas delegates, visitors and speakers.

Walkability
No other town in Britain has such a concentration of meeting facilities, accommodation, shopping areas and tourist attractions. Once in Brighton, delegates can easily get around on foot.

Conference Facilities
The Brighton Centre East Wing has recently been completed, adding to the building's flexibility and breakout capacity. Meetings from 300 to 5,000 can now be accommodated, with banqueting for up to 1,500. The Dome Complex and Brighton Metropole Hotel each have conference facilities for up to 2,000 delegates, the latter also possessing 8000 sq. m. of exhibition space. In addition, we have over 20 hotels with in-house conference facilities, plus the University of Sussex and Brighton Polytechnic, which can offer over 1,000 bedrooms on their campuses for conference delegates.

Accommodation
From 5-star luxury to friendly guesthouses, there are some 2,500 bedrooms within a 10-minute walk of the Brighton Centre. We operate a computerised accommodation bureau to take the headache out of finding suitable rooms for delegates, whatever their budget.

Advice and Assistance
The award-winning team in Brighton's Conference Office provides impartial advice on venue selection, plus a whole range of services to help in the organisation of your conference. Social programmes, bid support, and the provision of literature are examples of where we can help.

Fig. 6.7 (a) What Brighton has to offer as a conference venue

exhibitions, sometimes employ special conference organisers to make all the necessary arrangements for them. The following account describes the work of a conference organiser.

'After establishing the aim of the event which I am to organise, I find out as much as possible about the delegates who will be attending. From my research, I will select the venue to suit them and the budget. It may be necessary to find an audio-visual company to help with the presentations. If delegates are to be accompanied, an interesting partners' programme has to be devised in parallel with the right mix of social events and free time. Then there are the thousands of miscellaneous arrangements to be made, from choosing the menus and wines to arranging seating plans.'

EXERCISE

Imagine that you are a conference organiser. Describe the type of facilities which would be required for the following events. Do not forget accommodation and catering, and activities for people in their spare time, if required.

(*a*) A one-day reunion of 20 women who served in a particular section of the Women's Royal Army Corps during the Second World War. They will want to look at some home-movies shot during the war and some will be accompanied by their husbands, who will not be attending the reunion itself.

*Brighton
nference Centre*

(b) The Agricultural Machinery Show. A one-week international exhibition of tractors, combine harvesters, and other items of mechanical equipment. 100 000 visitors are expected.

(c) The annual conference of the Trades Union Congress. As well as the main conference, there will be a series of smaller debates, and an accompanying exhibition. The event lasts for four days.

CASE STUDY

Business tourism in France

France is one of the world's top business tourism destinations, and Paris is the city which hosts the greatest number of international conferences every year. What are the reasons for France's success in this domain?

Figure 6.8 shows an extract from a French Government Tourist Office publication describing France's business tourism facilities.

TASKS

1 What evidence is there in the text that there is a spin-off for *leisure tourism* from the business tourism which takes place in France?

2 List the examples of new technology and other facilities offered by conference centres in France. For each example, give reasons why it is important to the smooth-running of a conference.

3 What is meant by the phrase 'purpose-built conference centres'? What would the *opposite* of a purpose-built conference centre be?

ASSIGNMENTS

1 Conduct a class survey.
(a) Divide the class into groups of six.
(b) With one person in each group writing down the information, let each member of the group give as many examples as they can of the attractions which they most enjoyed at the last place they visited, either on holiday or on a day trip.
(c) Divide the attractions into the six categories given at the beginning of this chapter.

France is one of the major countries hosting international conventions and meetings. Literally hundreds of conferences are held every day at special venues, conference halls or hotel meeting rooms, in large and small towns, in seaside and mountain resorts, and even in the depths of the French countryside. Riverboats and ships are interesting alternatives and there are even conference train coaches for hire, courtesy of French Railways!

One of the reasons for France's popularity is that it is **easily accessible from all parts of the world.** The number of organisations whose headquarters are based in France is staggering – there are more here than anywhere else.

France has recently seen the development of a number of **excellent conference venues and convention hotels.** Still more are presently under construction to meet the growing demand. Professional conference organisers are on hand in the resorts and towns to ensure that events are properly planned and managed.

Conference delegates often like to extend their stay in France by a few days. There are countless fascinating and highly **enjoyable tours** available throughout France for before or after that convention. These can include technical study trips and meetings with French counterparts, which can be incorporated into the official programme.

Naturally **Paris** is the leading French destination for international conferences, closely followed by the Riviera-Cote d'Azur. Large cities such as **Montpellier, Strasbourg, Lyon, Bordeaux** and **Grenoble** also offer good conference facilities and are famous for their preeminence in the worlds of politics, tourism, and science. Several other cities and resorts are also well equipped to accommodate conventions and meetings with the greatest of ease.

For over ten years, Paris has been universally acknowledged as the world's premier convention city. All the necessary infrastructure is in place: several mainline train stations with high-speed rail links, international airports, motorways that fan out to link the capital with the rest of Europe, superb conference facilities for every kind and size of meeting, and excellent hotels. Finally, the French capital is proud of its fine cultural heritage, its long history of scientific research, and its large and active business community.

The Paris Convention Centre can handle the largest international conferences, with a set of conference rooms of varying sizes that can accommodate 50 to 4,000 delegates. There are 50 committee rooms and business suites. Every modern technical facility and service is to hand, including simultaneous translation, colour Eidophore and closed circuit television. The Centre also includes shops, restaurants, bars, a bank, post office, pharmacy and press office. There is a direct coach service to Charles ·de Gaulle Airport and central Paris is a short taxi ride away.

West of Paris, **the Centre for New Industry and Technology (CNIT)** has been designed to accommodate meetings, exhibitions and trade shows in the vast La Defense complex. There are many other conference venues for hire in Paris, and most major hotels provide good meeting facilities for 100 to 1,000 delegates.

The sophisticated French Riviera is also an ideal convention or conference destination. The area is renowned worldwide for its fine weather, ease of access, excellent facilities and the high standard of service provided in its many hotels. That's not all: the beautiful scenery and artistic heritage all around mean that non-delegates need never be bored and can take advantage of the many excursions and activities on offer.

The two main conference venues are **Cannes** and **Nice.** Both resorts offer state of the art convention centres and additional meeting facilities in the major hotels. They are served by the **international airport of Nice-Cote d'Azur,** which enjoys good road links to the main coastal resorts. **The Palais des Festivals et des Congrès** in Cannes can accommodate up to 2,400 delegates in its main hall and, because it was only opened a few years ago, it can boast the very latest equipment necessary for audiovisual presentations, product launches and exhibitions.

Banqueting arrangements for up to 1,200 can also be made, and there are in addition several good restaurants and bars, a press office and parking for 900 vehicles.

The Acropolis Centre in Nice is the largest in Europe and was opened in 1984. It can accommodate up to 4,500 delegates at a time. The main auditorium seats 2,500, and there are several meeting rooms available complete with the most up to date equipment on the market. The Acropolis can also provide 43,000 square feet of exhibition space, a press office and a television studio. Functions can also be held : drinks parties for up to 4,000 guests, or sit-down meals for up to 2,000. Nice, Cannes and other French Riviera resorts can also offer meeting rooms in the larger hotels.

Purpose-built conference centres are for hire in many major French cities. In Strasbourg, **the Palais de la Musique et des Congrès** can host conventions of up to 2,000 delegates, and the **Palais des Congrès** in Bordeaux can seat 1,000 in comfort in its main auditorium. **Grenoble's Palais des Congrès** has facilities for 1,200 delegates, Lyon's new venue can accommodate the same number... **Lille has a Palais des Congrès** that can host 1,000, and the resorts of **Deauville** and **La Baule** can also welcome up to 1,000 delegates. Several other towns and resorts are suitable venues for smaller scale meetings and business seminars.

Whichever venue you select for your conference in France, you can be sure of good service and helpful advice. Your working sessions and leisure hours will be enhanced by that inimitable French flair, and there's no doubt that when the time comes to return home, every delegate will be sorry to leave the beautiful country that is France.

g. 6.8 *France's business tourism facilities*

urce: French Government Tourist Office

(d) Which were the most popular categories? To show the results, each member of the group should draw a bar chart.

(e) Compare the results of all the groups.

(f) Discuss within your groups what you think the results would have been for:
- very young children
- teachers or lecturers
- middle-aged Americans visiting Britain on holiday.

2 The arrival of leisure pools in Britain has not pleased everyone. The Amateur Swimming Association is concerned that leisure pools may turn us into a nation of splashers rather than swimmers, and that by making water sports first and foremost into a *fun* activity, the emphasis on competitive standards in swimming is being lost. Others claim that the fitness aspect of swimming is lost in leisure pool activity.

Conduct a class debate: imagine that an old-fashioned, though busy, swimming pool in your own area is to be closed down for a year, in order to be converted into a leisure pool. When it reopens, it will have waterslides, wave-machines and fountains. The cost of admission will rise from the present £1.00 per session to £4.50 for the whole day. Instead of attracting visitors from the immediate area only, people will come from a radius of 10 miles to use it.

Divide the class into two equal sides, one to argue in favour of this development, for example, from the tourist's point of view, and one to argue against it, as a resident in the immediate locality.

3 Suggest a place in your own area where people either do an unusual job, or make an interesting product. Imagine that you are the person responsible for advertising your area in order to attract visitors. Write a letter to the manager or owner of the place you have thought of, suggesting that it be opened up to visitors.

Describe briefly what the visitors could be shown, assuring the person you are writing to that tours would not interfere with the business of the place. Emphasise the advantages of the place becoming an attraction.

4 As a group, draw up a list of attractions and business facilities in your own area. Try to think of attractions from each of the six categories. Let each member of the class select *one* of the built attractions or business facilities, and use that as the basis of a project. For each place, find out:
- how many visitors it had last year
- where they came from
- the average length of stay
- how many people work there, both full-time and part-time
- what jobs they do

Draw a map of the area, showing the position of facilities in relation to the town.

Write up your project, including any advertising material produced by the attraction or business facility.

7

TOURISM PROMOTION AND TOURIST INFORMATION

After reading this chapter, you should have a clear understanding of:
- the importance of tourism promotion,
- how countries promote themselves overseas in order to attract tourists,
- how tourism is promoted internally within countries,
- the role of tourist organisations,
- how Tourist Information Centres contribute to tourism promotion.

Tourist destinations can only be successful if they attract enough customers or tourists. The different sectors of the tourism industry at any destination depend for their success on tourists coming to them in large numbers, and spending money. Without tourist spending, many transport, accommodation and catering facilities and tourist attractions would go out of business.

Any destination, whether it is a country, or a region within a country, or even a single town or resort, must work hard to attract visitors, in order to be successful in tourism.

Tourism promotion is the name given to the business of persuading tourists to visit a particular destination, i.e. working to attract visitors to a particular country, region or town. It is not usually enough for a destination to have beautiful scenery, comfortable hotels, a variety of tourist attractions and good transport networks. People need to be told about the destination and encouraged to visit that one in particular, rather than any other place. Tourism promotion is concerned with making potential visitors aware of a destination and persuading them to choose it in preference to any other.

Promotion is so important to tourism that most destinations have established official organisations which are responsible for encouraging people to visit them.

National tourist organisations

Most countries who wish to attract international tourists to themselves have national tourist organisations, all of whom work in a similar way to the British Tourist Authority. The aim of the British Tourist Authority is to promote incoming tourism to Britain from abroad, by convincing residents of other countries that Britain has much to offer the tourist. Because it is responsible for promoting the whole country, it is called a national tourist organisation.

The BTA was established in 1969 through an Act of Parliament, and is financed through central government. It is based in London, but undertakes promotional activity abroad through overseas offices situated in countries around the world. The locations of these offices are shown in Fig. 7.1.

BTA staff working in overseas offices aim, through the work they do, to:

1 increase the number of visitors to Britain from abroad;
2 encourage overseas visitors to spend more money in Britain;
3 persuade overseas visitors to spend more time exploring the less well known parts of Britain, including areas of high unemployment;
4 promote London as a major tourist destination; and
5 persuade visitors to come to Britain all year round, and not only during the summer.

How do they do this?

To find out how the BTA offices work, we shall take the office in Sydney, Australia as an example. Australian tourists visit Britain year after year,

Fig. 7.1 BTA office worldwide

despite the long journey that is involved. They come for many reasons; either to visit friends and relatives, on business, or simply to spend time in a country where the people share the same language, interests and outlook on life. Whatever the reason, Australian tourists are big spenders.

Figure 7.2 shows the number of visits to Britain from Australia between 1988 and 1991, and the spending levels of Australian tourists in Britain.

Figure 7.3 shows the regions and countries of stay of Australian visitors to Britain, as compared with those of *all* visitors to Britain ('world') in 1990.

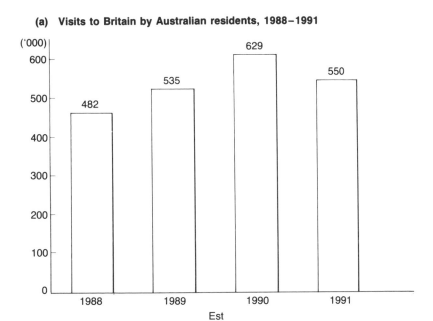

(a) Visits to Britain by Australian residents, 1988–1991

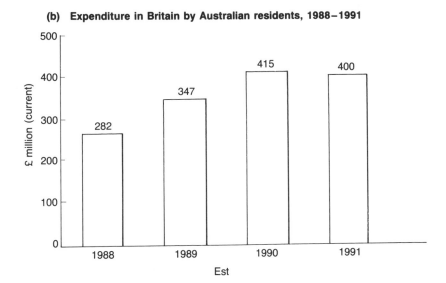

(b) Expenditure in Britain by Australian residents, 1988–1991

g. 7.2 (a) Visits to ritain by Australian sidents (1988–1991)) Expenditure in ritain by Australian sidents (1988–1991)

urce: British Tourist thority

	World (excl Irish Republic)			Australia		
	Staying visits	Over- nights	Spending	Staying visits	Over- nights	Spending
	'000	'000	£m	'000	'000	£m
Base:	16 705	184 896	7 330	629	14 253	414
	%	%	%	%	%	%
England:	90.1	88.6	90.3	97.1	86.1	85.6
London	57.2	39.1	55.4	68.2	31.0	45.4
Rest of England:	45.5	49.5	34.9	58.0	55.1	40.2
Northumbria TB	1.8	1.4	1.0	3.2	3.4	1.9
Cumbria TB	1.4	0.8	0.5	4.3	3.2	1.8
North West TB	5.5	4.4	3.0	9.5	5.9	4.9
Yorks & Humbs TB	5.0	4.0	2.5	10.7	5.1	3.1
East Midlands TB	3.5	2.8	1.7	5.9	2.8	2.3
Heart of England TB	6.9	4.7	3.9	10.9	5.8	6.3
East Anglia TB	5.3	4.8	3.2	8.2	4.8	4.0
West Country TB	7.4	6.0	4.2	16.2	7.0	4.8
Southern TB	5.3	4.9	3.3	7.7	3.6	2.0
South East TB	10.9	9.3	6.6	15.4	9.2	5.6
Thames & Chlts TB	7.4	5.9	4.7	9.3	3.5	3.3
Channel Islands (A)	0.2	0.2	0.1	0.4	0.6	0.2
Isle of Man (A)	0.1	0.1	0.1	0.1	0.1	0.1
Unspecified	0.1	0.1	0.1	0.2	0.1	*
Scotland	8.9	8.1	7.1	17.0	8.5	9.6
Wales	3.8	2.8	1.7	12.1	4.5	3.8
Northern Ireland	0.4	0.4	0.3	0.7	0.8	0.7

Fig. 7.3 *Region and countries of stay by visitors to Britain*
Source: British Tourist Authority

EXERCISE

1 Look at the map showing the cities where BTA has overseas offices. In how many different countries outside Europe can BTA offices be found? Name the cities of each of these offices.

2 Look back at the aims of the BTA. Is the BTA office in Sydney successful in achieving aims 1–3? Give reasons for your answer.

3 Why do you think spending and visitor numbers fell in 1991?

The BTA office in Sydney has a staff of nine people, to promote Britain as a tourist destination for Australians. However, there is strong competition from the 57 other national tourist organisations operating in Australia, all of whom are actively promoting their countries, and trying to tempt Australians to spend their holidays in places such as Hong Kong, Singapore, the USA, and New Zealand.

How does the BTA persuade Australians to choose Britain?

Many Australians decide to visit Britain after reading newspaper or magazine articles written by Australian journalists who have been on BTA-organised visits to Britain. BTA organises about 50 such press visits or 'educationals' every year from Australia, paying for groups of writers to visit all parts of Britain, in order to encourage them to write articles about their trip when they get back. Many of these articles persuade the Australian readers that a holiday in Britain would be a good idea.

The BTA office in Sydney also sends out a number of short press items to Australian newspapers and magazines every month. These are usually in the form of a story about some interesting event which is to take place in Britain, or about a new hotel or a new tourist attraction.

BTA staff also attend ten travel trade shows a year in Australia. At each travel show, they run an exhibition stand where they give out brochures and leaflets on Britain to the thousands of people who enquire at the stand for information. Again, the BTA is in competition with all the other national tourist organisations who have exhibition stands at these shows.

BTA Australia ceased to have an advertising budget in 1989, as the result of a Head Office decision. The rationale behind this was that the BTA had very good press relations with magazine and newspaper editors and could secure, for a lower budget, significant positive media exposure from press visits. (However, as the Australian economy has gone into decline since 1989, so has the number of publications being produced as well as the number of travel pages available. This has tended to put BTA Australia at a disadvantage, at a time when its competitors are allocating *increased* resources to the Australian market.)

Finally, the Sydney office of the BTA gives out information on Britain and specially printed brochures such as 'Australian's Royal Britain' to the 50 000 enquirers a year who contact them with questions about Britain as a tourist destination.

Figure 7.4 shows two members of staff dealing with enquiries from members of the Australian public calling at the BTA Sydney office.

Each of the overseas offices of the BTA works in a similar way to promote Britain as a tourist destination to the people living in the countries in which the offices are located. They also play the part of 'shop windows' for Britain, places where people can telephone or call in person for information on Britain. Residents of these countries ask a variety of questions about Britain

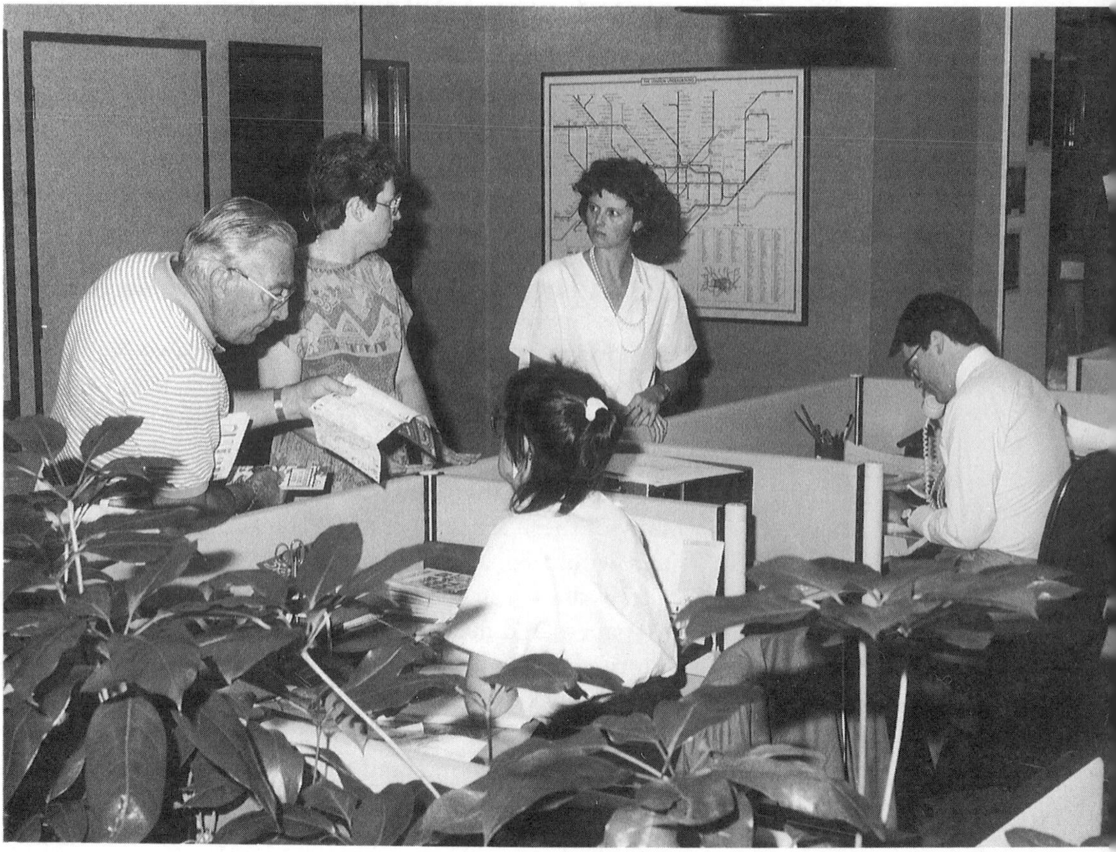

Fig. 7.4 The BTA office in Sydney, Australia

when they are planning their trips. For example, Americans may ask where in Britain they can spend the night in a castle; Germans may want to know if they can buy unleaded petrol in Britain for their cars and Japanese people may want to know if there will be Japanese-speaking guides available to show them around Britain's main tourist cities. BTA staff in the overseas offices must be able to answer all these questions and, hopefully, persuade the enquirers that Britain has just what they are looking for.

In the same way that the BTA works overseas, other countries' national tourist organisations provide information and run advertising campaigns in Britain, in order to persuade British people to visit the countries they represent. For example, while the BTA is busy trying to persuade Australians (and people living in many other countries) to come to Britain as tourists, the Australian Tourist Commission is working hard to convince people in countries all over the world that Australia is the ideal tourist destination. The ATC is based in Sydney and has overseas offices in Auckland, Frankfurt, Los Angeles, New York, Tokyo and Singapore, as well as London.

The staff of the Australian Tourist Commission's office in London work hard to promote Australia to British people. Their activities follow a similar pattern to those of BTA staff overseas:

- they staff the busy ATC stand at the World Travel Market in London, Britain's leading travel trade exhibition;
- they run cooperative advertising campaigns with major Australian tour operators, in British magazines and newspapers;
- they organise a Visiting Journalists Programme, arranging for representatives from film, print and broadcast media to visit Australia and to publicise what they see, when they get back to Britain; and
- they run a series of holiday 'roadshows' throughout Britain, aimed at telling travel agents all about Australia making it easier for these agents to sell holidays in Australia to their clients.

How effective has the ATC been in attracting visitors to Australia? In a recent study entitled *Marketing International Tourism to Australia*, the authors, Crouch, Schultz and Valerio, made the following observations:

'Although the total number of inbound visitors to Australia remains relatively low by international standards – largely due to Australia's isolated geographical situation – inbound tourism has experienced very healthy growth rates . . . Few dispute the fact that 1988 was an exceptional year when Australia hosted Expo and celebrated 200 years of settlement. But the high growth rates began a few years before 1988. A number of factors have been proposed as determinants of this growth, including international terrorism in the mid-1980s, which seemed to reach a peak in 1986, sending tourists to destinations which were perceived to be safe; the growing popularity of Australian films and music abroad, particularly the international popularity of the feature film *Crocodile Dundee*, the devaluation of the Australian currency through the 1980s; and the Chernobyl disaster in 1986.'

Despite all of the above factors, which have worked in favour of inbound tourism to Australia, the Australian government continues to fund the marketing work of the ATC, to the sum of A$63 million in 1990–91.

Figure 7.5 (a) and (b) shows the number of international visitors to Australia between 1980 and 1990, together with visitor expenditure and length of stay for 1990.

EXERCISE

1 In which countries of the world do the BTA and the ATC both have offices? Why do you think they both choose these countries in particular to promote their own countries?

2 Which three regions of the world have seen the largest increases in the number of tourists they sent to Australia between 1980 and 1990? Can you explain the reasons for the growth in visitors from these particular regions?

ARRIVALS OF OVERSEAS VISITORS

Country of Residence	1980	1985	1989	1990	1990
Canada	28,500	40,900	54,200	53,700	2%
USA	111,400	196,500	260,700	250,700	11%
UK and Ireland	131,500	158,900	285,100	288,300	13%
Europe (excl UK/Ireland)	112,300	142,000	245,600	260,100	12%
Japan	48,800	107,600	349,500	479,900	22%
Asia (excl Japan)	89,900	163,400	321,000	348,100	16%
New Zealand	307,100	245,300	449,300	418,400	19%
Other	75,100	88,000	114,900	115,700	5%
Total	904,600	1,142,600	2,080,300	2,214,900	100%

Purpose of Visit

	1980	1985	1989	1990	1990
In Transit	67,300	79,600	78,600	70,200	3%
Convention	17,600	20,100	25,400	32,500	1%
Business	112,700	158,000	230,800	231,100	10%
Visiting Relatives	263,900	287,100	459,900	456,000	21%
Holiday	360,200	500,000	1,107,000	1,233,700	56%
Other	82,900	97,800	178,600	191,400	9%
Total	904,600	1,142,600	2,080,300	2,214,900	100%

Source: Australian Bureau of Statistics, Cat No 3401.0

Fig. 7.5 (a)

Country of Residence	US & Canada	Japan	Other Asia	NZ	UK & Ireland	Other Europe	Total
Average expenditure in Australia	$2,061	$1,551	$2,103	$1,351	$2,242	$2,477	$1,858
Average expenditure per day	$69	$119	$54	$59	$39	$50	$58
Average number of nights in Australia	30	13	39	23	58	50	32
Total number of nights in Australia (million)	8.6	5.9	12.2	8.8	15.6	12.5	66.1

Source: BTR, International Visitor Survey, 1990.

Fig. 7.5 (b)

3 Suggest an explanation for the relatively low daily expenditure of visitors to Australia from the UK and Ireland.

4 Comment on the average number of nights spent in Australia by visitors from the various regions, and suggest explanations for the differences in these averages.

More than one official organisation in Britain is responsible for tourism promotion. Because Britain itself is made up of separate nations, each has its own national tourist board, also established through Acts of Parliament. While the BTA promotes Britain as a whole overseas, the English Tourist Board, the Scottish Tourist Board and the Wales Tourist Board are responsible for encouraging British tourists to visit the three countries they represent. As well as promoting their own countries to British people, these three tourist boards work to spread the benefits of tourism, by encouraging British people to visit the less well-known parts of these countries and to make their trips at off-peak times, so that the tourist season is stretched.

The English Tourist Board is based in London, the Scottish Tourist Board in Edinburgh, and the Wales Tourist Board in Cardiff. Each of them runs a range of promotional and advertising campaigns in Britain to tempt people to visit them for a holiday, business, or a short break. Londoners travelling to work on the underground, for example, see advertisements inviting them to 'get away from it all' by spending some time on holiday in Scotland.

As well as undertaking this type of advertising, each of the three national tourist boards publishes annual guides on holidays in England, Scotland or Wales, and distributes these through travel agencies. In this way, for example, a person in Aberdeen can go into their local travel agency and book a holiday in Torquay from a brochure on England, in the same way that they can book a holiday in Spain straight from a brochure. Figure 7.6 shows an ETB publication, *Let's Go*, which gives details of off-peak short breaks in England.

The STB and WTB also have powers to give financial assistance in the form of grants to tourism businesses in their countries. Grants of this kind are used for many purposes, such as adding leisure facilities to hotels, building coach parks, or helping to finance the building of new holiday centres. In this way, the tourist boards help improve the tourist facilities and amenities in their countries.

To sum up, therefore: while the BTA is promoting Britain overseas, to encourage international tourists to visit Britain, the ETB, STB and WTB are promoting England, Scotland and Wales to British people as well as making sure that when tourists arrive, they find all the facilities that they need.

The situation in Northern Ireland is different. The Northern Ireland Tourist Board was created by an Act of Parliament in 1948 'to promote the development of tourist traffic in Northern Ireland, and to encourage persons

Fig. 7.6 *Front cover of an ETB brochure for short breaks*

who reside elsewhere to visit Northern Ireland'. In other words, the NITB is responsible for promoting Northern Ireland overseas, and it has offices in Britain, the Irish Republic, New York and Frankfurt, for this purpose. Within Northern Ireland itself, the NITB concentrates on improving and developing tourist facilities and amenities.

Regional tourist organisations

Most countries, including Britain, have smaller, more localised organisations which are responsible for promoting specific regions of those countries to people who live in other parts of the same country, as well as overseas. For example, in the USA, each separate state, such as Texas or California, has its own regional tourist organisation which promotes that state throughout the USA.

England, Scotland and Wales each have their own networks of regional tourist organisations. In England, there are 12 Regional Tourist Boards.

Each of these Regional Tourist Boards was set up by the ETB in the early 1970s to promote specific areas of England. Unlike the ETB and BTA, they are not wholly supported through central government funds but have three sources of income:

● funding from the ETB;

1. Cumbria

2. Northumbria
(Cleveland, Durham, Northumberland, Tyne & Wear),

3. North West
(Cheshire, Greater Manchester, Lancashire, Merseyside, High Peak District of Derbyshire).

4. Yorkshire & Humberside
(North, South and West Yorkshire and Humberside).

5. Heart of England
(Gloucestershire, Hereford and Worcester, Shropshire, Staffordshire, Warwickshire, West Midlands).

6. East Midlands
(Derbyshire, Leicestershire, Lincolnshire, Northamptonshire, Nottinghamshire).

7. Thames and Chilterns
(Bedfordshire, Berkshire, Buckinghamshire, Hertfordshire, Oxfordshire).

8. East Anglia
(Cambridgeshire, Essex, Norfolk, Suffolk).

9. London

10. West Country
(Avon, Cornwall, Devon, Somerset, Western Dorset, Wiltshire and the Isles of Scilly).

11. Southern
(Eastern Dorset, Northern Dorset, Hampshire and the Isle of Wight).

12 South East England
(East Sussex, Kent, Surrey, West Sussex).

7.7 Regional tourist board areas in England

- contributions from the individual county and district councils which they cover;
- membership fees from tourism operators, such as hoteliers and tourist attraction owners, who pay to become members, so that they can have a say in the running of their Regional Tourist Board and use its services.

Each Regional Tourist Board runs a series of promotional campaigns for their region using similar techniques to those of the BTA for the whole of Britain when campaigning abroad. These include publishing regional guides, inviting travel agents and press to visit their region, running advertising campaigns in the media, and attending travel shows with their own exhibition stands. For example, the Heart of England Tourist Board developed a new overseas promotion group in 1987, made up of county councils in the region, Birmingham International Airport and Coventry City Council, to promote the Heart of England region at overseas travel exhibitions. In this way, the group hopes to persuade more international tourists to visit their region for leisure and business.

Scotland has 32 Area Tourist Boards to cover the country and promote the individual regions, as well as ten district councils which are involved in tourism promotion. Wales has three Regional Tourism Councils. The regional tourist organisations for Scotland and Wales are shown in the following maps.

All of the regional tourist organisations in Britain strive to persuade British people to visit other parts of their own country, and to persuade visitors from overseas to try new places as well as the more obvious tourist destinations such as London, Edinburgh and York. Like the BTA and the other national tourist boards, they also work to persuade tourists to take more holidays and short breaks at off-peak times, in order to spread the load more evenly throughout the year. Many of the bright and attractive holiday brochures produced by regional tourist organisations feature spring and autumn breaks and emphasise the excellent value of holidays at those times of year.

EXERCISE

1 What do the following abbreviations stand for?

(a) BTA (c) STB (e) ATC (g) NTO.
(b) ETB (d) WTB (f) HETB

2 Which one of the official organisations in question 1 is responsible for promoting England, Scotland and Wales overseas?

3 Look at the following list of official tourism promotion organisations and divide it under two headings, national tourist organisations and regional tourist organisations:

The Yorkshire and Humberside Tourist Board
The English Tourist Board
The Barbados Board of Tourism

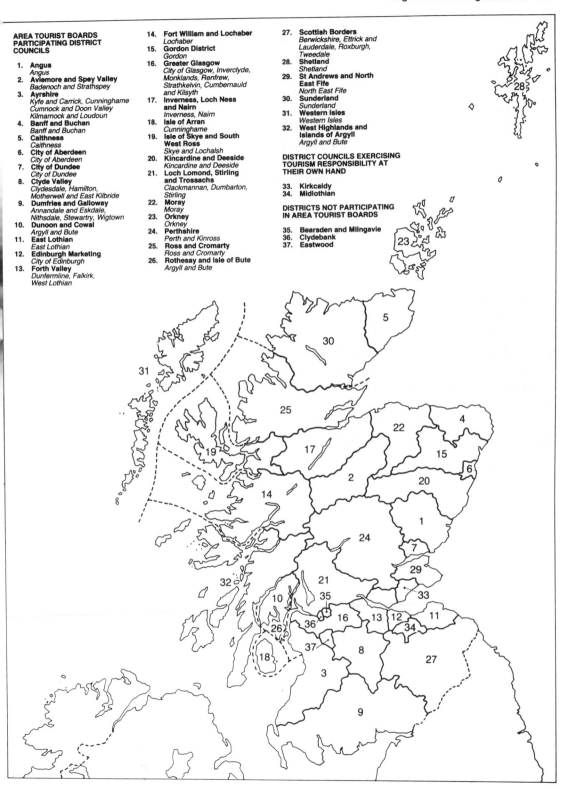

AREA TOURIST BOARDS PARTICIPATING DISTRICT COUNCILS

1. **Angus**
   Angus
2. **Aviemore and Spey Valley**
   Badenoch and Strathspey
3. **Ayrshire**
   Kyle and Carrick, Cunninghame
   Cumnock and Doon Valley
   Kilmarnock and Loudoun
4. **Banff and Buchan**
   Banff and Buchan
5. **Caithness**
   Caithness
6. **City of Aberdeen**
   City of Aberdeen
7. **City of Dundee**
   City of Dundee
8. **Clyde Valley**
   Clydesdale, Hamilton,
   Motherwell and East Kilbride
9. **Dumfries and Galloway**
   Annandale and Eskdale,
   Nithsdale, Stewartry, Wigtown
10. **Dunoon and Cowal**
    Argyll and Bute
11. **East Lothian**
    East Lothian
12. **Edinburgh Marketing**
    City of Edinburgh
13. **Forth Valley**
    Dunfermline, Falkirk,
    West Lothian

14. **Fort William and Lochaber**
    Lochaber
15. **Gordon District**
    Gordon
16. **Greater Glasgow**
    City of Glasgow, Inverclyde,
    Monklands, Renfrew,
    Strathkelvin, Cumbernauld
    and Kilsyth
17. **Inverness, Loch Ness and Nairn**
    Inverness, Nairn
18. **Isle of Arran**
    Cunninghame
19. **Isle of Skye and South West Ross**
    Skye and Lochalsh
20. **Kincardine and Deeside**
    Kincardine and Deeside
21. **Loch Lomond, Stirling and Trossachs**
    Clackmannan, Dumbarton,
    Stirling
22. **Moray**
    Moray
23. **Orkney**
    Orkney
24. **Perthshire**
    Perth and Kinross
25. **Ross and Cromarty**
    Ross and Cromarty
26. **Rothesay and Isle of Bute**
    Argyll and Bute

27. **Scottish Borders**
    Berwickshire, Ettrick and
    Lauderdale, Roxburgh,
    Tweedale
28. **Shetland**
    Shetland
29. **St Andrews and North East Fife**
    North East Fife
30. **Sunderland**
    Sunderland
31. **Western Isles**
    Western Isles
32. **West Highlands and Islands of Argyll**
    Argyll and Bute

DISTRICT COUNCILS EXERCISING TOURISM RESPONSIBILITY AT THEIR OWN HAND

33. **Kirkcaldy**
34. **Midlothian**

DISTRICTS NOT PARTICIPATING IN AREA TOURIST BOARDS

35. **Bearsden and Milngavie**
36. **Clydebank**
37. **Eastwood**

Fig. 7.8 Regional tourist board areas in Scotland

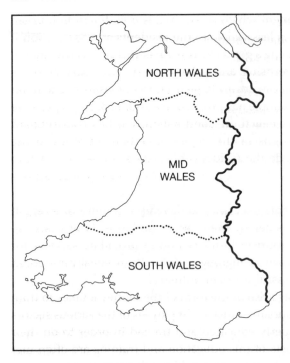

Fig. 7.9 Regional tourist board areas in Wales

The South Wales Regional Tourism Council
The Netherlands Board of Tourism
The Hawaii Visitors Bureau
The Tourism Development Corporation of Malaysia
The Singapore Tourist Promotion Board
The Cumbria Tourist Board
The Kenya Tourist Office
The Comité Départemental de Tourisme du Nord (Pas de Calais).

4 Which regional tourist organisation is responsible for promoting the area in which you live?

Local tourist offices

On an even more local scale than the regional tourist organisations, individual towns, cities and districts have set up their own local tourist offices to promote tourism to the places they represent. In Britain, most of the first tourist offices were established in seaside resorts and historic cities such as Blackpool, Bournemouth, York and Chester. These were supported by the local authority of their town or district, and paid for through the rates. Most local tourist offices around the world are financed in this way, through rates or local taxes, as opposed to national government funds.

Tourist offices come under a variety of titles: for example, The Brighton Resort Services Department, The Dallas Visitor and Convention Bureau, the

Torbay Tourist Board, the Birmingham Convention and Visitors Bureau, Northamptonshire Tourism, The Melbourne Convention Bureau, the London Tourist Board and Convention Bureau. Those using the word 'convention' in their titles are emphasising the fact that they wish to attract business as well as leisure tourists.

Today in Britain, several hundred different tourist offices exist, many of which are successfully engaged in promoting places not traditionally associated with tourism.

Since the early 1980s, many cities, towns and districts have set up their own tourist offices to keep in line with the growth in importance of tourism as an industry. These places have often begun by giving themselves catchy slogans in order to tempt the tourist to visit them. Examples of these include:

- Aldeburgh, The Resort of Infectious Charm
- Folkestone, Spacious and Gracious
- Ironbridge, Birthplace of the Industrial Revolution
- Plymouth, Pearl of the West
- Keswick, A World of Activities at Your Feet

Nottingham, 'the City of Lace, Legend and Life', also promotes itself as a tourist destination through the local authority's Tourism and Public Relations

g. 7.10 Promoting *ottingham at the orld Travel Market in ndon*

urtesy: Nottingham City *uncil*

Office. The city succeeds in attracting over 900 000 visitors a year, mostly tourists who come on day trips or to spend a few days on a short break in the city, home of the legendary Robin Hood and his arch enemy the Sheriff of Nottingham. They visit the city's many museums, shops, sports facilities, and often find their way to 'The Trip to Jerusalem', the oldest pub in the world or to the new Robin Hood Centre.

Telling Britain – and the rest of the world – about the many attractions which Nottingham has to offer is the responsibility of the tourism promotion staff of the city's Tourism and Public Relations Office. These staff undertake a wide range of promotional activities to attract leisure and conference visitors to Nottingham. They arrange tours of the city for visiting journalists; they represent Nottingham at major travel shows and exhibitions in Britain and overseas; they provide the press and other media with information on what is happening in Nottingham that would interest visitors and they produce a wide variety of leaflets and brochures about Nottingham's attractions and facilities – many in French and German as well as English.

In 1992, Nottingham's tourism staff were heavily involved in promoting the city's Civil War celebrations. King Charles I declared war on Parliament at Nottingham Castle in 1642 with the raising of his standard. To mark the 350th anniversary of the outbreak of the Civil War, a number of events took place in Nottingham throughout the summer of 1992, including battle re-enactments, a Civil War exhibition in Nottingham Castle, and a re-creation of the raising of the King's standard.

Figure 7.10 shows the modern-day Sheriff of Nottingham promoting the city at the World Travel Market in London.

Tourist information

One very important way in which countries, regions and individual towns promote themselves and what they have to offer the tourist is through Tourist Information Centres, or TICs as they are called.

Tourists need information about what is available, in order to get the most from their holiday or business trip. Most countries which welcome tourists, therefore, have a network of TICs in major towns and cities to provide visitors with information on a variety of topics, such as which bus to catch, where to take a sightseeing tour, which local carnivals and festivals are on, where to eat, and where to stay. TICs can be managed by the national or regional tourist organisations or by the local tourist office, depending on which country the tourist is in, but they are almost always paid for out of the public's money and the tourist rarely has to pay for information.

Britain has more than 700 TICs offering a free, nationwide service. Most of them are run by the local authorities in which they are situated. However, the regional and national tourist organisations are also involved with the

Fig. 7.11 A TIC assistant giving information to two visitors in Gloucester

training of TIC staff and keeping them supplied with uniforms, display material, brochures and leaflets. The service is free and the people working in them can answer questions and provide information on tourist attractions within a range of 80km (50 miles) of their centre, or within the scope of a day's excursion. They have all the information that makes a holiday or a day out a success such as which restaurant is likely to provide a high chair for baby, which garage to call when the car breaks down, the best place for a picnic, a walk or a scenic drive and which stately home does not involve too much walking for the elderly.

In addition to the information on transport and tourist attractions, Britain's TICs carry details of accommodation from camping sites to five-star hotels. Most have lists of local accommodation which they are happy to send out on request to people making telephone enquiries, or which they give out to personal callers.

Two accommodation services are available:

(1) Local bed-booking service. TICs offering this service will make a reservation for the visitor at a local hotel or guest house. This is a service which is useful for visitors who have just arrived in town and who need accommodation but do not want to spend too much time looking around at different hotels. The TIC will do all the work for them: looking through their lists to find a place in the visitor's price range, and then telephoning to make the booking.

(2) Book-a-bed-ahead service. This is a helpful service for tourists who are travelling around from place to place. By going into the TIC in one town, they can book a room in a hotel or guest house in the next town they are planning to visit, even when it is hundreds of kilometres away. The first TIC will make a small charge for telephoning the TIC in the tourists' next destination.

TICs in Britain can be found in a variety of locations. Some are situated in railway stations, airports and ports so that tourists can get information as soon as they arrive; many are in town halls or libraries; some are situated in major tourist attractions, and some can even be found in large stores such as Harrods and Selfridges in London. In 1989, 10.7 million British adults used the services of a TIC in Britain.

CASE STUDY

The Singapore Tourist Promotion Board

In 1990, the number of international tourists visiting Singapore passed the 5 million mark for the first time, with visitor arrivals up 10.2 per cent over 1989.

The Singapore Tourist Promotion Board promotes tourism to Singapore through its overseas offices in 12 different countries and every year produces a report on its activities. The following article shows some extracts from its annual report for 1990–1991.

Sharing the Singapore experience

Through its worldwide marketing efforts, the Singapore Tourist Promotion Board reaches out to potential and repeat visitors through a range of creative campaigns with the consistent message that Singapore is an exciting tropical destination which delivers modern Western comforts, but not at the expense of its Asian soul.

With award-winning videos, print and television advertising, innovative promotions, joint campaigns, public relations and quality publications, the Board injects the colours, cultures, cuisines and crafts of Singapore into its key markets worldwide.

New print advertising in Australia updated both consumers and the trade on exciting new developments, while in Italy, Japan, Scandinavia, the United Kingdom, USA and Germany, the successful 'Singapore: The Most Surprising Tropical Island' campaign continued. In France, audiences in six major cities caught a glimpse of Singapore through a colourful cinema commercial. Within Asia, Singapore's image as a fun-filled activity-packed destination was reinforced through the advertising campaign 'Singapore: the World's Most Colourful City'.

Joint advertising promotions with Singapore Airlines and the Civil Aviation Authority of Singapore also enabled the Board to widen its advertising reach.

But while advertising can suggest warm welcomes, exciting attractions and a host of creature comforts, the suggestion becomes more tangible through personal experience and contact.

As in other years, the Board's primary efforts were concentrated on taking a taste of Singapore to markets as far flung as Stockholm and as close as Asean*.

At major trade shows including the World Travel Market in London, the Internationale Tourismus-Bourse (ITB) in Berlin and the Borsa Internazionale del Turismo (BIT) in Milan, this sampling of Singapore encourages major tour operators to continue their commitment to the destination. Australia received special attention with a ten-day promotion covering Melbourne, Perth and Sydney, updating the travel trade on both new attractions and old favourites.

The Board also focused on its key markets in Asean and Asia, mounting a host of direct-mail campaigns, special promotions, competitions, workshops and seminars, many linked with the expansion of air links.

Complementing these trade initiatives was a full programme of media educationals for 622 international print, television and radio journalists and film crews. Like the tourist, the journalist whose experience of Singapore has been both professionally and personally satisfying makes a powerful ambassador for Singapore tourism, reaching out to a wide audience.

With tailor-made itineraries, designed to meet the specific interests of the media and their readers, the Board not only highlighted new attractions, but introduced journalists to Singapore's many colourful stories and exciting facets.

(*The term 'Asean' stands for 'Association of South East Asian Nations' and refers to the six-country political association comprising Brunei, Indonesia, Philippines, Malaysia, Singapore and Thailand.)

TASKS

1 List the different media used by the SPTB to promote Singapore to overseas markets.

2 At whom are the various 'trade initiatives' aimed, and why?

3 Why do you think Singapore Airlines and the Civil Aviation Authority of Singapore carry out joint advertising promotions with the STPB?

4 Visitor arrivals figures for Singapore's top 10 markets are given in Fig. 7.12 (*a*). Which continent provided the greatest growth in visitors to Singapore between 1989 and 1990?

5 Figure 7.12 (*b*) shows a month-by-month record of UK visitor numbers to Singapore.
(*a*) Which are the busiest and the quietest times of the year for UK visitors?
(*b*) How might this be explained?
(*c*) How would you describe the general trend concerning UK visitors to Singapore?

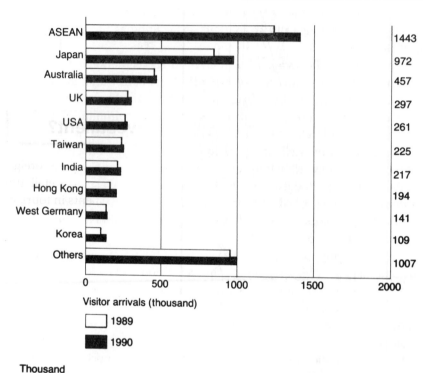

Fig. 7.12 (a) Top ten visitor-generating markets 1989 and 1990

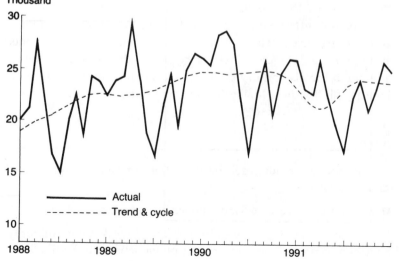

(b) Visitor arrivals to Singapore, 1988–199

7.13 Singapore

ASSIGNMENTS

1 Promoting your town

A representative from your school or college has been invited to join the staff of the local tourist office, to help promote the town or district in which the school or college is located. Before he or she leaves to take up this position, the class has the opportunity to come up with original and interesting ideas for how the town or district could be promoted. The local tourist office is particularly eager to run a new campaign aimed at attracting *young* visitors.

Working in groups, produce a plan containing ideas for advertising campaigns, new publications, and other promotional materials which could be used to attract young visitors to your area.

Consider each of the following:

- what does your area have that is unique, and which might appeal to young people?
- has any celebrity or historical figure been born there?
- are there interesting places to visit?
- does your area offer exciting entertainment or leisure facilities?
- can you think of a catchy slogan to catch the eye of tourists?
- are there any overseas connections which would help your area attract international visitors, for example town twinning?

A member of each group should then present the group's plan to the whole class for discussion.

If time is available, groups could produce real brochures or even short videos to demonstrate their ideas for promoting the area.

2 Role-play the following situation.

You will need to obtain some brochures about the local tourist attractions and accommodation in your area, as well as railway or bus timetables.

Two participants are required: one to play the TIC assistant and one to play the visitor.

The visitor enters the TIC, visiting your area for the first time and having just arrived by train. He or she wants to find out where to stay, where to eat out, and what there is to see in your area. The TIC assistant welcomes the visitor and provides the information that is required. The visitor intends to spend only one night in your area before continuing on his or her tour. The TIC assistant emphasises that there is much to see and do in your area, and tries hard to persuade the visitor to consider staying a little longer in order to see the place properly.

Conduct a class discussion on how the roles were played.

- was the TIC assistant welcoming enough?
- was the visitor persuaded to spend more time in the area?
- could anything more be done in order to provide the visitor with a better service?

8

THE IMPACT OF TOURISM ON THE ENVIRONMENT

After reading this chapter, you should have a clear understanding of:
- the importance of the environment to tourism,
- the ways in which tourism and the environment can benefit from each other,
- the ways in which tourism can harm the environment,
- the importance of tourism planning and management.

The environment in which tourism takes place is important to the quality of the tourist's experience. Both the natural environment in the form of land, water, plants and animals, and the man-made environment, which includes buildings and streets, form the foundation of the tourism industry. In the absence of an attractive environment, tourism rarely succeeds, because this is one of the vital things which tourists look for in a destination.

Often, it is the environment itself which initially attracts tourists to a destination: for example, the warm, sunny beaches of the Mediterranean and the breathtaking scenery of the Lake District. Any town or city hoping to attract visitors will take steps to improve its image such as planting flowers and creating attractive areas. When this happens, the residents also benefit from the environmental improvements. Sometimes it is the environment that encourages tourism developers to build hotels and tourist attractions in particular locations: Center Parcs chose Sherwood Forest as the location of their first British holiday centre partly because of the beauty of the surrounding environment and the presence of a lake for watersports. However appealing an individual hotel or tourist attraction may look in itself, it will rarely be built in a location which lacks an attractive environment. Visitors like to look out upon attractive views from their hotel windows and to drive through unspoilt, pleasant scenery as they approach their final destination. As the environment is so important to tourism, it might be reasonable to expect that tourism developers – those responsible for building tourist accommodation and attractions – would take care to ensure that the environment was properly cared for and preserved. This, however, is not always the case as tourism and tourists can have a great impact on the natural and man-made environment which is not always beneficial and can be quite harmful.

Tourism can have two different types of impact on the environment where it takes place:

1 Tourism and the environment can exist together in **harmony**, when tourism benefits the environment in some way.
2 Tourism and the environment can exist together in **conflict**, when tourism damages the environment in some way.

Tourism and the environment in harmony

When tourism and the environment exist together in harmony, the environment benefits from tourism (and, of course, tourism benefits from the environment). There are many examples of this relationship, most of which fall into one of two types of benefit to the environment: conservation and rehabilitation.

Conservation is the preservation and sensible use of the natural and man-made environment. Conservation and tourism often go together hand in hand.

Many historic monuments and archaeological sites have been saved from destruction because of the great interest in these from tourists. Many hundreds of historic houses in Britain would be no more than ruins or would certainly have been demolished long ago if they held no value as tourist attractions. Not only grand, stately homes and castles have been rescued in this way. Beamish Museum, near Newcastle, is an open air museum which includes a large number of more humble buildings, such as miners' cottages and shops dating from the beginning of the 20th century. These have been saved from demolition because of their value as tourist attractions. Each building has been dismantled brick by brick and then rebuilt on the site of the Beamish Museum, where they have been furnished and fitted out as they would have looked a hundred years ago.

Throughout the world, the natural environment, too, has benefited from tourism in a variety of ways. Some East African states, such as Kenya and Tanzania, have established huge national parks and game reserves for the conservation of their wildlife, the best-known ones being the Masai Mara and the Serengeti. They have done this in the knowledge that wildlife is one of the most important natural resources which attract tourists to East Africa. The national parks and reserves have led to the protection of many species which may have otherwise been destroyed through uncontrolled hunting. Today, Kenya has 13 national parks and 24 national reserves, representing around 7.5% of the total area of the country. Not only does tourism provide a reason for the conservation of the natural and man-made environment, it can also provide the money which pays for the conservation: part of the income from tourism can be used to preserve the environment. Many of Britain's parish churches and cathedrals use the donations they receive from visitors to carry out essential repairs and restoration work, for example.

Rehabilitation describes what happens when a building or an area is given a new life and is 'reborn', as something quite different from its original state. While conservation involves preserving the environment in a form as close as possible to its original or natural state, rehabilitation involves a major change of use of the environment. Many buildings and areas have been saved by tourism through their rehabilitation as tourist attractions or as tourist accommodation.

CASE STUDY

Brougham Hall

The newspaper article on p. 132 describes Brougham Hall, a stately home which has been rehabilitated as a tourist attraction.

TASKS

1 Explain why Brougham Hall is an example of tourism benefiting the environment through rehabilitation, as opposed to conservation.

2 Which word in column 1 of the article means the same as 'rehabilitation'?

3 Give a brief description of what you think the natural environment around Brougham Hall looks like, and say why this is important in attracting visitors.

The world is full of examples of individual buildings and whole areas which have been given a new lease of life by the tourism industry as a result of rehabilitation as tourist attractions or accommodation. Derelict factories have found new lives as museums; industrial land has been converted into the locations of lively garden festivals; and a variety of castles and stately homes falling into disrepair have been given new lives as accommodation for tourists. Such examples demonstrate how tourism can benefit the environment by saving what otherwise might have been lost completely.

Sweeping clean 'new' Brougham

A FEW YEARS AGO, Brougham Hall, near Penrith, was a forgotten and derelict landmark. At Easter, hundreds of visitors spent a day out there enjoying the displays, craft 'demos' and the views over Lakeland.

And this time next year, visitors will also be able to explore the first Lakeland museum, see woodcarving and stonemasonry and watch a goldsmith at work. As well as the present salmon-smoking house - where people can watch, learn and best of all taste - there should also be a factory making hand-made chocolate, furniture restorer and ceramics exhibition.

In fact, Brougham Hall, former home of the Lords Brougham and Vaux, will be alive again, a centre of attraction and a centre of activity.

Impossible

But just a few years ago, this renaissance was impossible, unthinkable, unimaginable.

Brougham Hall, described in 1672 as a 'Hall, fyne house, byre and meldoer' dates from the 15th century and has been the scene of some of history's more unusual events.

It was a vantage point near the scene of the last battle on English soil in 1745 - when Bonnie Prince Charlie was defeated by the Duke of Cumberland. The Great Reform Act of 1832 was largely drafted here by the first Lord Brougham, an eccentric yet notable Lord Chancellor.

Land speed

The world's first land speed record was recorded here, by a Brougham carriage fitted - incredibly enough - with an electric motor engine. And it was here that Edward VII found tranquillity and the fourth Lord Brougham (the man who broke the bank at Monte Carlo - twice) lived in such extravagance that bankruptcy soon followed.

Since 1934 the hall has been empty and partially demolished. A trickle of tourists and local people would come to admire the ruins and the views but the future for Brougham seemed more in the lap of the gods, rather than the hands of its admirers.

In 1986, Christopher Terry - an admirer since he discovered Brougham Hall back in the sixties - acquired the hall with a view to rebuilding and enlivening the area as a tourist attraction that will, within a couple of years, be among the top ten in Cumbria.

£1 million

Eventually, the restoration project will demand an investment of over £1 million, although the first stage, costing some £250,000 is now complete.

The ETB assessed its potential - 20 full time and 17 part-time and seasonal staff will be employed - and awarded development grant aid of £48,600 to help the project proceed.

Pedigree

As a theme/heritage attraction, Brougham Hall will also boast a *son et lumiere* portraying its historical 'pedigree': it will encourage local craft employment and provide the sort of tourism attraction that is a rarity these days - a venue that combines 'tabloid' history with serious environmental and architectural appreciation.

Tourism in Action,
ETB

EXERCISE

Divide the following examples into two groups according to whether tourism has benefited the environment through (*a*) conservation or (*b*) rehabilitation:

- the establishing of national parks in Britain
- the conversion of the Orsay railway station in Paris into a museum
- the reopening of some coal mines in Britain as tourist attractions
- the building of a visitors' centre close to Hadrian's Wall, the proceeds from which pay for archaeological work being undertaken nearby
- declining monasteries being taken over by the Spanish government and turned into 'paradores' – tourist accommodation.

Tourism and the environment in conflict

Much of the damage done to the environment as a result of tourism is caused simply by the volume of visitors arriving at destinations which are not used to supporting people in such great numbers. As tourists seek more exotic and remote destinations, the likelihood of the environment suffering as a result becomes even greater.

The natural environment rarely escapes damage where large numbers of tourists are found. The quality of water and air and the amount and diversity of vegetation and wildlife are inevitably affected in some way.

The Mediterranean Sea has to cope with vast amounts of waste material, not only from industrial processes but from the tourist developments which crowd its shores. Untreated sewage, harmful bacteria and petrol spillage from boats all combine to cause harm to aquatic plants and wildlife, as well as to the tourists who swim in it. Vegetation also suffers in areas of high tourist intensity as constant trampling and crushing by feet and car wheels can lead to erosion and to the disappearance of fragile species. Many footpaths in Britain, are being widened to such an extent that the surrounding areas are suffering serious erosion. Walkers along paths such as the Pennine Way are responsible for trampling the vegetation at the sides of the path, particularly in wet weather when they wish to avoid the muddy conditions of the centre of the path. This has led to the disappearance of the grass and plants along the paths' sides and to the subsequent loss of topsoil, thereby creating erosion. In some cases, the volume of walkers has made necessary the construction of concrete or wooden paths, in order to prevent this widening effect.

Sand-dunes play an important part in protecting islands and coasts from wave and wind force. Plants growing in sand-dunes bind the dunes together and save them from being swept inland by the winds sweeping in from the sea. Trampling, and the building of beach accommodation along the coasts, disturbs this system of protection and can lead to damage to farming land. As sand dunes play a particularly important role in the defence of Holland against the elements, most dunes there are fenced off to the public, who are allowed access to the beaches by a few narrow paths only.

Forests, too, are vulnerable to the impact of tourism. The danger of forest fires increases as more tourists escape into the countryside for picnics and camping holidays. The thoughtless lighting of one bonfire can lead to the destruction of vast ranges of forest and wildlife. Tree felling to make way for tourist facilities, ski slopes and ski lifts represents another way in which forests suffer.

Wildlife itself, despite being protected in national parks and safari parks, is often the victim of tourist development. As well as suffering a loss of habitat wherever tourist facilities and roads are constructed, wildlife is affected in other ways by the influx of tourists to their regions. Although the hunting of animals by tourists has largely been replaced by the viewing and photographing of them, even these activities can have a harmful impact. The effect on animals and birds of large numbers of tourists driving around and photographing them at close range can lead to great disruption in their lives. Feeding and breeding patterns are interrupted as different species are prevented from laying their eggs in their usual places or hunting for food, undisturbed.

More deliberately destructive is the (usually illegal) trade in wildlife trophies which leads to the slaughter of elephants, zebras, rhinos and other animals whose hides, etc., are valuable as tourist souvenirs.

CASE STUDY

Cruelty to chimpanzees

The following newspaper article gives details of a cruel practice involving the use of animals to make a profit out of tourism.

The chimpanzee is listed as a vulnerable species as poaching and destruction of its West African rain forest habitat continue to cause its numbers to shrink. Their illegal import into Spain to be used as props by holiday photographers further threatens the survival of the entire species. It also means intense suffering for the chimpanzees who are used in this extremely cruel way.

The full page newspaper advertisement shown in Fig. 8.1 was produced to draw attention to this scandal.

TASKS _____

1 Apart from the danger to the species and the cruelty involved in the use of baby chimpanzees in this way, what other reason is given to

Holidaymakers can help save chimps

THE ILLEGAL IMPORT of baby chimpanzees to Spain for use by holiday photographers has resulted in the death of thousands of this vulnerable species, the World Wildlife Fund estimates.

WWF has launched a campaign to stop the chimp trade, and is asking everyone going on holiday to Spain and the Canary Islands to tell WWF if they see beach photographers abusing chimps in this way.

It is illegal under a European Community regulation to use chimpanzees for commercial purposes, and as new members of the Community, Spain is now obliged to comply with the law.

THREAT

Latest estimates are that 200 young chimps are being used in Spain and the Canaries. But at least 10 animals die in the jungle or in transit to Spain for each baby that arrives alive, posing a serious threat to a species already at risk of extinction because of habitat loss.

WWF HAS PRINTED 300,000 copies of a leaflet requesting holidaymakers not to be photographed with chimps, and to notify WWF were and when they see it being done. The leaflets are being distributed nationwide by AA Travel offices and WWF supporters groups.

WWF intends to make a formal complaint to the European Commission at the end of the summer, using the evidence from British tourists. This could result in Spain being taken to the European Court.

WWF warns that because the chimps have been imported illegally, they have not been medically examined and can carry diseases such as hepatitis, rabies and dysentery which humans can catch.

"Thousands of tourists face a risk of infection, for the sake of a gimmicky holiday snap with a sad little chimp," says Tessa Robertson, one of WWF's conservation officers.

"They don't have any idea that the parents are shot so the poachers can capture the baby – and then when it's too old to be appealing to holidaymakers, it in turn is cold-bloodedly killed by the photographers who have used it to make a lot of money. we are determined to stop this trade.

Greenock Telegraph, 20 July 1987

discourage tourists from having their photographs taken with these animals?

2 How can tourists help to prevent such cruelty?

3 Can you think of any other animals which are used, in Britain or overseas, to make a profit from tourists? Think of rides on the beach, for example.

The man-made environment, too, is affected by tourist development as well as by the tourists themselves.

Long before tourists arrive at the destination, the environment may be damaged or degraded by the uncontrolled building of vast 'concrete jungles'

What's there to smile about?

They shot his mother.

They tore him from her breast.

They shot his father, brothers and uncles.

They smuggled him into Spain in a box with eleven others.

He lived.

They snapped off his teeth with pliers.

They force feed him on tranquilisers. Not much else.

They work him 16 hours a day, seven days a week.

They earn about £200,000 a year out of him.

They think he's not cuddly enough now he's four.

They're going to slit his throat the day after tomorrow.

They'll be using a new chimp the day after that.

STOP CHIMPANZEES BECOMING EXTINCT. REFUSE NEXT TIME A PHOTOGRAPHER IN SPAIN ASKS YOU TO POSE WITH ONE. REPORT THAT PHOTOGRAPHER TO THE POLICE. (THE CHIMP PROBABLY CARRIES RABIES, HERPES, TUBERCULOSIS OR DYSENTRY.)

Fig. 8.1 A newspap[er] advertisement produced to draw attention to the cru[el] treatment of chimpanzees

which do not fit in with the existing architecture, and which are not even appealing in themselves in terms of design.

The worst examples of this are the solid rows of hotels which are often developed along coastlines, to the extent that the beach and the sea are almost blocked from the view of those living in the original coastal towns, now lost behind these high-rise sea view hotels. Such development which does not fit in with the natural environment or the existing buildings is often labelled 'architectural pollution'. Tourism is responsible for many examples of this, as poorly-designed buildings, out of proportion and out of character with their surroundings, are hastily erected, not only in coastal resorts, but in city centres, too, which are especially vulnerable if they are rich in architecture of past centuries.

Traffic is also a problem where tourists prevail in large numbers, and both coastal resorts and towns and cities suffer as a result of the increased volume of cars, taxis and coaches, and the accompanying air and noise pollution. A shortage of parking can also lead to frustration for those living or working at the tourist destination, as well as for the tourists themselves.

The volume of tourists and their vehicles can have a major impact on the man-made environment. Congestion on the streets, queues in shops and overcrowding on buses and trains are the inevitable consequences of the mass influx of tourists into towns and cities which are not equipped to deal with them. Conflict between visitors and local residents can result, as can conflict between those making a profit out of tourism and those not directly connected with the local tourism industry, but who have to put up with the impact it has on their environment.

EXERCISE

1 Tourism has been described as 'a factory without a chimney', by people who claim that it is an industry which produces wealth and yet which is clean, compared to industrial manufacturing processes. Discuss whether or not you think this claim for tourism is accurate.

2 It has been said that 'tourism often destroys the very thing it comes to see'. Discuss what you think is meant by this.

Planning and managing tourism

Many of the worst effects tourism can have on the natural and man-made environment can be controlled, or prevented altogether, through intelligent planning for tourism development and through sensible management of tourists and tourist facilities. In this way, the negative effects of tourism on the environment can be minimised.

Both local and national governments can control tourism development through the use of planning controls and regulations, which limit developers' scope of building. In many countries, particularly in the developing world, high-rise hotel development is banned in locations which are close to 'unspoiled' villages, in order to protect local inhabitants. Some local authorities have passed planning regulations which preserve open spaces along beach fronts, to avoid the solid 'hotel wall' effect. Other local and national governments insist on 'low-rise' developments for tourist facilities and other buildings in locations along their coastlines or in areas of natural beauty or historical value.

The impact of traffic can also be controlled through regulations. A successful way of protecting villages and small towns from the worst effects of vehicles is to ban them altogether. The pretty town of Lindos on the Greek island of Rhodes is an example of this. A car and coach park has been built on the outskirts of the town, and visitors to Lindos must leave their vehicles at that point. From there, the only available means of transport is a donkey!

Where tourist facilities have already been developed, it takes skilful management of visitors to minimise the negative effects they can have on the environment. Popular tourist attractions are particularly vulnerable because the pressure of too many visitors can eventually damage or even destroy the attraction. Stonehenge is an example of this where visitors are now restricted in how close to the ancient monument they can go, to prevent further defacing and chipping away of the stones by irresponsible visitors to the site.

Visitors must be managed in order to minimise the impact they have on tourist attractions. Here is an example of what can be done.

At a Roman fort which is in danger from the vast number of tourists who visit, the stones are increasingly being damaged by wear and tear from the visitors walking around, and the grounds constantly trampled because the paths are so congested. The visitors too, are unhappy with the situation: at certain times of the day, and particularly at weekends, there are long queues to enter the car park and again to enter the fort itself; the presence of so many other visitors spoils the experience of seeing a piece of history and with so many visitors it is only a matter of time before someone falls from the high walls as a result of the number of people in such a limited space.

Those responsible for managing the fort have four main techniques which they can use to remedy this situation:

(1) They can make the fort less 'user friendly', i.e. make it more difficult to reach, for example, by moving the car park further away, and making visitors walk further before they get to it.

(2) They can control the visitors further by insisting that they are shown round the fort by a guide on groups, as opposed to wandering around freely.

(3) They can create a new tourist resource close to and related to the fort, to distract visitors away from the fort itself. An example might be to construct a visitors' centre or museum where visitors can see an exhibition on the history of the fort and look at articles found by archeologists digging at the site.

(4) Finally, they can charge higher admission fees or charge different prices according to the time of day, day of the week, and time of the year. They might even decide to allow free entry to visitors on weekday mornings during autumn and winter, to spread the numbers of tourists more evenly throughout the year.

CASE STUDY

The Albert Dock, Merseyside

The extract which follows is taken from a tourist brochure entitled 'Discover Merseyside 1988'.

The multi-million pound restoration of Liverpool's historic dockland is spearheading the renaissance of Maritime Merseyside.

Shopping pavilions, restaurants, office and conference facilities, a Maritime Museum, watersports and riverside promenades have already transformed a group of waterfront Victorian warehouses into one of Britain's most exciting tourist attractions, Albert Dock. Its warehouses and dock basins, restored by the Merseyside Development Corporation and the Arrowcroft Group, attract three million visitors a year.

Liverpool began as a muddy tidal creek and became the Empire's second port. Its history is charted in one of the exhibitions at the Merseyside Maritime Museum.

The Museum also has floating exhibits, working displays, demonstrations, a unique 'Emigrants to a New World' gallery and a Maritime Records Centre. In the Maritime Park there's a reconstructed Piermaster's House and working Cooperage, Pilotage House and Boat Hall, a schooner and pilot cutter.

The Tate Gallery opens at Albert Dock in May. Sister to the Tate in London, the Gallery houses the National Collection of Twentieth Century Art and will feature special international exhibitions.

The Mersey Ferries are one of Liverpool's oldest waterfront activities. Started in 1150 by the Birkenhead monks, ferries run frequently between the historic Pier Head and Wirral.

The former P & O passenger terminal at Prince's Dock, close to the Pier Head, is now Liverpool Museum's Large Objects Collection and has working models of cars, coaches, engines and machines. The Museum has also developed one of only four Technology Testbeds in the country, to explain the principles of basic science with display models.

Watersport activities are fast becoming one of Maritime Merseyside's most exciting attractions. The Liverpool Watersports Centre, based at Albert Dock, is putting the restored dock basins to new use with activities such as sailing, rowing, canoeing and wind surfing.

*8.2 Maritime
Merseyside 88*

TASKS

1 What is the other word which describes the renaissance of the dock as a tourist attraction?

2 Public and private finance was used to bring about this development. Who supplied (a) the public finance (b) the private finance?

3 Many leisure facilities are mentioned in the extract. What evidence is there in the extract that Albert Dock will also be used for business tourism?

4 The Merseyside Development Corporation is backed by national government finance. Why do you think the government is investing money in the Merseyside region?

5 Can you think of any other former industrial waterfront areas of Britain which have also now become tourist attractions?

CASE STUDY

The Loggerhead Sea Turtle

The loggerhead sea turtle's survival as a species has been threatened by the march of tourism. The following article describes the fate of this turtle.

Report maps turtles' sea of troubles

With recent reports suggesting that even prime 'blue flag' Mediterranean bathing beaches are far more polluted than official statistics suggest, pity the poor Mediterranean turtles, which have to put up not only with the pollution, but also with massive human disturbance of their breeding beaches and a growing threat from fishing.

In June, MEDASSET (the Mediterranean Association to Save the Sea Turtles) and Herpetofauna Conservation International funded two German zoologists, Dr Max Kasparek and Professor Wolfgang Baumgart, to survey possible turtle breeding beaches along the Syrian coast in the Eastern Mediterranean. One previous breeding site, at Ras el Basit, was found to be crowded with people, surrounded by tourist installations and busy with boats offshore. Not surprisingly, turtle tracks were absent there.

Two tracks were found on another 29km stretch near the Lebanese border, but the sea here was heavily polluted, and in places there were piles of plastic garbage up to a foot thick on the beach. Only on a beach south of the town of Latakia were there frequent signs of turtles, including endangered green turtles, with 24 sets of tracks counted in one day along 12km of beach.

Kasparek and Baumgart recommended that the nesting beach at Latakia should be protected, especially from tourist and industrial development (buildings are already sprouting up close to the beach). They also urge that the Syrian government should be given strong support to solve the immense sewage and rubbish-disposal problems along its coast, though with the present political situation in the Middle East, that may be a forlorn hope.

Certainly, Mediterranean countries with far less intractable political problems still seem unwilling to protect the sea turtles. In Turkey, for instance, the reprieve for the 150–200 turtles nesting in the Dalyan estuary seems to have been only partially effective. The Turkish government, anxious to find favour with the EC, which it hopes to join, declared the beach a 'special environment protection region', and drastically reduced plans for a 3200-bed hotel.

But now a smaller tourist development of two restaurants, six toilets and a first-aid station is being built along a 500-metre stretch of this beach. And although building work was supposed to stop during the turtle breeding season, tractors continued to deliver building materials throughout the summer and regularly drove over the turtle nesting area. And at the opposite end of the beach, the abandoned hotel site is being used as a large car-park.

Reports to MEDASSET suggest that the 'environmental-protection rangers' appointed by the government to patrol the turtle beach, rarely leave the vicinity of the restaurants, and that tourist parties are regularly landed on the beach at night – to 'stroke and cuddle the turtles', according to one English tourist – while the four night-time guards are nowhere to be seen.

At the largest nesting concentration of loggerheads in the Mediterranean, at Laganas Bay on the Greek Ionian island of Zakynthos, things are little better. Each year, up to 800 turtles try to return to breeding beaches, most of which have been overrun by tourist development, and their nocturnal egg-laying trips ashore are disrupted by the noise of low-flying aircraft and the glaring lights of hotels, tavernas and discos.

By presidential decree, umbrellas, sunbeds and all the paraphernalia of the basking tourist are restricted to 300 metres of the lower shore, but Lily Venizelos of MEDASSET reports that this summer more than three times that length of beach was in regular use. She claims that the Zakynthos prefect – the leader of the local administration – has 'lost control' of the beach.

But Venizelos sees some optimistic signs too. In Zakynthos, a new organisation, ZEMELDICA, which includes local landowners, has been set up to protect and study the turtles, and, despite the misgivings of some conservationists, it seems to be encouraging real local enthusiasm for turtle conservation. Then there is the conservationist's secret weapon: tourist power. At Dalyan, the vast majority of complaints about the lack of protection for turtles comes from the tourists themselves – the very people in whose name the breeding beaches are being destroyed.

And MEDASSET has circulated a letter sent by the Greek ambassador in London to his government this July in which he claims 'there is a distinct danger that the matter of the sea turtles of Zakynthos will get entirely out of hand, with unforeseen and incalculably damaging consequences for tourism specifically and for our country more generally'. Venizelos says that the ambassador has yet to produce any response which would reassure her that the Greek government is taking his warning seriously.

Nevertheless, despite a 25 per cent increase in the Zakynthos tourist trade this summer, in an otherwise disastrous year for Greek tourism, it does seem that the spectre of beach boycotts and protest letters just might offer some hope for the Mediterranean's beleaguered turtles.

Michael Scott
BBC Wildlife Magazine, November 1991

In 1987, the Greek Government, under international pressure, passed a law to protect the turtles nesting in their country. Laganas Bay on the Greek island of Zakynthos is now the most important known remaining nesting area for loggerhead turtles in the Mediterranean. The tourist industry itself has helped spread awareness of the turtles' plight. The text which follows is taken from a leaflet produced by the World Wide Fund for Nature, for distribution to tourists travelling to Zakynthos.

Please
Help us to Protect
the Loggerhead
Sea Turtle
of Zakynthos

Many visitors to Greece will have heard of the
loggerhead turtles, which come ashore every year
to lay their eggs on the sandy beaches of Laganas
Bay on the island of Zakynthos (Zante). The turtles
have been following this annual pattern for millions
of years – long before Man began to use the
beaches for his own activities. Today, however,
these magnificent creatures are in danger of
becoming extinct, as the ever increasing number of
tourists causes nesting sites to be destroyed and
the nesting turtles to be disturbed.

Laganas Bay is now the most important known
remaining nesting area for loggerhead turtles in the
whole of the Mediterranean.

HELP US TO KEEP IT THAT WAY.

IN JANUARY 1987, after appeals from caring people all over the world, a law was passed which provides strict protection for the turtles and their nesting beaches.

HERE'S HOW YOU CAN OBEY THE LAW AND HELP THE TURTLES AT THE SAME TIME

1. Please do not use the protected beaches of Laganas Bay between sunset and sunrise. This is when the female turtles leave the sea to lay their eggs and when the baby turtles hatch. Noise disturbs and disorientates the turtles, and can prevent them from laying their eggs.

2. Do not take motor vehicles, including motor cycles, mopeds and bicycles, onto the protected beaches. Their use is prohibited.

3. A new law for sea traffic has just been passed, which prohibits all boats in one sector of Laganas Bay. This same law limits the speed of all boats in a second sector of the Bay. Visitors should check with the Sea Turtle Information Stations or the Port Police for specific details.

4. Do not dig up turtle nests – it is illegal. Please do not make sand castles or dig any kind of hole, as you could inadvertently disturb a nest with fatal consequences for the developing eggs. Even such structures dug nearer the water's edge can obstruct nesting females and baby turtles trying to reach the sea, so please level the sand before you leave the beach.

5. Baby turtles should never be handled or carried to the sea. Although it may look an impossible task for the tiny creatures, it is vital to their biological development that they reach the sea on their own.

6. Lights disturb and disorientate the nesting females and discourage others from coming ashore. Lights are fatal to the hatchlings, causing them to become disorientated and to wander aimlessly, unable to find the sea. You can help by encouraging the hotel and restaurant owners to eliminate lights on the beach.

7. Do not stick beach umbrellas into the sand of the turtle nesting zones. This is now prohibited because it can destroy eggs buried underneath. The nesting zones are usually 15-30 metres from the water's edge.

8. Please do take empty cartons, tins and any other rubbish with you when you leave the beach. Remember that such garbage can obstruct the free access of the turtles to and from the nesting sites.

9. During the day the beach can be used for sunbathing and swimming, but please do avoid the nesting zone (about 15-30 metres from the water's edge) where most nests are found.

WWF UNITED KINGDOM WOULD LIKE TO THANK

Greek Islands Club
Olympic Holidays
Portland Holidays
Greek Connection
Manos Holidays
Airlink Holidays
Worral & Moore Ltd

for their vital help in distributing this leaflet to visitors to Zakynthos.

Specail thanks to:
Airtours
Ilios Island Holidays

for financial help with the production of this leaflet, as well as helping to distribute it.

WWF United Kingdom would also like to thank:

Friends of the Ionian and Sea Turtle Survival for their help in the preparation of this leaflet.

WWF – the World Wide Fund for Nature – is the largest international nature conservation organisation in the world. WWF United Kingdom is one of the 27 national and associate organisations working around the world to protect our threatened environment.

TASKS

1 Why has the population of loggerhead turtles decreased so dramatically around the Mediterranean?

2 Why did the Greek Government pass the law protecting the turtles?

3 Give three examples of actions which the law has made illegal.

4 What kind of companies provided the funds to help print the leaflet and helped distribute it to visitors to Zakynthos? Why do you think they agreed to do this?

The following is an extract from Sunmed's summer brochure, 'Go Turkey'.

" Turkey...keeping it lovely "

Turkey is one of the last unspoilt areas of the Mediterranean and we'd like to see it stay that way. We're not so naive to believe that tourism won't have an impact on Turkey, because that's inevitable. What we do want to avoid is Turkey becoming another Costa del Sol. We certainly don't want to be associated with the destruction of beautiful creatures like the endangered Loggerhead Turtle and Monk Seal, so along with other responsible operators we've been putting pressure on the Turkish Government. This pressure resulted in one of the last nesting areas of the Loggerhead turtle being declared a conservation area. The pressure has also started to affect building controls - we don't want the coastline to be littered with tasteless hotels any more than you do. As a traveller to Turkey we ask you to use your common sense when it comes to buying souvenirs and taking local 'trips to see the turtles'. Together we can keep Turkey lovely.

g. 8.3 Extract from brochure on Turkey

5 What do you think is meant by 'what we do want to avoid is Turkey becoming another Costa del Sol'?

6 What has the Turkish government done to protect the loggerhead turtle, and why has it done this?

7 Why does the brochure recommend using 'common sense when it comes to buying souvenirs and taking local trips to see the turtles'?

Fig. 8.4 A female loggerhead turtle on nesting beach on th Greek island of Zakynthos.

Courtesy: J Sutherland/W Wide Fund for Nature (UK

ASSIGNMENT

1 Conduct a class debate.

An abandoned abbey in the countryside close to your area has been falling into a state of decay for some time. It receives a few visitors each day, mainly ramblers who discover it by accident on their country walks and who stop to admire the beauty of the ruin which is situated in a quiet, secluded spot.

Your local council has now decided that the abbey is to be turned into a tourist attraction. They are going to charge a small entrance fee, build a car park and a visitors' centre nearby and improve the over-grown road which currently leads to the abbey. The project will provide jobs for six people, excluding those who carry out the work involved in rehabilitating the site and building the facilities.

Divide the class into two sides. One should take the view that this development is a good idea, and that it will give people an appreciation of their own local history, and save the abbey from falling into further disrepair. The other side should argue that this development will spoil the magic and sense of mystery and tranquillity which currently surrounds the abbey, and that the abbey should therefore be left alone.

9

THE IMPACT OF TOURISM ON THE ECONOMY

After reading this chapter, you should have a clear understanding of:
- how investment in tourism is necessary for new tourist destinations,
- the costs of tourism,
- the difference between visible and invisible imports and exports,
- the ways in which tourism benefits the economies of destinations,
- the role of the tourism industry in a country's balance of payments,
- the effect of tourism on a country's employment,
- how profits from tourism can be lost to other countries, outside tourist destinations.

We have seen how tourism is expanding in all kinds of communities and countries throughout the world, and how, if the current rate of expansion continues, tourism will be the world's largest industry of all by the year 2000.

Why is it that so many countries in the developing as well as the developed world are taking great steps to build up their tourism industries? Why are so many different towns and regions in Britain making strenuous efforts to develop facilities which will attract visitors from other parts of Britain and from abroad? The answer is that tourism has the potential to bring great wealth and prosperity to countries and to regions within countries.

The first and most important reason for tourism development is almost always the various **economic benefits** which tourism can bring to a destination.

This chapter explores the main impact which tourism can have on the economic systems of destinations which attract large numbers of visitors. The first part examines the investment in tourism which must be made in order to attract visitors or tourists in great numbers, and the second examines the various economic benefits or returns which a thriving tourism industry can bring. Finally, the question of precisely who benefits financially from tourism is discussed.

Tourism investments – the costs of tourism

Chapters 3–7 described the various sectors of the tourism industry in general – travel and transport, accommodation and catering, and leisure, recreation and business facilities. These, together with tourism promotion, are the elements which add up to a complete tourism industry anywhere. The various sectors are interdependent, and must work together to attract and serve the customer of the tourism industry.

Destinations need to spend money in order to prepare themselves for tourists, long before those tourists arrive. Even those places which are rich in heritage or natural attractions such as temples, stately homes, areas of outstanding natural beauty, or long sandy beaches must spend money in order to attract tourists in the first place, and then cater for them once they have arrived.

Spending money in this way, to attract tourists and to cater for their needs represents **investment** in tourism. Such investment creates part of the impact which tourism has on the economy of a country or a region, as it takes money out of the destination's economy. Because this spending represents a drain on the finances of a country or region, tourism investments are also known as the **costs** of tourism, i.e., the costs to a destination of attracting and catering for visitors.

What kind of spending is necessary to build up a tourism industry? Or, in other words, what are the costs of tourism?

The island of Iota

Iota is an imaginary island in the Pacific. In the past, the island has operated on a subsistence economy based on agriculture. Now the island's Government has decided to develop tourism as the main part of its economy.

EXERCISE _____

Comparing the drawings of Iota in Fig. 9.1, 'before the arrival of tourism' and 'after the arrival of tourism', list the main investments which were made, under the three headings:
• travel and transport
• accommodation and catering
• leisure and recreation

_____

These visible investments in tourism are sometimes known also as **tourism infrastructure**, or the physical changes which must be made in order to cater for visitors. Most of these costs arise long before the benefits from tourism start to flow in.

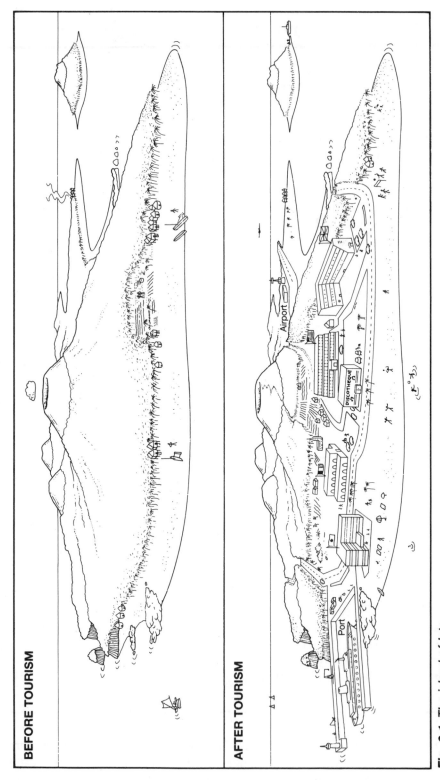

BEFORE TOURISM

AFTER TOURISM

Fig. 9.1 The island of Iota

The other type of investment which is required is investment in tourism promotion. Although this is less visible to the residents at a destination it is of equal importance to having a good tourism infrastructure. As was shown in Chapter 7, tourism advertising and promotion are necessary before a potential tourist destination can attract large numbers of visitors. The Iotan Government in the above example has invested in a Tourist Board to promote Iota overseas as an attractive new tourist destination. The Iota Tourist Board mounts advertising campaigns in the media of certain countries in the developed world to persuade the residents of those countries to travel to Iota for a holiday. Without such investment, the hotels and tourist attractions of Iota could remain empty.

So far, only the investments necessary to **develop** a country or a region for tourism have been considered. Many more investments or costs are involved in maintaining a tourism industry and in providing services for tourists. These costs are known as **ongoing costs**. They are equally important to the operation of a successful tourism industry.

Some of the ongoing costs arise in the form of the money it takes to train the staff who work in the tourism industry. Employees of the various sectors of tourism need to be properly educated and trained in order to do their jobs professionally. The costs of this education and training are often met by the governments of destinations and paid for through taxes.

Other ongoing costs arise in the form of the additional public services which must be provided for tourists. Roads and parks must be maintained, sewerage facilities and extra police and fire protection must be paid for and tourism promotion must be sustained to keep a destination in the media, in order to keep attracting new tourists and bring back those who have already visited. All of these costs are usually met through the money provided by the residents or taxpayers who live at these destinations.

Tourism returns – the benefits of tourism

The main reason why governments, local authorities and private companies are prepared to invest so much in the development and maintenance of a tourism industry is the range of economic benefits which tourism can bring.

This part of the chapter examines the economic benefits of tourism and the way in which their impact in the economy of a destination may be measured.

Foreign exchange and international trade

Almost every country in the world has to **import** goods, materials, and services from other countries. To pay for these imports, a country must earn exchange by **exporting** other goods, materials and services. This system of importing and exporting is known as international trade.

A country can earn foreign exchange through two kinds of exports: visible or invisible exports. Visible exports are physical goods which can be seen, touched and weighed as they pass through the ports of one country, heading for another. Timber, sugar cane, washing machines and cars are all examples of visible exports. By contrast, invisible exports are not physical goods, but services provided by one country for another. For Britain, examples of invisible exports include banking services provided by British banks for overseas customers; the fees paid to a British playwright in exchange for his play being performed in the USA; the shipping of foreign goods by a British vessel; or fees paid by overseas clients of British architects, lawyers or accountants in return for their advice and expertise.

Tourism is also regarded as an invisible export because it has the potential to bring in foreign exchange to a country, through the provision of services to overseas visitors. These services are provided in the hotels and restaurants and other enterprises which cater for overseas tourists. Tourism, therefore, as an invisible export, brings in foreign exchange to a country, in the same way that the export of coal, iron-ore, televisions or wheat would. The potential of tourism to earn valuable foreign exchange is often the main reason why destinations choose to develop that industry.

After the services provided by financial institutions such as banks, tourism is Britain's second biggest invisible export.

Taking the earnings from inbound tourism as a percentage of the total earned by a country from the export of goods and services (visible and invisible exports), the relative importance of tourism to that country as an earner of foreign exchange can be measured. The greater the percentage, the more important tourism is as a form of export.

Figure 9.2 shows the contribution of tourism to the total foreign exchange earnings of those countries which are members of the OECD, the Organisation for Economic Cooperation and Development.

EXERCISE

1 List, in order of importance, the six European countries for which tourism is most important in earning foreign exchange.

2 What is the effect on the relative importance of tourism in countries, such as Britain, which have many varied forms of export?

3 Why are earnings from *domestic* tourism not counted as exports for particular countries?

4 In 1991, the United Kingdom earned approximately US$12.5 billion worth of foreign exchange through tourism. Use a calculator to work out the total earned by the UK from all its exports that year.

	%
Austria	18.9
Belgium-Luxembourg	2.4
Denmark	6.0
Finland	3.6
France	5.6
Germany	2.1
Greece	21.1
Iceland	5.5
Ireland	4.5
Italy	7.3
Netherlands	2.1
Norway	4.1
Portugal	16.4
Spain	25.1
Sweden	3.7
Switzerland	8.1
Turkey	13.1
United Kingdom	3.7
Canada	4.1
USA	5.4
Australia	7.5
New Zealand	8.3
Japan	0.8

Fig. 9.2 *Tourism receipts as a percentage of all exports (1988)*
Source: OECD Balance of Payments Division

Tourism and the balance of payments

In the same way that individuals have bank accounts, so too do individual countries. People with bank accounts can pay money into the account and take money out, each time making a transaction. People try to take less out of their bank accounts than they pay in, to avoid going 'overdrawn'.

The current account for a country is a record of that country's economic **transactions** during a period of time (usually a year). Those transactions are composed of **credits** – money coming *into* a country through the exporting of goods or services to other countries – and **debits** – when the country *imports* goods or services from other countries, causing money to flow out of that country. The balance of payments on a country's current account is calculated by subtracting the value of the country's debits from the value of its credits. For example:

Country A		Country B	
Balance of payments		*Balance of payments*	
Credits (exports)	$6500 (bn)	Credits (exports)	$7450 (bn)
− Debits (imports)	$5450 (bn)	− Debits (imports)	$9650 (bn)
	$1050 (bn)		− $2200 (bn)

Fig. 9.3

The example above shows that country A has exported more than it has imported and so has a positive balance of payments, or a **surplus**.

Country B, however, has imported more than it has exported, and so has a negative balance of payments, or a **deficit**.

Every country wants to have a surplus rather than a deficit in its current account. A thriving tourism industry can make a great contribution to a country's credits by bringing into that country large amounts of foreign exchange.

Many countries are now investing in the development of their tourism industries in order to attract the foreign exchange which can help their balance of payments accounts show a surplus. Tourism's potential contribution to a country's balance of payments as an earner of foreign exchange has been widely recognised throughout the world. Many developed as well as developing countries would have major balance-of-payments deficits if it were not for the income they earn from tourists visiting them from other countries.

Nevertheless, residents of a particular country also spend money overseas on tourism in other countries, which also has an effect on the current account of their own country. When British residents go on holiday to Italy, for example, this is equivalent to Britain *importing* from Italy. British currency or exchange leaves the country to be paid to Italian businesses (such as hotels and restaurants) in the same way that it does when a British family buys an Italian car or an Italian washing machine. Therefore, when a country's residents travel overseas, the money which they spend represents a **debit** on the balance of payments because money is leaving the country to be spent abroad.

It is interesting to compare the amount spent by a country's residents on tourism outside that country with what tourists from overseas spend in that country. This is known as calculating the **travel balance**, which indicates to a country whether international tourism as a whole − into and out of that country − contributes a credit or a debit to its balance of payments. In other words, the travel balance shows whether more is spent on tourism in a country by visitors from overseas than is spent by the same country's residents when they travel abroad, or vice versa. Figure 9.4 shows the travel balance and balance of payments for three hypothetical countries.

Country	Total earnings from inbound tourism (£ billion)	Total spent by country's residents on overseas travel (£ billion)	Travel balance (£ billion)
A	600	750	− 150
B	400	200	200
C	750	650	100

Country	Travel balance (£ billion)	Balance of payments (£ billion)
A	− 150	− 350
B	200	250
C	100	− 150

Fig. 9.4 The travel balance and balance of payments

The first table shows how the travel balances for the three countries are calculated: the amount spent by each country's residents on overseas tourism is subtracted from the country's total earnings from inbound tourism.

The second table sets the travel balance for each country beside that country's balance of payments.

EXERCISE

1 Three statements describe the effect of the travel balance on the overall balance of payments account of countries A, B, and C from the previous table.

Which country (A, B or C) is being described by each of these statements?
  (i) The travel balance has made a balance-of-payments deficit even worse.
 (ii) The travel balance has been a significant factor in reducing a balance-of-payments deficit.
(iii) The travel balance has improved a balance-of-payments surplus.

2 Country D earns £100 billion from inbound tourism, and its own residents spend £300 billion on overseas tourism. It has a balance of payments of £150 billion. Calculate the travel balance for country D, and describe the effect of this on its own balance of payments.

3 Explain how a country with a negative travel balance can still have a balance-of-payments surplus.

Figure 9.5 shows the progression in Britain's travel balance during the 1980s, in £millions. The bar chart indicates the tendency of the British to spend increasing amounts on outbound tourism, year after year. While Britain's tourism receipts also increased in general during that decade, they failed

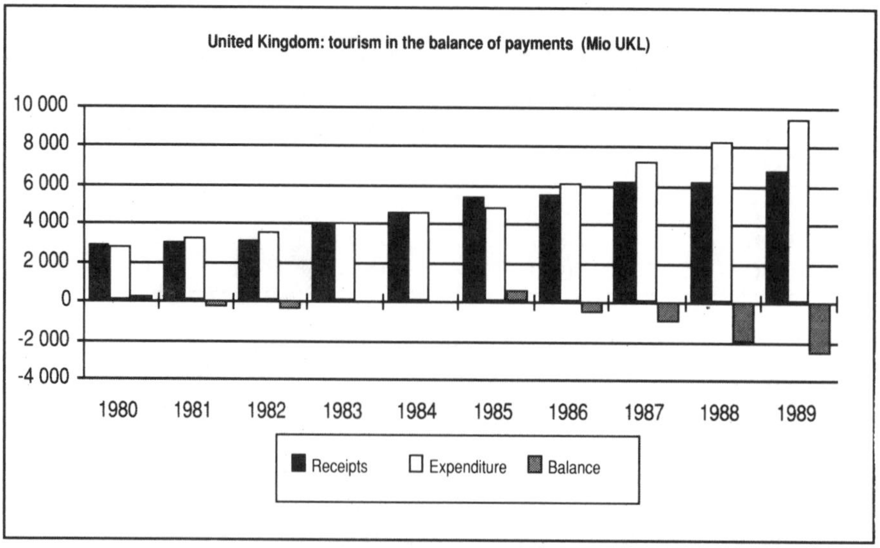

United Kingdom: tourism in the balance of payments (Mio UKL)

Fig. 9.5 *The progression in Brita travel balance*

Source: Eurostat, *Tourism Europe*, Trends 1989

to keep up with the growth in expenditure on foreign travel by the British, and as a result the travel balance went deeper into deficit.

Tourism and employment

Another characteristic of the tourism industry which helps it to have a beneficial impact on economies is its capacity to create employment for large numbers of people, of different skills and levels of ability.

The tourism industry is labour-intensive, meaning that it depends largely on the people working in it, as opposed to machinery and technology.

For this reason, it is much cheaper to create jobs in tourism than in other industries such as manufacturing or new technology. One hotel may employ between 200 and 300 staff, but a distillery on the same site may cost much more to build (because of the expensive plant and technology involved) and require only half a dozen skilled technicians to operate it. Much less **capital investment** is required to create a job in tourism than is required to create a job in another industry. In Britain, it is generally accepted that the cost of providing a job in tourism through investment is approximately two-thirds the national average cost of creating a job in this way.

The wages and salaries of the people employed in tourism can also benefit other industries. For example, a waiter may save up and buy a car or a refrigerator, creating business for manufacturing industries and shops. In this way, the benefits of tourism can spread throughout the entire economy of a destination.

Another way of measuring the importance of tourism to the economy of any country is to calculate the number of jobs in the tourism industry as a percentage of total employment in that country. The higher the percentage, the more important tourism is to the employment market in the economy.

Even within the continent of Europe, there are great variations in the percentages of tourism jobs given as a proportion of total employment, from country to country. As would be expected, the percentages are highest in those countries whose economies are very dependent on tourism; while in countries with more mixed economies, the percentages are lower. In countries such as Spain, Portugal and Greece, almost one in ten workers are employed in the tourism industry. By contrast, in other, northern European countries less dependent on their tourism industries (for example, the Netherlands and Belgium) employment created by tourism represents only 2% or 3% or all jobs in those countries.

Tourism employment and skills is discussed in greater detail in Chapter 11.

Who benefits from tourism investment?

We have seen how governments welcome tourism because it brings foreign exchange and jobs with it. We shall now examine in more detail the important issue of where the financial returns from investments in tourism actually go.

Who invests? – the island of Iota

Figure 9.6 shows in more detail the island of Iota, developed as a tourist destination.

EXERCISE

1 What was the source of finance for some of the tourism developments?

2 What does this imply will happen to some of the profits from tourism on Iota?

3 Iota has no mineral wealth, no manufacturing industry and can only grow enough to feed the local population. Make a list of imports which the island will have to make to keep the tourists happy.

Tourism benefits the economies of countries because it is an invisible export, bringing in foreign exchange. Anything which causes the profits from tourism to drain away from the place where the tourism occurs is known as **leakage**, because the benefits leak away to other countries.

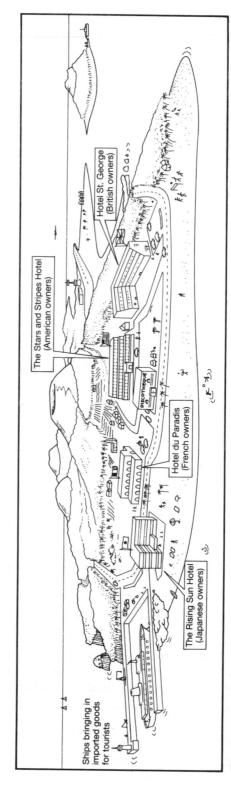

Fig. 9.6 *The island of Iota, developed as a tourist resort*

Leakage can occur in four ways:

(1) The materials required to develop the infrastructure for tourism may have to be bought from other countries. This means that an island such as Iota may have to import construction material, for example, from elsewhere.

(2) Tourist facilities such as hotels, and the airlines which bring in tourists may be owned by companies based in other countries. Therefore the profits from running these leak overseas to these other countries.

(3) Food and drink for tourists and the manufactured goods (such as souvenirs) which are needed may have to be imported from other countries. Some tourists are inflexible in their habits and want the same things on holiday which they find at home. Every time such items are imported into a tourist destination, some of the benefits from the invisible exports are lost to that country.

(4) Some of the people working in the tourism industry may be from outside the destination, sometimes from the countries who own the hotels, for example. Alternatively, foreign workers may be employed because the skills required to work in the tourism industry are not available in the local population. Wages paid to foreign workers represent another form of leakage, because part of the money earned may be sent home, and not spent in the local economy.

The extract which follows is from a report on Third World tourism.

The extent of food imports, for example, is one of the most striking characteristics of the Caribbean tourist industry: a recent study showed foreign exchange leakage associated with hotel food purchases in Jamaica to be 54.2%. As much as one-third of the food bill of most luxury hotels goes for imported food. However, the inability of Jamaican agriculture to supply hotels with a greater part of their food needs is simply part of a larger problem.

In Mauritius, tourism is the third biggest foreign exchange earner after sugar and textiles, but how much of these earnings are retained within the country? An analysis of 1980 data by the World Bank showed that only 9.1% of all gross foreign exchange earnings were retained if various kinds of outflows were taken into account.

The UK and Third World Tourism

EXERCISE

1 Why do you think leakage is a bigger problem for developing countries than it is for developed countries? Give as many reasons as you can.

2 The more profits and wages from tourism that leave a country and the more that has to be imported to satisfy the tourists, the less the country benefits from the tourism industry, and the less it helps that country's

current account. Write a paragraph giving reasons why you think the benefits from tourism should go to the people living in the country where the tourism actually occurs.

Leakage from tourism also occurs in Britain. Some of the profits from tourism in a particular region leak out to other regions in Britain, and some leak out of the country altogether.

EXERCISE

1 Working in groups, list the big companies operating in the tourism industry in your own town or region. Note any tourism facilities which you think may be owned by companies based in countries outside Britain. Examples might be hotels, restaurants, fast-food outlets, tourist attractions, and transport facilities.

2 Can you identify any other ways in which profits from tourism in Britain leak overseas? Think of the items which visitors to your area buy in the shops. Where do the souvenirs come from, for example?

Minimising leakage

The more profits and foreign exchange which remain in the tourist destination, the better it is for that country's prosperity and balance of payments. Governments and tourism developers can make decisions about how they develop their tourism industry, which keep the leakage from tourism to an absolute minimum.

The island of Beta

The neighbouring island to Iota is Beta. The government of Beta has developed tourism in such a way that most of the profits remain on the island, and a minimum of imports are needed to keep the industry going.

Tourists stay in village communities, in houses built using traditional methods and materials. Visitors experience life as the local inhabitants do, and eat the same ethnic dishes of the island. The local population is fully involved in the running of the tourism industry, including producing the souvenirs which are made exclusively by local craftsmen.

EXERCISE

Write a short paragraph comparing the type of tourists likely to be found on Iota with the type of tourists most likely to be found on Beta.

CASE STUDY

Investing in tourism in Tyne and Wear

Tyne and Wear is the conurbation which surrounds the two famous shipbuilding rivers in the North East of England, with the sixth largest concentration of population in Britain. Economic difficulties have resulted from the contraction of its old heavy manufacturing industries. Tyne and Wear is, however, making great efforts to replace these old industries with new ventures, including tourism.

The following are some extracts from a handbook, entitled *Invest in Tourism – Tyne and Wear.*

A great place to invest

The tourism and leisure industries are expanding in Tyne and Wear. The amount of spending by consumers is impressive and growing, and the amount of investment in new development is also increasing. If you are thinking of some form of investment, Tyne and Wear merits very serious consideration.

It has a large population, many fine tourist attractions, and all the facilities you would expect of a major conurbation, including all the services you will require for successful development – advertising agencies, financial services and expert advice of every kind. As a regional centre of government, the professions and the media, it contains all the important decision-makers and contact-points you may have to refer to.

Tyne and Wear is well connected by road, rail, air and sea – having invested heavily in its communications in recent years. Newcastle Airport is rapidly expanding: rail services are already excellent and shortly to improve further: there are fast modern road links: and the traditional connections by sea to Scandinavia are maintained. The Metro rapid transit system is Britain's greatest success story in public transport in modern times.

The message is that Tyne and Wear is a convenient and well-equipped area for you to invest in.

The role of tourism

For some time it has been apparent that tourism and leisure have an important role to play in the return to prosperity in Tyne and Wear, for they are two of the industries that are leading the comeback, both in terms of new investment and of jobs. The tourism industry is already large and important here, and the potential for growth is outstanding. At present Tyne and Wear attracts 1.8m domestic tourists in a year, who stay over 5m nights and spend over £53m. In addition about 130,000 foreign tourists stay for some 1.2m nights and spend in the order of £27m. So the total for holiday visitors is about £80m per annum. Day visitors number almost 4m annually, and their expenditure is estimated at £16m. Business tourism has always been particularly important in Tyne and Wear, and will remain so. Conference business alone is estimated to produce over £6m spending, each year. Finally,

Tyne and Wear, as a major centre of population, attracts substantial numbers of visitors coming to see friends and relatives. Taking all these figures together, total spending is over £120m a year. This is an impressive total and one that is undoubtedly set to increase. Spending has shown significant increases over the last five years, and new initiatives now being prepared in Tyne and Wear give the promise of even better performance to come.

A new mood – better prospects

The public and private sectors are already investing substantially in tourism and leisure development. It is difficult to find a part of this conurbation which does not have projects under way or planned for the near future – new museums; Roman excavations and displays; restored theatres; sea-front developments; illuminations; dockside restoration schemes; live steam railways; new hotels; visitor centres – and there is scope for more. These and other items, if developed with flair and imagination, can bring rich rewards for the investor who is prepared to come in at the right time. The right time is now.

The best opportunities

As a result, Tyne and Wear now offers great scope for investment and development in tourism and leisure – in a wide range of possible ventures. The members of the TDAP believe that projects in the following categories enjoy particularly good prospects:

- riverside developments, including marinas and the presentation of maritime heritage themes
- further development of Roman and mediaeval history and heritage
- industrial heritage development – railways, shipbuilding etc
- conservation projects, and re-use of industrial buildings
- serviced accommodation – hotels, motels etc
- conference and exhibition facilities
- entertainment and sports facilities
- the licensed trade – restaurants, pubs, clubs
- mixed use developments

Invest in Tyne and Wear

TASKS

1 At whom is the information in this handbook directed?

2 Draw a bar chart to illustrate the information given on the spending of the different tourist groups who visit Tyne and Wear.

3 Identify (*a*) tourist projects already underway or planned for the near future, and (*b*) categories of projects which it is believed offer investors particularly good prospects.

To which of the sectors of the tourism industry do most of the investment projects in the two lists belong?

4 Why do you think the pattern of investment in Tyne and Wear is different from that necessary to develop the infrastructure of Iota?

CASE STUDY

Investment by Scandic Hotels and Ackergill Tower

Spending on investment in tourism infrastructure by the public or private sectors always creates a 'ripple effect' of benefits spreading out to other sectors of the economy. The most obvious example is the construction industry, which stands to gain from any decision to build a new airport, theme park or hotel, for example. However, any investment in new tourism facilities has the potential to create profits and employment in a wide range of manufacturing industries, as shown in the article in Fig. 9.7.

Tourism investment reports released earlier this spring showed the industry in a healthier state than many others. Against gloomy economic forecasts and international unrest, financiers were still finding funds for new schemes.

At the start of the year, in England alone, work was in progress on major tourism and leisure projects* worth an estimated £2,512 million, and confidence had been high enough in the second half of 1990 for work to begin on £482 million-worth of new projects.

There has been a high level of work started on new hotel projects in the last six months, the English Tourist Board reported, and the value of new hotels under construction – £980 million, on top of £300 million for extensions and refurbishments – was the highest the Board has recorded.

It made good news for jobs in tourism and construction. But those figures only tell part of the story. They are bricks-and-mortar figures: no lighting, heating, decorating, furnishings or equipment.

When a project manager takes over a shell building (or begins a refit) and goes shopping for furnishings, fixtures and equipment, he or she is spending anywhere from £4,000 to £9,000 on a bedroom with ensuite bathroom. For public areas consultants estimate around £400 to £800 per square metre, and for kitchens you can add another £600 to £700 per square metre.

These are, admittedly, ballpark figures. If it's a deluxe job the sky's the limit. If it's a budget project carefully monitored it can be far less. But, tot up the number of hotels built, refurbished or converted last year in England alone and that shopping list is large – and could have been largely bought from British manufacturers.

In some cases it was. And some of the shoppers were overseas groups who found it paid to buy British.

The 151-bedroom Scandic Crown Hotel, Gatwick, opened last November, spent approximately £40,000 on bedroom and bedroom-corridor carpets, and ordered them from Firths, in West Yorkshire. Bedroom fabrics came from Skopos in Bradford and the bill totalled upwards of £80,000.

The decision to place the contracts with UK manufacturers is down to Scandic itself, the largest hotel group in Sweden and expanding fast in Britain and other EC countries.

Within five years it plans 2000 bedrooms in Britain and so far has 1200, in Edinburgh, Gatwick, Docklands, Victoria and, most recently, Euston.

'In Sweden we have a strong tradition in textiles and we wished to put a high Swedish profile on the hotel. But when it came to it, labour costs in Britain are so competitive that we were able to place the contract here,' said Kenneth Astrom, general manager at Gatwick.

For furnishing and fitting public areas, the budget was £700,000, including £120,000 on kitchen equipment, which also came from British factories.

'In this hotel we used Swedish bedroom furniture, but we now know that we could get it cheaper in Britain, and we may well do so in future,' Astrom added.

At the Scandic Crown, Euston, opened on May 1, some of the hotel's most striking furniture has indeed been made in Britain.

Behind its neatly restored 19th-century facade in Upper Woburn Place – Grade II listed – the hotel's owner, Muirgold Ltd, has built a thoroughly high-tech property.

The decor, furniture and fittings, though, chosen by operator Scandic, are traditional Swedish – creating the feel of Stockholm Old Town in the lobby and echoes of 1850s Swedish provincial style in the restaurant.

To get the right rural 'feel', they might have imported the restaurant inch by inch. Instead they commissioned a North London workshop to recreate the wooden effect characteristic of old Swedish interiors, using white-washed oak furniture, flooring and panelling.

In fact much of the 'traditional Swedish' furnishing carries a made-in-Britain tag. Almost all the hotel's fabrics came from British factories, the majority of carpets were woven by companies like Hugh Mackay of Durham, and the cutlery is from Sheffield, despite Scandinavia's reputation for tableware.

At Ackergill Tower, in the far north of Scotland, 90% of the £1 million owners John and Arlette Banister spent on restoration and refurbishment went to British firms; and almost 60% of that was spent locally.

'The only things we bought overseas were Oriental rugs and a German boiler,' said Arlette. Local builders earned £500,000 for restoring the crumbling baronial hall (high above the Pentland Firth and little more than a haggis throw from the Queen Mother's Castle of Mey) and they delivered it on time in seven months.

Fitting out the 17 bedrooms, now used exclusively for incentive and other group bookings, meant more work for local craftsmen and suppliers, who restored and reupholstered all Ackergill's antique contents. By the time the tower opened in September 1988, it had specially made British mattresses, linen and towels; Caithness glass on the tables, and a Landrover, Rangerover and Discovery standing outside for guests to use after they fly up to Wick.

* Projects with a capital cost over £.5 million. Source: 'Investment in Tourism, July–December 1990', English Tourist Board.

Fig. 9.7
Source: BTA, *Horizons,* June 1991

10

THE IMPACT OF TOURISM ON CULTURE AND COMMUNITIES

After reading this chapter, you should have a clear understanding of:
- the cultural differences which can exist between tourists and the people who live at their destinations,
- how host populations can react to tourists,
- how tourism can influence the culture of host populations,
- the degree to which tourism leads to communication and understanding between cultures.

The previous two chapters examined the impact of tourism on the economy and on the environment. This chapter looks at a different, but equally important, kind of impact – the impact of tourism on the people who make up the communities living at tourist destinations, and the impact on their culture.

It is comparatively simple to *measure* the economic and environmental effects of tourism on a country or particular region, but the way in which the presence of large numbers of tourists affects the people who live in these areas is much more difficult to measure. In many cases, the effects are gradual, invisible and complex.

Changing attitudes of host populations

Imagine a self-contained, small community with a simple, basic lifestyle, living in a remote location visited by very few outsiders. The community has its own customs and traditions, and its own rules and standards of behaviour, which have changed very little for hundreds of years. All the members of this community have a special place in it and they are (generally speaking) happy and content with their lot.

Suppose next that the tourism industry discovers this location and quickly develops it for the tourists who suddenly arrive in droves. From then on, for the greater part of each year, the members of this community may be outnumbered by large numbers of wealthy, loud, fun-seeking tourists, whose lifestyle, expectations, appearance and customs are totally unlike their own.

It would be surprising if these people were unaffected by the experience of being surrounded by so many tourists who were completely different, in many important ways, from themselves. This section looks at some of the ways in which the attitudes and behaviour of individuals and communities at destinations are changed by the experience of tourism.

The name usually given to the inhabitants of a tourist destination is the host population. The host population is composed of all the people living in this area, not only those who make their livelihood from looking after the needs of tourists. For example, for overseas visitors to Britain, the host population is the entire British public.

Cultural differences

Because tourism involves the movement of large numbers of people from their normal places of residence to new locations, it has the potential to bring together in large numbers two groups of people who often have very little in common with each other: the tourists and the host population. These two groups can differ from each other in many important ways.

For example, two friends, Liz and Natalie, join the many thousands of British tourists who now visit Turkey each year. Liz and Natalie are both 18. They work in an office and have saved up all year for their two-week holiday in Turkey, and so are both determined to enjoy themselves and to relax and take things as easily as possible. They plan to see such sights as the ancient mosques, and to spend lavishly in the shops and bazaars, buying presents for friends and families. They have already spent much of their money on fashionable holiday clothes, and new cameras, personal stereos and sunglasses. Both Liz and Natalie are sociable and chatty, and they want to meet and get to know Turkish men and women of their own age. They are also excited at the thought of being away from their families and from such restrictions as having to be home by a certain time every evening. In addition they want to return to Britain with excellent suntans to show off, so they intend to spend much of their time stretched out on the beach, with as much skin as possible exposed to the sun's rays.

By way of contrast, the Turkish host population is, on the whole, a poor one in comparison with people living in such industrialised countries as

Britain. A large proportion of Turkish people work in agriculture, and their lives are harder and more primitive than those of British people. Those working in the tourism industry also work hard to earn a living. Turkey is a Moslem country and many Turks are very devout in their religion. Certain activities which are totally acceptable in Britain, for example, are forbidden or frowned upon by Moslems. Topless sunbathing is one of these, and visitors to mosques are expected to display reverence and respect in their dress, and to cover their heads if they are women. Women generally have less freedom in Turkey than in Britain. Marriage is often prearranged by parents, and, in small towns particularly, men and women socialise separately – men in cafés and women together at home.

EXERCISE

Liz and Natalie are on holiday in Turkey, with lots of leisure time and few responsibilities. They have plenty of money to spend on luxury items and gifts, and they are both free to socialise with anyone they choose. If they visit any mosques in Turkey, they do so because they are popular tourist attractions.

Anja is an 18-year-old Turkish girl who follows a religion which regards activities such as sunbathing as immodest and therefore forbidden, and which also forbids gambling and drinking alcohol. Although Turkish is her first language, she also speaks English, because she works with tourists.

Write a paragraph contrasting Anja with Liz and Natalie. Based on the information in the above two paragraphs, suggest as many ways as possible in which they differ.

Reactions of the host population to tourists

When large numbers of tourists such as Liz and Natalie come into contact with the host population of a country such as Turkey, there can be many different reactions on the part of the host population. Their attitudes and behaviour towards tourists can be expressed in various ways.

Hostility

Even peace-loving, naturally friendly host populations can react with hostility towards tourists who constantly clash with the traditions and customs of the country they are visiting. Too many examples of thoughtless or objectionable behaviour on the part of tourists, for example, entering a temple in nothing but beachwear, getting drunk in countries where the predominant religion forbids the use of alcohol, mocking traditional ceremonies, will, before long, cause members of the host population to respond with hostility towards tourists. The numbers of tourists alone can be enough to create hostility. In Hawaii, for example, where American and Japanese tourists outnumber Hawaiians by 5 to 1 in the summer, and overcrowding is at crisis point, tourist buses are regularly showered with stones and cries of 'tourists go home'.

Removal of charity

Formerly in many countries, hospitality has been a matter of honour, and even one's enemies had to be treated in a lavish and courteous manner if they were one's guests. Tourists arriving in such countries in the early days of tourism, were often amazed at how well they were treated by members of the host population who provided great quantities of free hospitality in the form of food and places to stay. In some parts of Greece, this attitude towards guests and visitors still survives, and is known as *xenophilia* – the love of foreigners. However, this traditional, generous attitude of the host population cannot survive when tourists start to arrive in great numbers. The relationship between the host population and the tourists becomes a commercial one, with tourism becoming a business and not a charity. As a result, the custom of giving charity to visitors either disappears completely, or the host population takes steps to protect itself from going bankrupt through its own generosity. Mount Athos is a peninsula in northern Greece upon which 20 monasteries from the tenth and eleventh centuries still survive. Women are forbidden to enter this part of the country, but until recently, any man arriving there was provided with free accommodation and food in the monasteries during his stay there. The monks refused any offer of money, but since the arrival of so many tourists in the early 1970s, the monasteries have no longer been able to cope, and a complicated system of permits and letters of permission has been established in order to limit the number of visitors.

An even worse impact upon the host population is sometimes created due to the residents' perception of tourists as being wealthy, extravagant spenders. A traveller returning from Egypt told the story of his attempts to photograph some peasant farmers who were gathering in the harvest. Thinking that this was a picturesque scene, he pointed his camera at them, but they, seeing him, immediately stopped harvesting and came towards him demanding money before they would allow themselves to be photographed. The traveller gave up the attempt, but was saddened at the thought that the only words of English which the peasant farmers knew were 'How much?'.

Here the host population has begun to charge money from tourists for something which, even in highly commercialised countries, would be given at no charge.

Imitation

Another possible response of the host population to tourists is that of imitation. Tourists can appear wealthy, successful and sophisticated, which may have the effect of causing younger members of the host population to want to be more like the tourists. They try to achieve this by imitating the tourists' ambitions and values. This can have a positive and beneficial impact: the Turkish girl who meets many tourists like Liz and Natalie may be inspired by their successful careers and independent thinking, and may in turn develop greater ambitions for herself and a determination to work harder in order to achieve these ambitions.

More often, however, the attempt to imitate the tourists creates problems for the host population. When tourism arrives in a country such as Turkey, many young people in particular become attracted to the 'bright lights' of the cities and resorts frequented by tourists. Consequently, many of them abandon their farming families and migrate to the tourist destinations to work in the tourism industry in the hope that this will not only enable them to spend more time in the presence of the tourists, but also help them to earn the money they need in order to buy for example, the kinds of clothes worn by tourists, and to be able to spend equally extravagantly. When families are split up and traditional patterns of work disrupted (particularly where sons and daughters are needed in order to work on the farm, for example), the whole community can be upset. Even greater problems are caused by those members of the host population who, in their desire to imitate the tourists' lifestyle, turn to crime in order to obtain money. The presence of a group of relatively rich and poor people in the same location can be a stimulus for crime, as the latter group attempts to match the spending power of the former. In recent years, the Costa Brava and Costa del Sol in Spain have suffered a crime wave, with muggings and thefts. Such crimes are made easier by the presence of so many tourists which increases the chances of the criminals escaping undetected, through the crowds. The saddest result of imitation is that those members of the host population who respond in this way are often left with dreams and ambitions which simply cannot be fulfilled in their own countries, and which leaves them disillusioned and discontented with their own lives.

EXERCISE

1 Why are the impacts of tourism, which have been discussed so far, more likely to be felt as a result of international than domestic tourism?

2 Why is hostility towards incoming tourists more likely to be felt by those members of the host population who are not employed in the tourism industry?

3 German tourists flying to Sri Lanka are shown a film in which Sri Lankan customs and traditions are explained, and which offers tips such as

'Do not pose for a photograph next to a statue of the Buddha. Each of these statues contains a relic of the Buddha, and is, therefore, considered sacred by the Sri Lankans, who object to photographs of them being taken.'

Discuss the reasons for showing this film, and suggest what advice for general behaviour should be included for tourists travelling to Turkey.

CASE STUDY

The Himalayan Tourist Code

The popularity of the Himalayas as a trekking holiday destination has risen sharply in recent years, bringing tens of thousands of tourists every year to a previously isolated and remote part of Asia. This influx of visitors now threatens to have a severe impact on the physical environment as well as the host population of those countries through which the Himalayan mountain range passes.

Annapurna, Nepal's most popular trekking destination, has proven to be particularly vulnerable to tourism's impacts. These are apparent from the vast tracts of forest depleted each year in order to fulfil fuelwood needs and accommodation for tourists. This has resulted in soil erosion and flooding. However, the host population itself is also at risk from the effects of the visitors, who now outnumber them each year. The 40 000 local inhabitants of Annapurna have for centuries carved the landscape according to their own way of life and have adopted their own distinctive cultural practices which are unique to this region.

In an effort to minimise the negative impacts of tourism in the Himalayas, a voluntary code of conduct was launched in 1991 by the British-based organisation, Tourism Concern, in consultation with the Annapurna Conservation Area Project. The aims of Tourism Concern are:

- to promote greater understanding of the impact of tourism on host communities and environments;
- to raise awareness of the forms of tourism that respect the rights and interests of people living in tourist receiving areas, promoting tourism that is just, sustainable and participatory;
- to work for change in current tourism practice;
- to enable tourists and travellers to travel with critical insight and understanding.

Tourism Concern has a special interest in drawing attention to the development issues raised by tourism in Third World countries.

The Himalayan Tourist Code suggests a series of 12 practical steps that

THE HIMALAYAN TOURIST CODE

By following these simple guidelines, you can help preserve the unique environment and ancient cultures of the Himalayas.

Protect the natural environment

▲ **Limit deforestation – make no open fires** and discourage others from doing so on your behalf. Where water is heated by scarce firewood, use as little as possible. When possible choose accommodation that uses kerosene or fuel efficient wood stoves.

▲ **Remove litter, burn or bury paper** and carry out all non-degradable litter. Graffiti are permanent examples of environment pollution.

▲ **Keep local water clean and avoid using pollutants** such as detergents in streams or springs. If no toilet facilities are available, make sure you are at least 30 metres away from water sources, and bury or cover wastes.

▲ **Plants should be left to flourish in their natural environment** – taking cuttings, seeds and roots is illegal in many parts of the Himalayas.

▲ **Help your guides and porters to follow conservation measures.**

▲ **When taking photographs, respect privacy** – ask permission and use restraint.

▲ **Respect Holy places** – preserve what you have come to see, never touch or remove religious objects. Shoes should be removed when visiting temples.

▲ **Giving to children encourages begging.** A donation to a project, health centre or school is a more constructive way to help.

▲ **You will be accepted and welcomed if you follow local customs.** Use only your right hand for eating and greeting. Do not share cutlery or cups, etc. It is polite to use both hands when giving or receiving gifts.

▲ **Respect for local etiquette earns you respect** – loose, light weight clothes are preferable to revealing shorts, skimpy tops and tight fitting action wear. Hand holding or kissing in public are disliked by local people.

▲ **Observe standard food and bed charges** but do not condone overcharging. Remember when you're shopping that the bargains you buy may only be possible because of low income to others.

▲ **Visitors who value local traditions encourage local pride and maintain local cultures,** please help local people gain a realisitic view of life in Western Countries.

The Himalayas may change you –
please do not change them.
As a guest, respect local traditions,
protect local cultures, maintain local pride.
Be patient, friendly and sensitive
Remember – you are a guest

Tourism Concern
Froebel College, Roehampton Lane, London SW15 5PU
Tel: 081-878-9053

10.1 *The*
alayan Tourist
le

can be taken by visitors to limit the problems caused by the impact of tourism on the environment and the host population. Ten thousand copies of the Code were printed by Tourism Concern and distributed to all British tour operators carrying visitors to the Himalayas. Copies were also sent to major ticket outlets, such as Campus, STA and Trailfinders, to ensure that they reach independent travellers, as well as those in tour groups.

Tourism Concern also encouraged tour operators to include the Code in their brochures, and requested publishers of tourist guides to the Himalayas to print the Code in future editions.

The Himalayan Tourist Code is shown in Fig. 10.1.

The impact of tourism on culture

The culture of a host population is often an important factor in attracting tourists to a particular destination. Many tourists are interested in experiencing a culture which is different from their own. The culture of a host population can take many different forms, but most examples fall into one of two categories:

(1) customs which have been created by the host population

(2) aspects of the host population's everyday life, their history and religion.

The first category of customs created by the host population, ranges from their arts and crafts, such as local dances, artefacts, costumes and other everyday objects, to special events such as festivals, colourful wedding ceremonies and carnivals. Almost every region of the world has its own traditional form of dance, from Spanish flamenco dancing to Maori 'Poi' dances: artefacts such as African carved wood masks, Tunisian rugs and locally made pottery make popular souvenirs, and events such as the famous Carnival in Rio de Janeiro ('the world's greatest party'), the Channel Islands' festival of flowers, or Bastille Day in France attract vast numbers of tourists.

Aspects of the host population's everyday life, history and religion include local or national traditions and customs, their work and leisure activities, and their forms of worship. Tourists love to take photographs of 'typical' scenes of the host population's life: these may include a picturesque group of old Greek peasants sitting around a table outside a 'taverna', a game of 'boules' in France, a colourful outdoor fruit and vegetable market in Barbados, or large numbers of Moslems kneeling at prayer facing in the direction of Mecca.

EXERCISE ────────────────────────────

From the following description of the island of Bali, taken from a holiday brochure, identify as many examples as you can of elements of Balinese culture which are mentioned in order to tempt the reader of the brochure.

BALI

Bali lies a thousand miles beyond Hong Kong and Singapore. It's a mathematical distinction that places this romantically unspoilt island in a geographical context which often seems more Polynesian than Eastern, with the Pacific rather than the Orient on the nearest horizon.

One of the green islands of the Indonesian chain, set amid the warm currents of the Java Sea, Bali, the 'Morning of the World', is unlike any other destination in these pages, with a hint of the world of Gauguin in the velvet breezes that temper the island's tropical setting.

Some 80×50 miles at its widest, Bali will confound cynics with the beauty of its scenery; its jade green rice-terraces and palms; volcanic mist-wrapped peaks; pastoral landscapes and thatched villages; and its gentle, artistic people, whose many Hindu festivals and temple processions will leave dazzling memories.

Spare some time to leave the palm-shaded, reef-protected beach at Sanur (with its flying-fish and colourful Balinese outriggers) to explore the mysteries of the island – Besakih, the holiest shrine, on the slopes of sacred Mount Agung; the holy springs and temples of Tampaksiring; Karangasem, with its beautiful lakes and gardens; Kintamani and mount Batur; picturesque Ubud village, and Denpasar, the tiny capital where you can shop for carvings and batiks. And visit performances of the classical Barong, Legong and Monkey dances, where the rhythms of the island *gamelan* music capture the haunting magic of strange, beautiful Bali . . .

Tradewinds Asean Brochure

EXERCISE ────────────────────────────

1 The photograph in Fig. 10.2 shows an example of a form of dance which is unique to Britain. What is the name by which it is known? Give an example of another form of dance unique to Britain or to a particular region within Britain.

2 Give two examples of each of the following which is unique to your own region or to another region of Britain.
- a special event or festival
- an artefact
- a traditional costume

- a leisure activity or sport
- a custom or tradition

The many different aspects of a particular country's culture have usually been formed long before the arrival of tourism. However, a host population's culture, when it becomes not only something for the host population itself, but also a form of tourist attraction can undergo some extreme changes. Some of the effects of tourism on culture are beneficial, but most are judged to be harmful.

Beneficial impacts

All over the world, traditional arts and crafts are dying out, as generations of people with particular skills are replaced by generations who do not learn these skills because they are thought to have become irrelevant to their modern way of life.

Because tourism creates an interest in these particular forms of culture, it can help in preserving traditional arts and crafts from being lost altogether. A famous example of this is that of the Canadian Inuit, or Eskimo, art of

Fig. 10.2 Tradition dancing in Englan Morris dancing

Source: Britain on View

carving. Before the arrival of European tourists in Canada, art was something of minor importance only to the Eskimo, and not at all a main feature of their lives. Tourism created a great demand for souvenirs, and the host population responded by producing high-quality carvings in soapstone, of figures representing central themes of their culture, such as the animals they hunt. The carvings reflect aspects of the traditional life of the Eskimo, and are now the principal way in which the host population expresses the qualities of its own culture. Without the arrival of tourists and tourism, and the demand for souvenirs, this particular Eskimo craft may have been lost forever. Instead, the traditional art form has been given a new lease of life through tourism, and the new generation of skilled craftsmen and craftswomen has created fulfilling and profitable employment.

Crafts in Britain have also benefited from the attentions of tourists. Traditional hand-made artefacts are sold throughout the country in shops or craft centres, keeping alive skills which are part of the pre-industrial heritage of Britain. An example of a different kind of skill is that of thatching, shown in Fig. 10.3.

Thatched cottages have for a long time been popular with domestic and inbound tourists, who regard them as an essential part of the traditional

ig. 10.3 *Thatching*

ource: Britain on View

village. Owners of houses with thatched roofs, on the other hand, are only too well aware of the expense and hard work involved in creating and maintaining such roofs, rather than the modern alternatives such as slate or tile. Yet the popularity of thatched roofs among tourists has been one of the factors responsible for the continuing demand for the ancient thatchers' craft in Britain. Some thatchers have even found employment in the USA where thatched roofs have become a status symbol, after being discovered in Britain by American tourists.

Harmful impacts

Nevertheless, while tourism can help to preserve the culture of a host population, more often the effects are harmful. One possible effect of tourism on culture is trivialisation: when aspects of the host culture become a degraded and commercialised form of entertainment for tourists. There are many examples of this kind of impact. One is seen in the Bedouin feasts which visitors to Tunisia are encouraged to attend. The Bedouins are a desert tribe of Tunisia with their own ancient customs which include, on special occasions, elaborate feasts around the campfire, accompanied by their own singing and dancing under the night-sky of the desert. The feasts have deep religious and symbolic meaning for the Bedouins, and are an important part of Bedouin culture.

The ceremony of the Bedouin feast has now been hijacked by the tourism industry and transformed into something designed to appeal only to the tourist in search of an evening's entertainment. Every night of the week, all over Tunisia, bus-loads of tourists arrive at the scene of 'Bedouin feasts' which are carefully stage-managed and entirely artificial showbusiness performances, resembling the original Bedouin ceremonies in little but name. Wine and couscous is distributed liberally to the audiences, tourists are invited to indulge in belly-dancing with the performers, and the whole experience is all but devoid of any insight into real Bedouin culture. Such trivialisation of the host culture is found in tourist destinations throughout the world. Although most examples are in the developing world, the developed world does not escape these effects: 'Cockney nights' in London's West End, and 'Caledonian evenings' in Edinburgh, at which guests are given kilts to wear and haggis to eat, have become commercialised to the extent that they now trivialise these traditional cultures from different parts of Britain. In all such examples, special events or aspects of the everyday life, history and religion of host populations are used as material for tourist entertainment which gives little real insight into the lives of the hosts.

The artefacts of a host population can also be victims of the harmful side effects of tourism. Traditionally, these have often been specially and carefully produced for particular purposes, such as religious ceremonies. An African mask would have been carved with great care to include particular details of special significance, such as an eagle carved on the upper part of the mask symbolising courage, or a half-moon shape indicating that the wearer is a wise man. When the masks begin to be purchased by tourists, however, changes begin to occur in the way in which they are made. The artist realises that tourists do not understand the symbolic significance of the details on the mask, and so the details are either left out or carved without care. Quantity rather than quality becomes the artist's main concern, while the tourist's concern is often whether the mask fits into their suitcase – a consideration which also changes the form of the mask. Traditional art then becomes what is known as pseudo-art. Two results occur: the artefact is changed, almost out of all recognition, from the original form, and the artist's level of skill in producing the masks is lost. Tourist destinations all over the world are full of such pseudo traditional artefacts. Often the artists take little pride in their art, and remember only dimly the time when they produced high-quality articles, rich in symbolic significance, to express their individual culture: Indonesian puppet figures, North African pottery, West African ivory carvings, and Maori 'tiki' figure carvings, are examples of this.

The tendency towards imitation which can effect the ambitions and values of the host population may also affect their culture. Members of the host population, particularly young people, can become attracted towards the culture of the tourists at the expense of further developing an interest in their own culture. This process is known as cultural drift because it involves one culture drifting into another. Cultural drift has turned the culture of some primitive, simple, host populations into 'Coca Cola' cultures, so that disco music, neon lights and cocktail bars begin to replace the traditional music and leisure activities of the host population. Language, too, can be affected in this way, when the language of the tourist threatens the survival of 'minority' or 'second' languages, such as Gaelic. In areas of Switzerland which receive large numbers of tourists, the Romansh language has declined in use much more rapidly than it has in those areas which receive few tourists. While tourism is not the only factor which leads to cultural drift (the cinema and television being others), it can have the effect of accelerating the process.

Tourism and communication between cultures

In 1961, a researcher into tourism wrote:

> Tourism has become the noblest instrument of this century for achieving international understanding. It enables contacts among people from the most distant parts of the globe, people of various languages, races, creeds, political beliefs and economic standing. Tourism brings them together . . . it leads to personal contact in which people can understand attitudes and beliefs which were incomprehensible to them because they were different.

The belief that tourism can help to bridge gaps and create understanding between different cultures and communities through the communication it makes possible is often held up as one of the positive effects of tourism in the world. By travelling and coming into contact with people different from themselves, tourists are said to achieve greater understanding of the host population, and vice versa. By this theory, tourism becomes a kind of educational process, and may be given the credit for such achievements as helping to maintain world peace, inspiring oppressed peoples to change their political regimes, and improving the situation of women in primitive societies.

Certainly, many people's attitudes are changed by holidays, and by the people whom they meet on their travels. But equally, many tourists return home, apparently unaffected by what or whom they have seen. The question is whether tourism leads to real communication between cultures, or not. This depends upon the type of tourism in question.

Figure 10.4 shows letters from two students on different holidays.

Dear Julia,

I'm lying beside the hotel pool writing to you as I tan under this blazing sun. Zios is a really great place. It really is home from home. The whole island is full of tourists and the beach looks really packed, so I spend most of my days here with the others beside the pool. Everything you need is right here in the hotel complex — food, drink, sports, entertainment, even some shops. We've met this other bunch of students from Leeds and we spend a lot of time with them having a good laugh and dancing in the hotel disco every night.

Last night before the disco got going, we had some entertainment from some Greeks who were paid by the hotel to show the guests how to do Greek dancing. It's all Greek to me! Maria, who cleans my room doesn't smile much, though. And she's a bit quiet, but she works hard.

Tomorrow we're all going on a coach tour into the mountains to a 'typical Greek barbeque' with as much wine as you can drink, free! Wish me luck!

See you soon,

Elaine

Fig. 10.4 (a) A letter from a student on holiday

Dear Stuart

I'm sitting in the Minerva Taverna drinking a huge glass of Ouzo as I write this letter.

Zios is a really great place, just as you said it was. I arrived here on the ferry boat 4 days ago. It was a relief to escape from all the other passengers who were heading for the big resorts on the other side of the island. This village is so peaceful, it's hard to believe that I'm on the same island as all those tourists. I've only spotted about 20 or so other visitors in this entire village.

When I got here, I went straight to the guest house at the address you gave me and rented a room. I told the landlady, Rosa, that I was a friend of yours and she remembered you straight away and asked if you were still studying at college. Her son Andreos and I came out to the Minerva Taverna the first night and he introduced me to his uncles and cousins. I practised a little Greek I have learnt, but Andreos came to my rescue and acted as interpreter. We spoke for a long time about what it was like in Greece during the Second World War and I told them about the television pictures I'd seen of the Blitz in London.

Yesterday, I took the local bus along the coast and then went walking in the mountains to visit the monastery I'd read about in my guide book. The monks were very friendly and I spent a couple of hours talking with them.

The whole holiday has been one big adventure so far.

All the best,   Andy

A letter from a [stu]dent on a different [holi]day

EXERCISE

1 List as many differences as you can between Elaine's holiday and Andy's.

2 Which involves more communication with the host population? Explain why you think this is.

3 Describe what can happen to a village such as the one Andy is visiting, if it is discovered by more tourists and, therefore, becomes a mass tourist destination? Write a paragraph describing the possible changes that would result.

Real communication between cultures is found less often in the mass tourism of huge, popular resorts than it is in the more personal tourism which often takes place 'off the beaten track'. The latter kind of tourism is more likely to offer the tourist opportunities to meet a wide range of members of the host population, and not only those serving his or her needs as employees of the tourism industry. Tourists using the same shops, bars and transport as local people are more likely to meet members of the host population on an equal footing, as opposed to only in the customer-employee relationship.

On the other hand, tourists who travel in groups and keep themselves securely inside tourist 'reservations' such as huge, self-sufficient, hotel complexes or holiday villages, are less likely to have any serious impact upon the host population as a community. If communication between cultures is limited, then so too is the impact which one culture can have on the other.

ASSIGNMENTS

1 Changing the Changing of the Guard?

The changing of the Queen's guard at Buckingham Palace may be the most famous ceremony in the world, as well as being a long-established London tradition. Led by their regimental band as the following photograph shows, the

Fig. 10.5 Changing the Guard at Buckingham Palace

Source: Britain on View

new guard marches into the palace forecourt in a colourful parade which attracts large numbers of sightseers.

Unfortunately, the crowds, especially in summer, are often so large that many tourists fail to get a good view of the ceremony. All they see of this spectacle is what they capture in the photographs they take by holding their cameras above the heads of other tourists. At present, the changing of the guard takes place only once a day, at 11.30 every summer morning, and on alternate days from September to March. It has been suggested that, to meet the huge demand from tourists who wish to see the ceremony, it should take place two, three, or even four times a day. Others, however, have dismissed this suggestion, saying that as it is traditional only to change the guard once a day in the summer, then it should stay that way.

Conduct a class debate on this issue, with one half of the class arguing that the guard should be changed more often to please the tourists, and the other arguing that the ceremony should be left as it stands now.

2 When two cultures – the tourists' and the host population's – come together, it is almost always the host population's which changes most, taking on characteristics of the tourists' culture. The tourists' culture is usually little changed. Conduct a class discussion on why you think this is the case.

CASE STUDY

The Tribal Alternative

Alternative travel is the name given to the kind of tourism that is as different as it can be from the 'mass tourism' of the overseas package tours.

Alternative travel is for tourists who like to do things differently, and who wish to spend less time with other tourists and more time finding out about the people living at their destinations and their culture. Tourists who choose alternative travel aim to avoid using special 'tourist' accommodation, transport, and other services, preferring to share those used by the population of the countries they are visiting. In this way, they hope to establish contact with the local population and to experience some aspects of their lives.

Many tourists choose this form of tourism because they are concerned about the negative impact which mass tourism can have on the culture of destinations. They feel that alternative travel has less of an impact on culture and communities.

The Tribal Alternative is a direct sell tour operator specialising in alternative travel. It focuses on people and their culture rather than on creating the comforts of the developed world in the Third World setting where the holidays are taken. Figure 10.6 shows details of the Tribal Alternative seven-week trip to India. The full trip costs £740 including travel within India (but excluding the cost of flying to Delhi from Britain), accommodation, meals and guides. Holidaymakers dine on regional cooking, meet local families and join in with cultural events.

Why we're different

After years of travelling the world's most exotic continent, we'd like to introduce you to the Asia we know.

Unlike other overland companies we don't spend endless days packed into trucks, isolated and uncomfortable. Nor do we pitch camp cut off from the heart of the local life and prepare English style food.

Instead we invite you to live amongst the people. In their homes, in the streets, on local transport and often far off the beaten track, you too can enjoy genuine first hand contact.

By living and travelling with our local friends you'll develop your own understanding of Asia and its political, social and religious traditions.

Accommodation & food

Throughout the trip, we'll be staying with local people whether in out-of-the-way villages and nomadic tribal hamlets, or in the sumptuous palaces of India's maharajas: enjoying excellent home cooking and popular local dishes, as well as the sophistication of Asian haute-cuisine.

Naturally our hotels and homes are carefully chosen for both their friendly atmosphere and their cleanliness.

Transport

We use public transport; buses and jeeps crammed with locals going to market, loaded with vegetables and livestock, where the dramas of daily life are chewed over with the betel-nut!!

Long journeys are taken over-night in luxury couchettes so you neither lose your sleep nor waste the days. (Mind you, the night life is colourful and well worth staying up for.)

And when the road and rail runs out, we'll take to camels in the desert, elephants in the jungle, boats in the tropical backwaters, and finally, we're trekking in the great mountains of Asia on foot.

India

There are few places on earth with the enormous variety India has to offer. Here is a mass of conflicting images; at once vast and crowded, extravagant and squalid, luxuriant and barren.

The seeming simplicity of modern urban existence contrasts with the intense subtlety of the ancient cultures which form the backdrop for all Asian lives.

The profusion of its splendid temples and palaces, abandoned cities and

Fig 10.6

ruins, marvellous art forms and strange religious festivals all crowd in on the everyday, giving local colour and vitality to each region.

The trip: Rajasthan to the deep south (7 weeks)

Week 1

From Delhi to the Yammuna River we visit Agra's famous fort and the spectacular Taj Mahal built by Emperor Shah Jahan as a monument of breath-taking grace and extravagance in honour of his wife. We catch it in the rising sun at its most serene. Nearby, almost perfectly preserved at the height of its splendour is the haunting abandoned city of Fatepur Sikri, the ancient Mogul capital.

From here we travel through Rajasthan, the 'Land of Kings'. Its exotic atmosphere extends far beyond the splendid desert palaces and fortresses to the people themselves in their vibrant costumes.

The rose-coloured sandstone of Jaipur, the 'Pink City' glows magically in the setting sun. This ancient walled city, the gem and art centre of India, combines the vitality of a state capital with the romance of its Mogul and Rajasthani heritage. Here as guests of the Maharajah we appreciate ultimate luxury as we relax in the opulence of his palace.

Week 2

Travelling through the desert, we visit the great fort in Jodhpur and sample local produce from its colourful bazaar. Jaisalmer, remote and seemingly out of the 'Arabian Nights', is perhaps India's most exotic city. Its magnificent temples and mansions are carved elaborately from the amber sandstone of which the entire city is built. A camel safari introduces us to the simple life of the tribal people as, with the touch of Hollywood we ride deep into the desert.

Week 3

A winding and arid route through desert villages brings us to Pushkar surrounding its holy lake and to the beautiful city of Udaipur. This cool oasis in the parched heart of Rajasthan, richly endowed with luxurious palaces has become a centre for local artisans.

Week 4

We experience life's dramas on the railway going south by couchette to more tropical climes. Here we explore the ancient Buddhist and Hindu cave temples of Maharashtra, famous for their remarkable sculptures and paintings.

Weeks 5 & 6

A local bus takes us to Pune, a spiritual centre today for many philosophies including the Rajneesh. The deck stages an enthralling world of activity as our boat ferries us to Goa (a former Portuguese colony), to one of its remotest beaches on the Arabian sea. Miles of white sand fringed with coconut palms; and nothing to interrupt the peace but the fishermen and local women bearing you tropical fruit! Well rested, the road continues through Karnataka to Mysore, the 'Sandalwood City' encompassed in the lingering aroma of woodcraft and incense production.

In Belur and Somnathpur we visit some of the world's most exquisitely sculptured temples. Built in the 13th century during the heyday of the Hoysala kings, they are still utterly breathtaking.

Week 7

Ootacamund in the Kunda Hills, with its old British flavour and cool fragrant eucalyptus forests, provides us with the ideal retreat.

Fig 10.6 cont.

11

TOURISM EMPLOYMENT AND SKILLS

After reading this chapter, you should have a clear understanding of:
- the types of employment created by tourism,
- the scale of tourism employment in Britain,
- the special characteristics of tourism employment,
- tourism skills.

Tourism employment

One of the reasons for governments around the world supporting tourism in their countries is the ability of the tourism industry to create employment wherever it flourishes. Some residents, too, are more prepared to tolerate the negative impact of tourism for the same reason.

It is estimated that tourism will be the world's biggest industry of all by the year 2000. As a labour-intensive service industry, tourism has the capacity to create jobs for large numbers of people of varying levels of skill, from top level executives to the semi-skilled and unskilled. Already, in Europe, 1 in every 12 workers is employed in the tourism industry: a total of around 35 million jobs. In Britain, the job-creating potential of tourism is acknowledged in the government's objective, through the activities of the national tourist boards, to develop tourism 'in regions of above-average unemployment'. This is the same reason why many local authorities try hard to attract to their regions investment in tourist facilities, such as hotels, leisure centres and other tourist attractions.

Tourism creates two types of employment:

(1) direct employment; and

(2) indirect employment

Direct employment is created for those people working in the various sectors of the tourism industry: travel and tourism, accommodation and catering, tourist attractions and business facilities and tourism promotion and information. These can be the 'front-of-house' staff who come into direct contact with the visitors, or 'behind-the-scenes' staff who, for example, cook, clean, or do office work relating to tourism. Anyone employed in any business or organisation whose aim is to provide tourists with information, travel, with a place to stay and eat, or with something to do or see is therefore in direct employment, created by tourism.

Indirect employment created by tourism refers to the jobs of those people who manufacture the goods and provide the services which are purchased by the businesses and organisations which serve the tourists directly. For example, factory workers manufacturing bedroom furniture for sale to hotels owe their jobs indirectly to tourism; a landscape architect who specialises in designing camping and caravan parks is also in a job indirectly created by tourism; and the same may be said of the people employed in a factory which produces uniforms for waiters and other hotel workers.

EXERCISE

Divide the following lists into examples of (1) direct and (2) indirect tourism employment:

(a) Ann is the manageress of a hotel restaurant.
(b) Alex makes ornaments out of shells and sells them to souvenir shops.
(c) Angela works for a company which installs computer systems in travel agencies.
(d) Amos is a redcoat entertainer at a holiday centre.
(e) Axel works as a tourist guide, showing visitors around his home town.
(f) Annabelle works as a conference organiser in a large international conference and exhibition centre.
(g) Alberto is a self-employed maintenance engineer, specialising in the servicing of fairground rides.
(h) April is the manageress of a food processing unit which produces boil-in-the-bag sauces and vegetables for use in hotel and restaurant kitchens.

Whenever tourism comes to a region, the wages and salaries earned by those directly and indirectly employed as a result of the tourism are spent on goods and services which, in turn, create additional jobs for a wide range of people. In this way, the prosperity created by the spending of visitors is filtered down through the local economy.

Apart from a general recognition that tourism brings employment and prosperity to a destination, there is little agreement among different tourism regions and countries on the ways in which this employment can be measured. While measuring the number of people employed in their police forces, for example, would be a relatively simple exercise for most countries, there are many difficulties involved in estimating the number of jobs created by tourism:

(1) The number of those who are indirectly employed in tourism is difficult to estimate, especially as some of them may be involved in producing goods and services for other industries, as well as tourism.

(2) Many people are employed in work which is only in part directly created by tourism: 50% of a leisure centre's customers may be visitors to that town, but the other 50% may be residents.

(3) Some people, particularly those in part-time or casual employment, work on an informal and unofficial basis and do not declare their earnings to the authorities: Greek families who accommodate tourists all summer may avoid declaring this income in order to avoid paying taxes on it and street traders selling souvenirs may operate on the same basis. Although such people as these are making a living out of tourism, they do not appear in tourism employment statistics.

(4) Many jobs in tourism are seasonal, only employing people for part of the year.

Almost every country measures tourism employment in a slightly different way from other countries. This lack of agreement makes comparisons of tourism employment levels between different countries very difficult and the figures that are available are often out of date and incomplete.

Tourism employment figures in Britain are estimated in the following way:

There were approximately 1.5 million jobs in tourism-related industries in 1990. This figure is higher than the number of men, women and children living in Birmingham. Figure 11.1 shows the progression in the number of tourism-related jobs in Britain between 1980 and 1990.

During the ten years up to 1990, the growth in numbers in tourism-related industries in Britain was 26.1%, compared to an actual *fall* of 0.6% in the total number of people in employment there. Within the tourism-related

	Restaurants, cafés, etc	Public houses and bars	Night clubs and licensed clubs	Hotels and other tourist accommo- dation	Sports and other recreation libraries, museums, art galleries	All tourism- related industries	*All service industries*	*All industries (Figures in thousands)*
1980	196	248	130	280	328	1183	*13 384*	*22 458*
1985	223	266	140	268	373	1270	*13 769*	*20 920*
1988	265	289	141	281	374	1350	*14 860*	*21 740*
1989	290	326	140	301	373	1431	*15 261*	*22 134*
1990	306	339	142	318	387	1492	*15 497*	*22 325*
Percentage changes:								
1980–90	55.8	36.5	9.2	13.4	18.0	26.1	*15.8*	*−0.6*
1989–90	5.5	3.9	1.4	5.5	3.8	4.3	*1.5*	*0.9*

Fig. 11.1 *Employees in employment in tourism-related industries, 1980–90 (Great Britain, thousand)*
Source: ED quarterly employment surveys

industries, the number of employees increased fastest in those ten years in restaurants and cafés – by 55.8%.

The importance of tourism employment to Britain is clearly seen in Fig. 11.2, which shows total employees in employment in 1990 in tourism-related industries alongside figures for a selection of other industries in Britain.

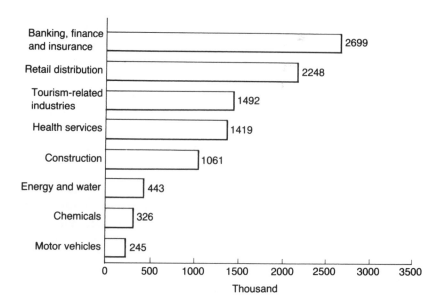

Fig. 11.2 Employees in selected industries June 1990

Source: ED employment surveys

Region of employment	1989		1981–89	
	Number of employees (thousand)	Per cent of total	Change in number (thousand)	Percentage change
South East	448.9	31	96.2	21.4
East Anglia	49.3	3	17.2	34.8
South West	145.5	10	37.6	25.9
West Midlands	115.8	8	23.9	20.6
East Midlands	87.6	6	24.1	27.5
Yorks & Humber	127.8	9	30.2	23.6
North West	168.6	12	25.3	15.0
North	84.9	6	10.3	12.1
Wales	71.8	5	15.0	20.9
Scotland	154.4	11	19.4	12.5
Great Britain	1454.6	100	299.1	20.6

Fig. 11.3 Employees in employment by region. Tourism-related industries (Great Britain)

Source: Census of Employment 1989

Tourism employment is on the increase throughout the country. The region where the most tourism jobs exist is in the South East, which includes London, and this is followed by the North West and Scotland. Figure 11.3 shows the number of tourism employees region by region, together with the percentage increase in their numbers between 1981 and 1989.

EXERCISE ————————————————————————————

1 Which regions saw the greatest increases in tourism employment during 1981 and 1989?

2 What evidence is there in Fig. 11.3 to indicate that tourism may be increasing in areas of above average unemployment in Britain?

Characteristics of tourism employment

Direct employment in tourism includes the variety of jobs done by people providing travel, transport, accommodation, catering, leisure and business facilities for visitors to their countries or regions. Despite this range of jobs, however, there are certain special characteristics of tourism employment which are common to them all. The combination of characteristics found in tourism employment is unique to this particular industry.

Work around the clock

Tourists need to be looked after 24 hours a day, seven days a week. They may arrive at their destination at 3am, on a night flight, and need to be met by airport staff and holiday reps. As the last tourist leaves the nightclub, hotel kitchens are coming to life as preparations are made for breakfast. Hotel desks are staffed throughout the night and the night-duty hotel manager is always at hand. Most roadside catering establishments never close. For this reason, shift work is an important feature of tourism employment. Many tourism businesses divide the day into three eight-hour shifts to provide the staff cover needed. Nevertheless, overtime is also common in tourism, in order to cover staff shortages or staff absences. Hours can be long and irregular or unsocial, meaning that they are outside the Monday to Friday 'office hours' routine.

Seasonal work

The working population in tourism tends to swell in number during the high season, and shrink back during the low season as tourist facilities close down and pay off staff. The proportion of seasonal to all year round employment is greatest in countries which depend largely on sunshine to attract visitors to themselves. In some Mediterranean countries such as Greece, for example, the vast majority of tourism-related employment is seasonal, lasting only for the months between May and October.

Seasonality is not such a large feature of tourism employment in Britain. There, 'seasonal variations', i.e. the difference between the number of those employed in the high and low seasons, is approximately 9% for the hotel and catering sector, this being the sector where the effect of seasonality is at its greatest. In other words, 9% fewer people are employed in hotels and catering establishments in winter than at the height of summer. This does not mean that these 9% are made redundant at the end of the high season: many of these people are students, for example, who return to school or college after working in summer jobs. Nevertheless, even in Britain, many thousands of jobs in tourism last for only four or five months of the year.

Work with people from other places

A barman on the Costa del Sol in Spain becomes accustomed to serving customers from a number of different countries every day. The customer in tourism is always someone from outside the immediate region where they might be on holiday or on a short break. Working in tourism, therefore, means coming into regular contact with large numbers of people from outside the region or outside the country to which the tourism staff belong. Tourist guides, tourist information centre staff, waiters, historic property managers are all examples of people whose job brings them into frequent contact with visitors. As well as bringing tourism workers into contact with people from other places, tourism employment can also introduce them to lifestyles and standards of living that are different from their own. The local peasant farmer's daughter who is employed as a waitress in a luxury hotel in Turkey; the American Indian family whose reservation is regularly visited by hundreds of camera clicking Japanese tourists; and even in Britain, the majority of those working in hotels begin their careers there without ever having stayed in a hotel as a guest, themselves.

Work in an atmosphere of enjoyment

One important characteristic which distinguishes work in tourism from work in other 'people' careers such as the police, social work, or even the undertaking business is that the customer in tourism has an expectation of enjoyment, fun and pleasure. Even business tourists expect to relax and enjoy themselves outside the hours that they are working. Naturally, this enjoyment is only made possible by the hard work of those employed to receive, feed, entertain, inform, and clean up for the tourists themselves.

The luxurious standards of living in some hotels are only made possible by the hard and often menial work of a whole army of staff. Processing hundreds of passengers onto a jet aircraft can be an arduous and stressful task for the airport staff and answering the same question for the hundredth time at the end of a long and difficult day can test the patience of any museum attendant. But the pleasure-seeking tourist expects at all times to be dealt with by staff who help to create the general atmosphere of enjoyment.

EXERCISE

Tourism employment has four particular characteristics. While other industries may share one or two of these characteristics, the combination of all four is unique to tourism.

For each characteristic that we have discussed, name as many other industries as you can which share the characteristic with tourism: e.g. work around the clock: hospital staff, and so on.

Tourism skills and attitudes

Perhaps more than in any other industry, the people who work in tourism are crucial to the success of that industry, in any part of the world.

Attractive hotels, excellent transport networks, and a number of interesting things to see and do will not, in themselves, succeed in attracting tourists if the people working in the industry do not come up to the tourists' expectations.

The skills and attitudes of those directly employed in all sectors of tourism are a major part of what visitors notice and what they remember when they return home.

The clumsy waitress who spills the soup, the coach driver who responds rudely to a passenger's enquiry, the tourist guide with a very poor understanding of the tourists' own language or the restaurant manager who deals badly with a customer's complaint will not impress the tourists who come into contact with these people. Too many instances of this kind of poor treatment may discourage them from returning to that destination, and they may carry bad reports of the place back home with them, discouraging others from trying the same destination.

Managers and owners of tourist facilities, as well as governments all over the world, realise that the people employed in tourism play a major part in determining the success or failure of the industry. For this reason, a great growth in interest has taken place in the skills and attitudes which come together to make a successful and professional employee in tourism.

In the same way that the industry has special characteristics which distinguish it from other industries, so too do those working in tourism need to demonstrate special skills and attitudes, the combination of which is unique to tourism:

Occupational skills

Occupational skills are the basic skills which enable people working in tourism to do their jobs competently. Chefs must be able to cook, airport staff must be able to check someone onto a flight, and a tourist guide must know how to show a group of visitors around a historic house. Much of the education and training which takes place in colleges, catering schools and company training centres is designed to provide these occupational skills. As new technology plays an increasingly important part in all sectors of tourism, constant re-training of staff is vital to keeping their occupational skills up to date. Some of the occupational skills necessary for certain tourism-related jobs are shown in Fig. 11.4.

Chef	prepare a meal for 20 people order supplies of food for the kitchen
Flight attendant/ air stewardess	serve meals to passengers sell duty-free goods
Travel agency counter clerk	use a computer terminal to book airline tickets advise customers on package holidays
Hotel receptionist	book guests into the hotel make up their bills when they leave
Theatre box-office assistant	sell tickets directly to the public answer telephone enquiries about the theatre's performances

Fig. 11.4 Occupational skills

EXERCISE

Give two examples of occupational skills for each of the following jobs in tourism:
• fast-food sales assistant
• waiter or waitress
• conference organiser
• tourist information centre assistant

Occupational skills differ from job to job, but there are certain skills and attitudes expected by tourists from all staff with whom they come into contact. The skills and attitudes described below are those looked for in all tourism staff who come into direct contact with visitors.

Customer relations skills

This is the name given to a person's ability to make a visitor feel welcome, properly looked after, and confident that they are receiving the standard of service they expect in the aircraft, hotel, or tourist attraction, for example. The need for tourism employees to have good customer relations skills is related to visitors' expectations of enjoyment and comfort, despite being away from home. They expect the tourism staff who serve them to be cheerful, polite and helpful at all times. Without a doubt, there are people working in tourism who genuinely enjoy meeting the public and responding to their needs, particularly in countries with a tradition of courtesy and hospitality towards visitors, or in destinations which receive few visitors and where tourists are still something of a novelty. For most, however, the ability to remain cheerful and co-operative to thousands of individual tourists every year is something to be learned and something which they regard as part of their professional attitude to the job, rather than something which comes in a spontaneous and natural manner.

Customer relations skills are at the heart of what managers and owners of tourist facilities expect and wish their staff to display in their dealings with customers. Staff are expected to behave in a welcoming and pleasant manner to tourists, particularly if they are the first members of staff with whom the visitors come into contact, such as hotel receptionists, or staff selling tickets at entry points to tourist attractions, for example.

It is also desirable for all staff, from the manager of a large hotel to someone selling ice-cream in a theme park to be courteous and polite in their dealings with visitors. Cultural differences are important here because different peoples around the world show courtesy and politeness in different ways. As tourists travel further afield to new destinations, they come into contact with cultures that differ from their own, and misunderstandings over standards of behaviour towards tourists inevitably arise. For example, European visitors to some Asian destinations have mistakenly formed the impression that the people working in the tourism industry there are reserved and curt in their dealings with them. By the same token, the courtesies and greetings which come naturally to American tourism staff – 'have a nice day', 'enjoy your meal' and 'you're welcome' – appear odd and extravagant to some European visitors. Yet both of these are examples of tourism staff from different cultures behaving in their own perfectly courteous and polite manner towards visitors.

The final way in which customer relations skills show themselves is in dealing with complaints. Even the best run tourism businesses receive complaints from time to time when visitors feel that something is not as it should be. Much of the training in customer relations skills worldwide is in the effective handling of complaints. This involves convincing the visitor that their complaint is being acknowledged and properly dealt with, and preventing it from escalating into a loud unpleasant argument which affects other people's enjoyment.

Information skills

Tourists need information on a variety of topics from travel directions to explanations of unfamiliar items on menus, where places are and what there is to see and do locally, and information on the history and traditions of the places they are visiting. Tourists tend to regard all those working in the industry as the source of answers to their questions, whether the person is a hotel doorman, a gardener working at a historic house, a waitress, the ticket collector on a train, or the manager of a holiday park. For this reason, the ability to understand what is being asked and to provide information and answers is regarded as an important communication skill for tourism staff everywhere. Most people working with tourists come to build up a range of knowledge about the place where they work and the surrounding area. In France the accumulation of such useful background information is considered so important that students studying tourism at college there, attend lectures on the culture, traditions and history of their own country as part of their course.

Great emphasis is also placed by tourism training staff on giving information as clearly and as accurately as possible. To illustrate this is an extract from a tourism training manual for employees dealing with overseas visitors, entitled *Welcome to Britain* (*See* Fig. 11.5).

A bad set of directions:
'Go out of here, follow the road called Bright Street until you get to the humped backed bridge. Turn right, no left, no sorry right, and walk as far as the gas works. The pub is at the back tucked away in a corner. You can't miss it!'

A better version:
'As you leave this building, turn left into Bright Street. Walk about 200 metres down to the bridge. The canal runs underneath and you'll see a number of boats by the bridge. Take the road to the right and follow it straight down to Ashley Gasworks. There's a big sign stretching over the road so you can't miss it. The Grey Duck Inn is 300 metres down the road on your left. It's timber-framed with a thatched roof. You'll see the car park first and there are usually plenty of people around. If you do get lost, ask one of the locals. They're very friendly.'

This might take extra time but not only will you enable the person to find the pub, you'll also show them you've done as much as you can to assist.

Fig. 11.5 *Examples of good and bad directions*

Foreign language skills

For staff working in countries wishing to attract overseas tourists, foreign language skills are greatly valued. The majority of tourists travelling to other countries need tourist guides, waiters and waitresses, hotel staff and transport staff who speak their language. While Japanese tourists want to be shown around London in their own language, British people want English speaking ticket sales staff in Indian railway stations, and Germans want to choose their Spanish restaurant meal from a menu printed in German.

The English language itself is important for communication between staff and visitors: a Norwegian tourist ordering a beer at a bar in Turkey will do so in English, the language which he and the bar staff are most likely to have in common. However, British people should not assume that they will be understood wherever they go overseas. Even in some developed destinations in Europe, the first foreign language spoken by the resident staff is not English but German. German tourists were responsible for discovering many new European destinations in the Mediterranean during the 1960s and 1970s and the residents of those places first learned the German language to make communication easier. There are still Greeks who speak both their own language and German, but not English, and there are resorts in places such as Majorca where the residents speak Spanish and German, or Spanish and French, but little or no English.

Nevertheless the importance of English as a common language of communication in tourism, as well as other fields, has meant that British and American people above all other nationalities have the highest expectations that overseas visitors will speak their language when they come to Britain or the USA. British tourists speaking English will be readily understood in any tourist information centre in the Netherlands, but only a minority of tourist information centres in Britain would be able to produce a member of staff who is fluent in Dutch. As more and more of Britain's overseas visitors are drawn from the Middle East and Far East countries, the need for British tourism staff to equip themselves with foreign language skills will greatly increase.

EXERCISE

Figure 11.6 shows how the French Ministry of Trade, Handicrafts and Tourism measures tourism employment in France.

1 As well as giving the number of employees in the different categories and their percentages, for what other area does the table show figures and percentages?

2 From the categories in Fig. 11.6, give two examples each of direct employment and indirect employment in tourism.

3 Compare this table with Fig. 11.1, Tourism Employment in Britain.
(a) Give three examples of employment categories which appear in Fig. 11.1 but not in Fig. 11.6.

Outlets run by firms (numbers at 31 December)	Establishments	%	Number of employees at 31 December	%
Construction and manufacturing				
Caravans and trailers	119	0.12	4008	0.74
Sports and camping goods	465	0.47	12271	2.28
Pleasure boating	474	0.48	3724	0.69
Retail Trade				
Sports and camping goods	3703	3.75	15790	2.94
Hotel and catering				
Other	13	0.01	39	0.01
Restaurants and café restaurants	31306	31.73	149975	27.95
Canteens	8627	8.74	63.949	11.92
Prepared food outlets	648	0.65	3983	0.74
Bars without entertainment	11392	11.54	27531	5.13
Cafés	5437	5.51	13839	2.57
Bars with entertainment	1546	1.56	7541	1.40
Cafés associated with another activity	3319	3.36	7724	1.43
Hotels with restaurant	18449	18.70	107894	20.11
Hotels without restaurant	3683	3.73	19701	3.67
Railway dining and sleeping cars	47	0.04	1182	0.22
Student and young workers' hotels	978	0.99	8915	1.66
Built accommodation	3048	3.08	32083	5.98
Lightweight accommodation	1231	1.24	8908	1.66
Total hotel and catering	89725	90.95	454177	84.66
Other				
Travel agencies	2318	2.34	17914	3.33
Spas and thalasso- therapeutic establishments	479	0.48	17385	3.24
Ski lifts	173	0.17	5689	1.06
Official tourist offices	1196	1.21	5478	1.02
Total	98652	100.00	536436	100.00

Fig. 11.6 *Employment in tourism: France*

Source: Economics of Tourism, Ministry of Trade, Handicrafts and Tourism, France

(b) Give three examples of employment categories which appear in Fig. 11.6 but not in Fig. 11.1.

(c) Describe briefly the main differences between the ways in which the British and French define their tourism industries for employment statistics purposes.

4 From the totals given, which country has the higher percentage employed in hotels?

Is it fair to compare the percentage figures for this in both tables? Give reasons for your answer.

CASE STUDY

Foreign languages for tourism employees in Britain

Earlier in this chapter, the ability to speak foreign languages was identified as one of the important skills required by many of those working in the tourism industry.

To what extent can non-English-speaking visitors to Britain expect to be understood in their own language while on holiday or on a business trip? The ability to speak languages other than one's own mother tongue differs greatly from country to country, even within the same continent, as shown in Fig. 11.7 (*a*).

Number of other languages	0	1	2	3+
Belgium	50	22	18	9
Denmark	40	30	25	6
Germany	60	33	6	1
Greece	66	27	5	2
France	67	26	6	1
Ireland	80	17	3	–
Italy	76	19	5	1
Luxembourg	1	10	47	42
Holland	28	29	32	12
Portugal	76	14	8	2
Spain	68	26	5	1
UK	74	20	5	1

Fig. 11.7 (a) Percentage of people who can follow a conversation in another language
Source: Eurobarometer 1989

The Chairman of the British Tourist Authority, William Davis, stressed the importance of foreign language skills for Britain's tourist industry in a recent article which included the following points:

Foreign language skills are clearly of great importance to the tourist industry. They help to make visitors feel welcome and add to the enjoyment of their stay. They are also good for business.

This has long been appreciated by people in countries whose language is not widely spoken elsewhere. We in Britain have tended to be more complacent, chiefly because so many visitors have an impressive command of English.

We are fortunate that it has become the language of the global marketplace, but it would be quite wrong to assume that we therefore have no need to learn other languages.

For almost half of Britain's incoming tourists, English is not their mother tongue. Many do not speak it at all, or know only a few basic words. Fear of not being able to communicate can be a formidable deterrent to travel. A great deal of business may be lost because of it.

There are many markets with great potential for the British tourist industry, such as Japan and the former communist countries of Eastern Europe. After next year, we will be part of a single European community of more than 320 million people, 82 per cent of whom do not have English as their native tongue. There is an urgent need to pay serious attention to the needs of the new customers we hope to attract in the years to come.

A number of organisations, I am glad to say, have taken action to improve the service they give to non-English-speaking tourists.

Attractions such as Warwick Castle, Beaulieu, Castle Howard, Shugborough Hall, and the National Portrait Gallery, have started language training programmes for front-line staff. Best Western Hotels have operated an exchange scheme for young staff with associate hotels in Europe to develop both language skills and cultural awareness. Harrods has opened a Japanese information desk for customers. British Airways has made major efforts to ensure that 'the World's Favourite Airline' can communicate effectively with its passengers.

The BTA, which has publications in 19 languages, has encouraged all this in various ways. It has, for example, produced a comprehensive guide called *Caring for the Japanese visitor* which offers advice on a wide range of subjects, including signposting and menus. But a great deal more needs to be done.

Source: Horizons, April 1991, B.T.A.

Figure 11.7(*b*) gives some good examples of British tourism organisations which have taken steps to improve the services they provide for non-English-speaking clients.

TASKS

1 According to the percentages given in the above table, which European countries are the most gifted and the least gifted, in terms of understanding more than one language?

2 Why is William Davis someone who should be concerned with the question of foreign languages skills of tourism employees in Britain?

3 Give examples of how British tourism organisations have taken steps to encourage their staff to improve their foreign languages skills.

BAA plc at Gatwick – BAA, which maintains airport facilities and employs porters, information desk staff, trolley attendants, security guards etc, has a policy of recruiting staff with language skills at all levels.

Information assistants at airports and public announcers all have competence in at least one foreign language and BAA will provide financial assistance towards the cost of a language course for any employee who can justify the training in terms of their job requirements.

BAA pays a language allowance of £179 per annum to mother-tongue speakers, recent language graduates and all other employees who can pass an examination set by the Institute of Linguists in two languages. Flag badges are then worn by staff showing which languages they can speak.

Brighton Borough Council – As a major centre for the teaching of English as a foreign language and with a large international conference centre, Brighton enjoys more than the average number of foreign visitors.

Staff recruited to the Brighton Tourist Information Centre must therefore have a working knowledge of at least two foreign languages and, within the Tourism Development Department, preference is always given to applicants with some language competence.

Brighton Borough Council also provides publicity leaflets and information in French, German, Spanish, Italian, Portuguese, Dutch and Japanese.

British Airways – The airline, which has had a language policy for more than five years, aims to provide training for as many of its 6,000 cabin crew (including those on domestic flights) as possible in French, German, Italian and Spanish. BA has also begun training in Japanese and, after market research, is considering extending this to Portuguese, Arabic, Mandarin and Cantonese.

At present the airline's courses are custom-designed but in future distance-learning techniques may well be introduced to ease the problem of taking staff "off-line".

Records of the language skills of staff are kept on computer so that, whenever possible, staff with appropriate languages can be rostered on most flights. Performance in achieving this objective is continuously monitored.

BA also produces foreign language articles in its on-board magazines, and menus in the languages of destinations are provided for first-class travellers.

British Rail – After identifying the routes most likely to carry significant numbers of overseas visitors, such as Harwich and Dover to London, BR has produced taped announcements in French, German and Dutch to cater for travellers from the European mainland.

BR is also considering providing language centres with telephone information for overseas visitors.

Edinburgh Tourist Information Centre – Run by the District Council, the Tourist Office has a strong policy on language skills and for the past four years all new permanent information staff have been required to speak at least one European language.

The languages provided at the Office include French, German, Italian, Spanish, some Swedish, and some Gaelic, and the council pays for evening classes for staff wishing to learn a new language or brush up on existing skills.

Fig. 11.7 (b) *The services offered by some of the British tourism organisations for their non-English-speaking clients*

Source: Lost for Words, BTA 1990

Dealing with complaints

Some complaints are genuine, some are serious, some quite trivial. ALL should be investigated.

Tourism staff dealing with the public face-to-face can help to sort out any problems before they become too serious.

Several skills are needed to handle the range of queries or complaints that might be received.

Listening

Before you do anything, you need to LISTEN and make sure you understand what is being said. This avoids any misunderstandings and lets the visitor see that you genuinely care and want to help. Repeat the information and write it down if it helps.

Apologise

Whatever the problem always apologise first then see if you can sort it out.

Compare these two attitudes.

1 'I'm very sorry, Madam. I'll see what I can do to help'.
2 'What do you expect me to do about it? Write to the manager if you want to complain.'

APOLOGISING does not mean acknowledging that you are at fault nor does it make you appear weak. It can help to defuse situations and encourage the customer to be more reasonable.

Sorting out the problem

Usually it's not your fault. Something, somewhere has gone wrong but you are in the front line.

If you can sort out the problem, which may be a case of misunderstanding, then do so confidently and politely.

If the customer is still not satisfied, suggest you look into the matter carefully, or try suggesting alternatives.

Sometimes it is the customer who has made a mistake.

Don't ever say 'See, I told you so . . .'

Try 'I think if you just look at this again you'll see . . .'

Agreeing with the person is another good way of calming them down, usually because they expect you to rush to the defence of whoever is in the wrong!

Just letting them get it out of their system might be the only solution.

On all occasions never lose your temper

Fig. 11.8 Dealing with complaints

ASSIGNMENTS

1 Customer relations skills – dealing with complaints.

Figure 11.8 from a customer relations skills training manual suggests how to handle a complaint from a customer.

Role play the following situation:

A visitor to a waxworks comes to the manager or manageress to complain that his or her young child has been frightened and upset by the Jack the Ripper exhibition in the waxworks house of horrors. To add to the visitor's dissatisfaction, they were treated rudely on complaining to the attendant on duty near the exhibition in question, and are now extremely angry. The visitor complains loudly, demanding the entrance fee back, while some of the other visitors are witnessing this scene.

With a member of the class playing the complaining visitor and another member playing the manager or manageress, role play the situation, first with the manager or manageress beginning by responding 'What do you want me to do about it?', and then secondly with the manager or manageress beginning by responding, 'I'm very sorry'.

As a class, compare both approaches.

2 Applying for jobs in tourism.

The advertisements on pages 202–3 show a selection of jobs in the tourism industry in Britain.

Each member of the class should choose one of the advertisements and write an imaginary letter of application for the job, explaining:

(a) Why he or she is interested in working in that particular sector of the tourism industry.

(b) What qualifications he or she has for the job (these can be made up).

(c) What previous experience he or she has of this kind of work, through Saturday or holiday jobs for example (this, too, can be made up).

(d) What his or her general interests are.

(e) When he or she could start.

The letters may then be used to role play members of the class being interviewed for the jobs by the prospective employer. The class should divide into pairs, one person playing the interviewer and the other the interviewee and then exchange roles.

DIRECTOR OF CATERING

Blackpool Pleasure Beach Group
Britain's Number One Tourist Attraction

Blackpool Pleasure Beach Group currently operates three major Amusement Parks on the North West coast. Catering at all three sites is of great importance and includes the entire spectrum of food retailing, from fast food outlets to high quality restaurants, including nineteen licensed bars.

We seek an experienced, committed individual to assume overall responsibility for every aspect of our £multi-million highly seasonal catering operation.

The brief will be to achieve and maintain the highest possible standards whilst maximising turnover and profitability.

The Director of Catering will report to the Managing Director.

This is an important appointment within our group and will be rewarded by a first rate salary plus car and benefits package. A contribution will be made to relocation expenses.

To apply please write with full C.V. to Personnel Manager, Blackpool Pleasure Beach Ltd.,

Fig. 11.9 (a)

Fig. 11.9 (b)

WESTSHIRE DISTRICT COUNCIL
TORMINSTER SPORTS CENTRE
RECREATION ASSISTANT

Torminster Sports Centre is a dual use Centre which had new facilities added in the form of Squash Courts and fitness training room in June last year. In addition to this the Centre has a Main Hall, 15 metre Pool, small Solarium, Lounge Bar and vending facilities.

Due to internal promotion this junior management position has become vacant and would suit a keen committed individual wishing to progress up the management ladder.

This is a supervisory post with specific responsibilities for the day-to-day running of the Centre, supervision of staff and public, together with an input into the coaching programme. Previous experience in the leisure business would be desirable and applicants must hold a Pool Bronze Medallion or be training towards this award.

Preference will be given to those candidates holding coaching awards and having experience in the following areas, trampolining, squash, aerobics, fitness training and life saving.

39 hours per week to include daytime, evenings and some weekends.

The salary is fully inclusive of all enhancements.

For an informal discussion on the post, please contact Sarah Jones, Regional and Centre Manager.

Application forms and further details are available from the Personnel Section, Council Offices, Torminster, Westshire.

Westshire District Council is an Equal Opportunities Employer.

Fig. 11.9 (c)

GREEN HART HOTEL, THAMESTON

This famous hotel with luxurious bedrooms and varied conference facilities now requires

RECEPTIONIST

To carry out all reception duties including the operation of our Apricot computer, Regent switchboard and Puma Telex.

RESERVATION CLERK
9-5.30pm Mon-Fri

Operating a manual system at present we plan to transfer to a computerised system next year. Efficiency and friendly telephone manner essential as is an interest in all aspects of guest care and selling.

Uniform, meals and accommodation provided with excellent salary and career progression.

Apply to: **Reception Manager**
Green Hart Hotel
Thameston

INDEX

How to order

All books can be ordered through your regular bookshop or supplier. In case of difficulty, send your remittance, in full, to

Southport Book Distributors,
12/14 Slaidburn Crescent, Southport, Merseyside, PR9 9YF.
Tel: 01704 26881, Fax: 01704 506723.

If you would like further information about the full range of our travel and tourism titles, please contact the **Marketing Department** at our Harlow office:

Addison Wesley Longman Limited
Edinburgh Gate
Harlow, Essex
CM20 2JE
Tel: 01279 623437
Fax: 01279 431059

Information Technology in Travel and Tourism

GARY INKPEN

Director of Inkpen Associates, an independent IT consultancy firm

This book provides information on the latest IT systems used within the travel and tourism industry.

Specifically written to clarify the subject of IT within the industry, this book is up to date and addresses the key developments in supplier systems which are having considerable impact on the industry and which are crucial to the success and profitability of a company. Gary Inkpen's book is essential for those wishing to evaluate and implement the most suitable IT network within their own business.

The book is well written and easy to understand, with a number of graphical illustrations and explanations of technical terms. At the end of each chapter there are specially selected examples taken from real-life situations, together with questions to ensure effective revision. Answers are provided at the end of the book.

Key features

- first IT book for the travel and tourism industry available
- written for both the student and practitioner
- offers interesting real-life examples throughout
- excellent source of reference and information

ISBN 0 273 60229 2

Business Travel

ROB DAVIDSON

Visiting Lecturer in Tourism at the Universities of Montpellier, Lyon and Lille, and former Education and Training Manager at the British Tourism Authority

This is the first textbook to deal exclusively with the business travel sector of the tourism industry. *Business Travel*, written by an established and respected travel and tourism author, provides a comprehensive and up-to-date analysis of the business travel industry.

Beginning with an overview of the industry and its principal providers and customers, the six main chapters give a thorough coverage of each sector of business travel. In every case there follows an analysis of current trends, drawing on official statistics, articles from the press and published reports.

Each chapter contains detailed case studies drawn from business travel organisations and companies in Britain and overseas, including Berkeley Hotel, Gatwick Airport and Virgin Atlantic. These provide relevant illustrations of the information given and the issues explored.

Key features
- the first and only text dedicated to the business travel sector of the industry
- relevant to both the British and overseas educational market

ISBN 0 582 29476 2

Interpersonal Skills for Travel and Tourism

LISA BURTON
Open Learning Development Officer; formerly with Flexible Training Services

The text addresses the whole area of interpersonal skills and, through an expertly-written programme, investigates the skills needed to:

- create a professional impression with customers, face to face and over the telephone
- use active selling skills to increase sales of travel and tourism products
- deal with customer complaints in a professional manner which will satisfy both parties
- use a variety of methods of communication, written and verbal, and meetings, to communicate effectively with customers and with colleagues
- develop and enhance internal staff relationships through effective use of interpersonal skills
- use interpersonal skills to enhance the performance of staff

The book has been designed to enable students to interact with the text as far as possible. Each section of the book will include knowledge required to perform the required task, a series of exercises to enable readers to check their understanding, and activities which will allow the reader to put skills into practice in a real situation.

Key features
- as an ABTA Development Officer, the author has been actively involved with the development of the NVQ structure
- provides practical guidelines and exercises to practise interpersonal skills in the workplace

Contents
1 Creating a professional relationship with the customer: personal appearance / creating good rapport with the customer
2 Selling skills: questioning skills to identify customer needs / identifying opportunities to sell / using benefits to sell the product / closing the sale
3 Handling customer complaints and dissatisfaction
4 Communication skills: verbal communication skills / effective written communication / effective presentation skills for a promotional event
5 Internal staff relationships: the basics of assertiveness / providing feedback on staff performance / dealing with staff conflict / disciplinary and grievance procedures / counselling skills / running effective staff meetings

ISBN 0 582 27946 1

The Business of Tourism

4th edition

CHRISTOPHER HOLLOWAY

Professor of Tourism Management, Bristol Business School, University of the West of England

The Business of Tourism provides a basic understanding of the nature, structure and organisation of the tourist industry.

The book examines the role of tourism in the economic development of a country and explores the relationship between public and private sector tourism. The operations of each part of the industry – tourist attractions, carriers, accommodation, tour operation, retailing, tourist offices and ancillary services – are described in detail. Often overlooked aspects of the industry receive attention, such as the role of tourist guides and the importance of insurance, foreign exchange and credit.

Key features
- well-established bestseller
- each chapter has clear objectives, self-assessment questions and assignments
- numerous photographs, maps and diagrams included

What's new about the fourth edition
- thoroughly up to date throughout
- includes a new section on hospitality
- also covers travel retailing and support services
- addresses the issue of the social and environmental impact of tourism on the receiving country
- an update on the airline industry has been made to include the latest guidelines by the Civil Aviation Authority (CAA)

Contents
An introduction to tourism / The history of tourism: from its origins to the age of steam / Tourism in the twentieth century / The economics of tourism / Tourist motivation and behaviour / The structure and organisation of the travel and tourism industry / Passenger transport: the aviation business / Water-borne passenger transport / Road and rail passenger transport / The hospitality sector: accommodation and catering services / Visitor attractions and visitor management / Tour operating / Travel retailing / Ancillary tourism services / The structure and role of public sector tourism / Tourism design and management / The social and environmental impact of tourism / Bibliography / Index

ISBN 0 582 29042 2

Travel Geography

2nd edition

ROSEMARY BURTON
Senior Lecturer, Department of Town and Country Planning,
University of West of England, Bristol

This book has now been fully updated and specially altered to cater for vocational course requirements. It explains the distribution of tourism in the different regions of the world, looking at the geographical, social, political and economic circumstances that generate and control tourism.

Introductory sections cover the pattern of tourism worldwide, geographical resources for tourism, transport networks and future developments. In the following chapters four main regions are identified: Europe, Africa and the Middle East, the Americas, and the Pacific and Australasia. All the major tourism attractions and resources of each destination are covered as well as an in-depth explanation of why tourism develops in certain areas and not in others.

Key features
- provides superb maps and diagrams which illustrate each region discussed
- includes learning objectives and student activities in each chapter to aid student assessment and develop skills of information location and interpretation

ISBN 0 273 60203 9

The Business of Tour Operations

PAT YALE
Freelance Journalist

Business of Tour Operations is the only book available to provide an overview of the tour operations sector. It looks at the evolution of tour operations, examines a number in detail (for example Thomson, Air Tours and Owners Abroad) and explains the different types of operators.

The packaging of a product is explained, together with accommodation, travel and transfer arrangements. Also covered are the pricing of packages, the complexities of the brochure and marketing. The reader will understand how a tour operator's office is organised, about consumer protection, risks and the effects of tour operations on host destinations. Lastly, the book looks to the future and the impact of the EC Directive on package travel.

Key features
- the only book to investigate tour operations as a complete sector
- discussion points and assignments are offered at the end of every chapter

ISBN 0 582 27797 3

Tourism in Europe

ROB DAVIDSON
Visiting Lecturer in Tourism at the Universities of Montpellier, Lyon and Lille, and former Education and Training Manager at the British Tourism Authority

This book provides a sound appreciation of the current trends and issues influencing tourism throughout Europe. It complements textbooks which only examine tourism in the student's own country, and provides the wider context necessary for a full understanding of the subject.

Each chapter provides an in-depth analysis of a theme, such as transport or accommodation, drawing on up-to-date reports, statistical data and media coverage from different countries. Each chapter also includes detailed case studies on a theme drawn from a range of countries and branches of the industry.

Cases include Center Parcs, Budapest, the impact of the Madrid-Seville TGV route and the Channel Tunnel. The emphasis is on activity-based learning, with the inclusion of student exercises and assignments to develop understanding.

Contents
Europe and tourism / European Community legislation for tourism / Shrinking Europe: The European high-speed train network and the Channel Tunnel / New trends in accommodation / Theme parks in Europe / Business tourism in Europe / Tourism for all: social tourism in Europe / Small is beautiful: responsible tourism in Europe / European rural tourism / Open for business: tourism in Eastern Europe

ISBN 0 273 03829 X